CREEK

MARTIN CREEK

A Study on Nature, Starting a Ranch, and Building a Dream

Daryl Riersgard
Edited by Amy Pattee Colvin

Paperback: ISBN 978-1-7351215-1-2

Cover Photo: Daryl Rieirsgard
Cover Design: Amy Pattee Colvin
Editor: Amy Pattee Colvin

DEDICATION

This book is dedicated to Bobbi, a long-time friend, who has played a role in getting this book draft alive again. She and I have been good friends since our college days nearly fifty-five years ago. She has also been a dear family friend for this same amount of time.

Recently, she learned that I had an old book draft from fourteen years ago that was gathering dust on a back shelf. She was brave enough to ask to review the original manuscript. Soon thereafter, she responded with a loving spoonful of good comments that gave me the confidence I needed to move this book idea forward.

She has demonstrated an unwavering loyalty for the longest time, putting her into a special category of best friend. If this book should ever get to first base, she will deserve much of the credit.

Friends like this only come along once in a lifetime. I should also acknowledge that she was the one who came up with the book subtitle of Building a Dream. She knew many of the details involved in my twenty-one-month struggle to get my ranch infrastructure started.

CONTENTS

ACKNOWLEDGMENTS

This story is my autobiographical effort, where my focus is on one place and a brief period in time. Some of my favorite authors love to travel and then record their places, their miles traveled, and meeting people along the way.

Other favorite authors tended to find a single place and then put the microscope on the finer details. As I acknowledge in the first part of my book, I am beholding to authors such as Thoreau, Beston, Hubbell, and Heinrich. I seem to have found their works in the Nature section of various Barnes and Noble bookstores. It seems that my reading interests keep coming back to a common theme.

This section would not be complete without acknowledging the author Barry Lopez as I have long admired his writing style and his incredible vocabulary. My first book was a collection of short stories, very much influenced by his book called *Winter Count*.

Along the way, I found inspiration from the Montana cowboy poet by the name of Paul Zarzyski. Of all places, I met Paul in a cowboy saloon in Elko, Nevada. He flat challenged me to come out of my comfort zone and just start to write. He simply said, "you can do this." It matters not if it is classic poetry or a good non-fiction novel, just get up and do it.

So in 1996 and 1997, I decided to write about a bunch of things at once, kind of like mixing a blender full of a morning smoothie. My blender selection was going to simply focus on building a ranch from scratch.

As the subtitle says, also building a dream. This quest would take twenty-one months, a bit longer than I expected. At the same time, I am exposed to one of the most beautiful and quiet valleys in the Intermountain West.

This place is filled with a wild assortment of birds and wildlife. I am not a total newcomer to this natural element, but almost. So my story slows down enough to focus on what is right in front of me.

I can't live alone forever, so I must get out and meet the people who live around me, mostly hard-working ranchers. I write about them and the activities that they engage in. Finally, I try to lace this all together with some personal philosophy.

Since there is a fair amount of natural history in my book, I should acknowledge my close friend, Mike Janik, who was a willing coach on all things related to birds, mammals, and horticulture. While building my ranch house, I was also planting anything that would grow. I needed foliage, and Mike was my guy.

My final acknowledgment has to go to my hard-working editor, who realized that my tendency to jump from sub-topic to sub-topic might cause some readers grief, so she helped my draft with some serious re-organization. In addition to basic editing, she had a wealth of creative ideas that we exchanged freely via email. My story reads better thanks to her. She also did my front and back book cover. Amy Pattee Colvin can do it all. Best of all, Amy was fun to work with.

INTRODUCTION

Place is important, and therefore I took the initiative to find a meaningful spot where I could thrive for the balance of my life. Our world has gotten a bit crazy, and it seems that terrorism, illness, and fear of one another have permeated our travel and our lives. My home nest has grown empty, and my traditional office workdays are over. For all of these reasons, and more, I decided to find a spot that I could call home, a place that would satisfy both my needs as well as my free spirit. This new location also had to fulfill the need to get away from the madding crowd. As such, it was essential to find a spot where life was not crowded upon life.

The subject of this book is my transition to tranquility. This account is from the perspective of a guy, new to this location and landscape, which allows me to weave this net of stories from fresh eyes. The backdrop is a beautiful section of the upper Great Basin, Nevada. These reflections are limited to one special valley, which time may have forgotten—and forgotten implies a good thing. I aim to provide a positive narrative about this time and place, yet I would never wish to start a land rush to this beautiful locale. This place should stay just the way it is for as long as possible. So, don't think about moving here.

Many themes unfold concurrently, and the chronology is fluid. Through these words, you'll see me develop a rural ranch property. I will also slow down to a pace that allows me to smell the roses, or in this case, smell the sagebrush, and study the natural setting in which I now find myself. You'll be by my side as I take on the challenge of melding into a new community of ranchers, farmers, and the folks who generally support this way of life. This book allows me to digress and seek mental and thoughtful excursions that may crop up during the twenty-one months between April 2006 and December 2007. The landscape here offers up a great opportunity to describe the diversity of geography, the abundance of wild and natural things, the long culture of hard-working ranches, and the local people who make this place special.

As an upfront warning, I am not sure how much of this account will be considered deep or profound. I cannot guarantee any underlying purpose leading to any particular moral lesson. I no longer feel that I have anything to grouse about in life, so you'll find little to no raw emotion playing out in these pages. This is not a travel journal because I never intended to stray far from my new-found home. This will not be an elegy, except for some sentimental feelings that this local ranch lifestyle may be slipping away. Yet I hope I can paint for you, with words, the beauty of this place, and my profound feelings for it.

The site selected is in a quiet and peaceful valley, off the beaten path in northern Nevada. Finding the right place to call home has been one of life's most fulfilling adventures. Defining factors for most of us is where we live and how we live. This may be truer when you have hit that tenth or eleventh hour of your life-cycle clock.

This quest to find the right place to call home is easier said than done. For most of us, work and family seem to influence where we end up; however, the later stages of life may well afford a fresh perspective to get it right. To pursue this adventure begs a new set of personal priorities. Reshuffling these priorities is both reveling and life-affirming. My opportunity presented itself after my traditional work retirement. I may think I am retired, but the real work is about to begin. This fresh start for me really did constitute a new beginning. I had the freedom to do what I wanted as opposed to doing what I had to do. My new beginning called for the development of a fresh piece of rural property. I intended to build from scratch and get most of the work done in short order. For me, this development plan also presented an opportunity to share a story based on my first year or so. I desired to present a story based on a natural year; however, as the story started to tell itself, the time frame grew longer. This story chronicles the process of getting started and rooted in this valley.

A natural year is an approach described by many notable authors well before me. For my literary perspective, this approach started with Thoreau and *Walden Pond*, written between 1845-1847. A subsequent similar model followed eighty years later with Henry Beston and his 1927 account of a year on the great beach of Cape Cod called *The Outermost House*. More recently, Sue Hubbell in 1983 wrote, *A Country Year*, which described her small farm in the Ozarks. Her story chapters were entitled, Spring, Summer, Autumn, etc.

Thoreau said, "It is difficult to begin without borrowing." This is true for both literary purposes as well as practical purposes of starting any new project.

In the case of Thoreau, this literary device—a natural year—was not disclosed until early in Chapter two of *Walden*. It was referenced as a "convenience" that freed the author to follow the sequence of the four seasons. He started with summer, which then allowed him to end his book with the spring season. In his case, he started his natural year on the 4th of July.

Thoreau's efforts at Walden were about experiments in living, but on a smaller scale, and from a different direction, he offered other examples of his time. He specifically made the point that the purpose of his going to Walden Pond was not to live cheaply nor dearly there but to transact some private business, with the fewest obstacles. One of many annotators of Walden, Jeffrey Cramer, wrote that this private business was most likely the writing of what would become A Week on the Concord and Merrimack Rivers, a memorial tribute to his brother John, who died from lockjaw.[1]

My efforts here, will on occasion, follow the Thoreau pattern and, in other instances, work hard to differ from the Walden model. I see this pending challenge as a sort of transcendental opportunity to address the very best of my new community and lifestyle. If this book idea has merit, I will strive to make the publishing move quicker than the nine years it took Thoreau. But I may be wrong on my time estimate. I will also endeavor to exceed the number of book sales in the first year (256) that Thoreau accomplished. Lastly, I plan to build a ranch house larger than the ten-feet by fifteen-feet cabin in which Thoreau lived.

A year and one half before Thoreau moved to Walden Pond, he wrote in Paradise Regained, "We must first succeed alone, that we may enjoy our success together." I, too, will succeed alone as I start this project solo, leaving my wife, Becky, and grown kids behind in Reno.

The practice of being inspired by someone's earlier book is, of course, not uncommon. Thoreau was impressed with the book, The Human Body, written by James Wilkinson in 1851. "Wilkinson finds a home for the imagination...All perception of truth is the detection of an analogy; we reason from our hands to our heads." Understanding this was both a key and a confirmation of what he was trying to achieve in Walden.[2]

Emboldened by the Thoreau model, I, too, will report on living from day to day. My account will focus close to home. Unlike the travel authors, my sphere of influence will be right here. When I think of travel authors, I think of Barry Lopez. My emphasis will be on accurate impressions of this natural scene, where evocation is more important than storyline or drama. As the traveling author reports on his experiences away from home, this author will do the opposite. I will report on my stay at home and the phenomena of my intentional experiences here. I agree with Thoreau's belief that books must be read as deliberately and reservedly as they were written.

Thoreau took a flute with him to Walden, and Beston brought a concertina to his year on the beach. Since I have no musical talents, I came to this place armed with only my laptop and good intentions. As it turned out, there was little opportunity to fiddle around with any musical toys. I seemed to have my hands pleasantly full with the challenge of getting work done and, and in contrast, having the time and opportunity of doing nothing, if I so pleased. While it is true that music appreciation has long been a part of my life, musical talents have not matched my love of what music has to offer.

The following quote from the Beston book also helps set the stage for appreciating the elemental things associated with a special place,

> The world today is sick to its thin blood for lack of elemental things, for fire before the hands, for water welling up from the earth, for air, for the dear earth itself underfoot...the longer I stayed, the more eager was I to know this coast and to share its mysterious and elemental life. — Henry Beston Sheahan

In the case of the Beston book, he also used the controlling metaphor of the natural year to structure his book. He described the natural year, not as a great drama but rather as a ritual. The sun image seemed central to the story and the natural ritual. Even though Beston was thirty-six years of age, when he lived his story, it is considered by many to be a younger man's story because of the writing style that unfolded a sense of discovery along the way.

Again, nature played a key role in this story. He understood the psychic roots and the elemental need for man to seek out and respond to the wild nature that made up Cape Cod. According to the forward of this book, the Beston story is considered to be one of the classics of American nature writing. Beston's style was to finally leave his house on the beach with several notebooks full of material. He did not leave Cape Cod with a manuscript, either rough or finished. Even though he did not consider himself a naturalist, his practice of note-taking and observation certainly matched that of an expert field naturalist. His motivation was to get to know the coast and then to share its mysteries. This objective is similar to what I intend to accomplish at my new location.

In the case of Sue Hubbel's book, her chapters were also organized by the season. I have a few things in common with Hubbel in that my property is also surrounded by government land, we both have a deep appreciation for the beauty of our home location, and we are both doing it alone. We share the pattern of living alone with a singular purpose with dedicated time to focus on the story bubbling up from the world around us. The contrast only comes when you compare the age of these particular authors. Thoreau was relatively young when he wrote. Beston was in his middle years, and Hubbel was getting up in years. In my case, I was fifty-nine years old when I started this writing adventure.

To show how age is relative, consider the story about the retired Supreme Court Justice, Oliver Wendell Holmes Jr. When he was ninety-two, he paid a visit to a friend of his in New York City. His friend lived on the tenth floor, so he climbed the stairs for a visit. Later the two gentlemen decided to go to the street level for some fresh air. While there, Holmes spotted a good-looking young lady walking his direction. He paid close attention to her while she passed by and walked down the street in the opposite direction. Holmes never took his eye off this young lady. He commented to his friend, "Oh, to be eighty again." He also had a mustache to die for. He died in 1935 at age ninety-four.

Accordingly, I intend to discover and record a particular section of this part of beautiful Nevada. The above list of literary examples all feature locations east of the Mississippi. With my heart in the West, this book focuses on one part of the Great Basin of Nevada. The setting is the wildest landscape of the real West.

For my purposes, the real West is the Intermountain West, excluding urban California and the Pacific Northwest. My setting is the upper end of the old Great Basin, now most commonly associated with the borders of Nevada, Oregon, and Idaho. In some circles, this tri-border area has been called ION (Idaho-Oregon-Nevada). More specifically, my focus is on the perfect wide-open valley near the Oregon/Idaho border.

Between this rural property and the Oregon state line is a relatively untrampled section of national forest, with more than four hundred square miles of rugged terrain awaiting exploration. This section of the national forest is one of the least traveled in the U.S.

This quest will strive to be a "civil gathering of words"—a phrase borrowed from the last line of cowboy poet Paul Zarzyski's "Putting the Rodeo Try into Cowboy Poetry,"—or perhaps a world of words to describe this new setting.[3] My story describes not just the development of a small ranch property, but also provides a closer look at what Mother Nature provided here. A small dose of personal philosophy meanders through the book like a sun-dappled creek. My model for sharing a personal philosophy is patterned after William Kittredge and his book, *The Nature of Generosity*, published in 2000. Kittredge is mentioned not only because be serves as a model for introspective Western thinking, but because he was a product of this same upper Great Basin. This rural setting is subtly woven into his philosophical perspective. However, the Kittredge book is vastly different in that his perspective is global and makes no effort to focus on one place for any extended period.

A final piece of inspiration here, regarding Western influence, is my occasional reference to the wild and creative mix of words and rhyme of the Montana cowboy poet, Paul Zarzyski. Even the most reluctant cowboy can't help admire how Paul's words build a sweet picture for the brain to imagine. There is creative writing, and then there is the art of making your words dance. I even had the opportunity to discuss creative writing with Paul, over a beer at the Stockman's Hotel in Elko, Nevada. He was in Elko to perform at the annual Cowboy Poetry Gathering. In fact, I had just attended his performance an hour prior. That beer-bottle memory may have had some influence on my idea to write this book.

On one brief occasion, I had the chance to discuss the topic of writing with Paul Zarzyski. Paul walked in and took a barstool about three down from me. When I recognized him, I asked if I could buy him a beer. I moved down a couple of bar stools so we could better communicate. Since I bought the beer, I owned him for a brief amount of time. I made the comment that I had never tried creative writing before, and I was uncertain how this might work out. While creative writing was new, other types of writing were not. Between my Marine Corps years and my time in law enforcement, I was tasked with many different writing assignments. I think my kind of writing experience would fall into the category of technical staff writing. It had its own demands, yet was distinct from creative writing. Paul's comment back to me was that he could lock me in a room, and with his coaching, turn me into a writer of poetry. Unfortunately, I never got the chance to be locked in a room with his coaching.

For any of the millions of visitors to Nevada, the challenge is for them to imagine something other than the Strip in Las Vegas. Millions of visitors arrive and return home with an image of Nevada being a dry, barren landscape of alkaline sagebrush scattered in and around the finger-like mountain ranges, all arid and absent of either water or beauty. But to those of us who live here and especially those that are inclined to get out and explore, countless surprise locations offer some of the most striking natural beauty anywhere.

In May of 2006, I heard Mike White, hiker, and author, speak to this subject. Most people driving across Nevada on Interstate-80, the main route from Salt Lake City to Sacramento, will never have an understanding of or appreciation for the hidden beauty in Nevada unless they stop and search it out. Mike White is the author of 50 Classic Hikes in Nevada. His slide show featured the running streams, the wildflowers, and the panoramic views from his favorite hiking spots.

Even White points out the exceptional beauty of the green terrain in and around the Santa Rosa mountain range. For perspective, the Santa Rosa range is what I see when I look out my north windows. His book features several local hikes. I was particularly intrigued by Hike 6, Singas Creek. I was so eager to try this hike that I made the ascent to the trailhead on May 7th, 2006, only to find that the trek uphill from there was still snow-covered. I did not get back to finish this hike until the fall of 2006. It was well worth the wait as the aspen trees had laid down a fresh carpet of yellow leaves.

The cumulative influence of these above authors will be a guide for me through this natural year. This cross-section of authors has each influenced some aspect of this project.

Northern Nevada offers up surprises for those willing to search them out. While sagebrush grows in many areas, I don't know of any other place with the unique mix of landscape as this particular spot. My specific location offers beauty, both near and far, that I referred to when I mentioned the lost opportunity for most travelers. This stretch of landscape also has a certain resilience that belies its diversity.

The place of which I speak is Paradise Valley, a horseshoe-shaped valley with the opening to the south. More specifically, this book will center on the Martin Creek section of this valley, located in the far eastern corner of this magnificent landscape. As a friend once said, "they don't call this place Paradise for nothing."

On one extreme is the northwest corner of the valley where Cottonwood Creek forms on the east slopes of Santa Rosa Peak. This creek takes shape as multiple streams and springs converge into the main creek. The nearly ten thousand foot peaks offer variety to this Great Basin geography.

This corner of the valley is about seventy percent covered with mature aspens. The typical aspen is big enough that it would take a grown man's bear hug to reach around the diameter. The surrounding terrain offers a unique setting where nature is at its best, and bighorn sheep are still seen on these upper reaches.

On the other extreme side of this valley is my ranch property, overlooking Martin Creek. This year-round creek forms in the upper elevations of the national forest. It works its way first to the north, then angles around to the east, and finally is headed due south through the high rock canyon walls and eventually passing below my property. This creek is not insignificant; it runs for forty-eight miles before it drains into the Humboldt River. My acreage is on the west bank of this mountain stream. As the creek emerges from the rocky cliffs of the national forest, it opens into what the government maps call Adams Slough but what the locals call Muffler Meadow. From the upper elevation trails west and north of Sugarloaf, this panorama is magnificent, looking down into the lower elevation where the lush meadow is located.

As the snow melts from the higher elevations, it produces a watershed that looks like a raging river in the spring. The heavy flow observed during my first spring was related to heavy snowpack in the mountains. The water volume the following spring, when the snowpack was modest, was substantial but comparatively less. By midsummer, it turns into a mild-mannered mountain stream.

The water flow creates a peaceful waterfall sound, as the creek does a five-foot waterfall just below my ranch. This is the dominant sound, especially in the evening, when quiet becomes the norm. Competing for your audio attention are the cows in Muffler Meadow and the many birds that have found sanctuary here.

The birds include the usual hawks, ducks, vultures, sage grouse, chukars, crows, magpies, and numerous other small perching birds. Many of these birds will be described in more detail in subsequent chapters. The largest bird that most confuses my cattle dogs is the oversized wild turkey. My dogs are not used to scaring up a bird that is larger in size and weight than they are. These turkeys provide the wonderful classic turkey gobble sound. This vast array of complementary sounds provides part of the seasonal soundtrack for where I live.

As is often the case in rural Nevada, the immediate neighbors are not private property owners, but the federal government lands. I have the national forest immediately to my north, managed by the U.S. Forest Service. The Bureau of Land Management (BLM) manages the buffer land closest to my property. There are a few private property owners along the west bank of the creek; however, the larger ranch properties are situated in the heart of the meadow and, in many cases, immediately adjacent to Marin Creek or other prominent creeks.

All of these factors help define the personality and setting of my rural property. You don't have to live here long to be reminded that Mother Nature is in charge. At the same time, there is a brilliant mix of daily weather and seasonal contrasts. I spent much of my first year in awe of the beauty of the days and the geographic setting, reverently soaking in the combination of weather, natural landscape beauty, unusual abundance of wildlife, and purple Nevada sunsets. This is the place I have become fond of, and the place that unfolds in the following pages.

1: GETTING STARTED

Getting Started

With my own two hands, I will develop this ranch to the point that it provides all of the pleasures of *place*. You will hear me mention the condition of my working hands more than once. My station in life has reached the point where a sense of place is not just important but essential. Knowing that I have settled in will assure my psyche that I will never have to pack up and move again. Knowing that this is my place, I shall have no worries about investing myself totally.

I'd like to tell you how I selected this location. Of all the areas in the world where I might have ended up, I'll share with you why I'm here. I, at the age of fifty-nine, wish for this location to be my final home. The lifestyle that accompanies this new location will promote quality-of-life features important to me. While this story shares the advantages of this new lifestyle, it does not attempt to imply that it is right for anyone but me.

The August 2006 edition of *Men's Journal* did a feature titled, "This Land is Your Land." It looked closely at seven geographic locations considered to be quality-of-life locations. The magazine examples include:

1. Leadville, Colorado, Front range high country
2. Asheville, North Carolina, Blue ridge hill country
3. Silver City, New Mexico, High desert borderlands
4. Springfield, Missouri, The upper Ozarks
5. Lubec, Maine, The easternmost tip
6. Eureka, California, Humboldt County coast
7. Marquette, Michigan, The Upper Peninsula

On the downside, it is not uncommon for residents in one of these top-seven locations to lament the day that the secret got out and ruined it for the long-established locals.

I have long believed that many things in life happened for a purpose. This ranch location took a long time to find, and it happened at a point when I could dedicate full time to this development effort.

Considering that I grew up on the plains of North Dakota, that I traveled the world thanks to a Marine Corps' free ticket, and that I have lived in the four corners of this country, why did I choose this final destination? I don't need to describe those youthful years near the Canadian border because that task has already been accomplished thanks to the talented gentleman, Clay Jenkinson. He is from my birth state of North Dakota. This account of place and characters is contained in the book, *Message on the Wind*.

To provide background on how I acquired this place, I should retrace some of the events that helped shape me to the person that I am today. For more than two decades, I did carrier landings and jumped out of perfectly good airplanes as a special forces forward air controller. I not only flew helicopters in Vietnam, but I also experienced what it felt like to get shot down in a ball of fire and survive a gunshot wound. I flew my helo over the safari lands of Kenya, between Mombasa and Mt. Kilimanjaro, and I chased red kangaroos across the Northwest Cape of Australia.

I attended a NATO school in Poole-Dorset, England, and I graduated from the Naval War College in Newport, Rhode Island. I spent time at Harvard as a researcher for part of a think-tank strategic-studies group.

I participated in the rescue fleet that backed up the formal rescue attempt for the American hostages in Iran and, at the same time, learned what it felt like to land a helicopter on a carrier with sixty-foot waves crashing over the forward deck, during the Indian Ocean monsoon season.

I had the honor of being one of seven command pilots for President Reagan and the attendant privilege to attend a Christmas party at the White House, hosted by the President and First Lady.

I survived a mid-air helicopter crash at night over the Pacific Ocean and managed to get my crew of seven safely back to an island crash landing.

I had the chance to do staff work at the Pentagon, working for the Joint Chiefs of Staff, and I was lucky enough to be a readiness briefer for the Commandant of the Marine Corps and the Secretary of the Navy.

I had the opportunity to attend a key planning session at "the tank" with the President in attendance. I have spent lonely nights in the cold mountains of Korea as a military advisor.

I have spent multiple Christmases in Hong Kong during shore leave, dining with the British Royal Green Jackets, the same British unit that once burned our Capitol.

I have had a life of full adventure and excitement enough to last me a lifetime. It was good to get this all behind me because now it was time to shift gears for a different kind of lifestyle.

Except for the examples described above, my life could have been slightly boring. I appreciate the fact that my years, so far, have been filled with purpose and adventure—all good clean fun.

My Nevada connection started in 1972 when at the age of twenty-six, I flew over Lake Tahoe on the way to a military deployment at Naval Air Station, Fallon. I was so impressed by the flight over that beautiful alpine lake that I took time off to travel there and buy some land. I had never seen anything so beautiful before.

Years later, when my military travels were over, I found my way back to Tahoe, beginning an unsettled period of life. I was a single parent with a six-year-old son in tow, and my other two children were with their mother. I needed to find a second career, and I needed to find some stability because I had spent too much time traveling around the globe. By this point, I had lived or done duty on five of the seven continents. My priorities were changing quickly to things more domestic. No longer was I the number one priority, because there were now three children that took precedence. Lake Tahoe seemed like a fine place to settle and raise my family.

I lived in Tahoe with my son for seven years; then unexpectedly, my other two children came to live with us. Now my hands were really full. My new career took up way too much time, and I was frequently required to do mandatory overtime. During this wild ride, I met a Reno gal, and despite many hard lessons learned about marriage and relationships, I ended up with a new wife. I actually thought this marriage might work out. This Reno connection probably is the best way to answer my own question of "Why Nevada?" and why a community like Paradise Valley.

More specifically, why then, this part of Nevada?

My personal preferences were formed early on, with the old line that you can take a boy out of the country, but you can't take the country out of the boy. I knew that I wanted to retire to a ranch somewhere. I wanted that ranch to be a beautiful, remote, and special place. I wanted this location to be agreeable to not just myself but my wife as well—in case she stayed around.

By the end of 2004, I'd heard about a place called Paradise Valley. My wife's cousin had married into a Basque family that owned a large parcel of property in the valley. Their property was in the mountains rather than on not the valley floor. By the spring of 2005, Becky and I had our first opportunity to visit this thousand-acre spread, complete with a large comfortable lodge.

The beauty discovered during this single trip was all the introduction I needed to this region; I did not need to look further. In retrospect, this weekend visit was the turning point that motivated me to pursue land in this general area.

Before the summer season hit, I had hooked up with a fellow named Eddie out of Winnemucca, who was about to help me find the right spot. He showed me all the local options. By August of 2005, I'd made an offer on this seventeen-plus acre parcel.

It did not take many years of living in Nevada to realize that this is a wild and independent state. It likes to do things—such as gaming, prostitution, embrace less restrictive laws—its own way. Moreover, Nevada has plenty of wild and wide-open places. I like the different attitude about doing business and protecting certain lifestyles, even if we are the only state on this path. I like the free-thinking, if not stubborn, approach of the old native Nevadans. I married into one of these older Nevada families, and at that point, I was pretty well hooked on Paradise Valley.

Fortunately, my wife and I shared similar likes and dislikes. We were looking for paradise, and by golly, we found it.

Now let's take a closer look at what I need to accomplish at this location because I have a lot of work ahead and not much time to get things done.

For land that was only purchased last fall, the spring challenge is to get started with development. I have had the winter to think, plan, and sketch.

This property came with electric power and a reliable two-hundred-forty-five foot well. The power line to my property is the next to the last connection on the power grid. My only neighbor to the north is without grid power, and he likes it that way. As I took ownership of this land, I needed to make minor repairs for both the power source and the water source. As a condition of sale, I did have a water sample tested. The report came back positive with a side note that I would no longer need to take iron supplements because my well would provide all the iron my body might need.

The first task was infrastructure development. Based on lessons learned from my previous house construction experiences, I knew the importance of building the shop/storage shed first. This shop was critical for storage, keeping tools out of the weather, and for staging all the stuff needed to build a ranch home. With this priority clearly in mind, I set out to find a contractor who could do the work.

Thanks to a winter where snowfall was unusually plentiful, the start of spring was pushed into mid-April. Closer to Reno, the weather measuring station near Mt. Rose Summit reported over thirty-five feet of fresh snow after March 1st. This apparent record is also reflected in the snow-capped mountains to my west and north. This year's snowpack was significant, and therefore, the spring and summer watershed will be plentiful.

ᴧᴧᴧ ᴧᴧᴧ ᴧᴧᴧ
ᴧᴧᴧ ᴧᴧᴧ ᴧᴧᴧ

As of April 23rd, I managed the first symbolic step to building my forty-foot by fifty-foot shed. On this date, my near neighbor, Joe, was scheduled to move dirt with his large vintage caterpillar. Unfortunately, shortly before that date, Joe had an industrial accident on the ranch where he works, resulting in four broken bones and a foot the color of a purple Nevada sunset. Because of this misfortune and mistiming, Joe's sore foot was not capable of pushing the heavy foot pedals on the old cat.

We cut a hole in the wire fence separating our two properties so that the cat could get to my job site. This shortcut also kept us out of trouble with the county road people, who wouldn't like to see cat tracks scarring up the dirt-gravel county road. Eventually, this shortcut trail was cleaned up, and we even installed a fancy gate separating our two properties.

Despite the injury setback, Joe fired up the old diesel engine. Against this loud backdrop, Joe barked out basic instruction as to which of the eleven levers and pedals did what. Unfortunately, the diesel noise drowned out his words. I tried to look attentive, although his coaching was now just a matter of lip reading. Little did I know that after five minutes of coaching, Joe was going to turn this 1940 bulldozer over to my control; it felt a little bit like my first flight in a CH-46 helicopter, lots of noise, and many controls to figure out. This preliminary step took Joe only ten minutes.

This experience took me back to 1969 when my flight school instructor handed me the controls of a military helicopter and told me to hover without cutting down any trees nearby. The only two significant differences were weight and speed. This cat was constructed out of heavy steel and therefore weighed just a little bit less than Mount Rushmore. The good news is the fact that at top speed, you can outwalk this slow and heavy machine. How could I go wrong?

Joe came along for the ride as I started the trek across a streambed and through the sagebrush. I found the task reasonable until I decided to engage the front dozer blade. Blade control proved to be the challenge. In learning blade control, I managed to carve out some waves in the ground. Sometimes my blade went too deep, and sometimes I could see air between the bottom of the blade and the brown earth. So once again, I was learning something new. Running this cat was not just a task, but a new mini-adventure.

Joe then showed me how to skim off the sage growth from its ground anchor. He explained that I needed to remove this vegetation; otherwise, it would prove to be bad for ground compaction and the future of my shed/shop cement floor. By this time, his sore, broken foot was done for the day. Now it was my turn to wrestle this large yellow and rust-colored machine.

Seven and a half hours later, Joe came back to check my progress. For the most part, I took a sizable off-camber building site and made it level, not counting a few ground waves that reflected my skill learning curve. In the course of the workday, the weather shifted from a cool flannel shirt morning to a tee-shirt midday, to an ominous late afternoon dark storm cloud that provided both a small electric show as well as a mild rainfall. Judging from the amount of heavy metal in this cat, I had to assume that I was the best lightning rod around. Since I did not see any lightning strikes closer than the Old Mill Ranch, I gambled and continued to work. At this point in my life, I had gotten pretty good at risk-taking.

Caterpillar Work

Joe promised that if his foot recovered a bit, he would put a finishing touch to my dirt work the next day, as the contractor demanded a smooth surface before he started work the following week. However, Mother Nature was in control, and the next day's work was rained out. What was nice looking level dirt on Sunday night was gumbo mud on Monday morning. Just a mild setback while we wait for some sunshine to dry us out.

As the first hard labor was now underway, I had time to contemplate the significance of my age as I undertook this large ranch development project.

Ironically, the previous week, public radio did a segment on the effects of age on activity and quality of life. The surprising findings included the fact that people in their 60's and 70's are not retiring to the rocking chair, but undertaking new activities and new challenges. I am part of the boomer generation and fit this age bracket. I seem to be living the life they described.

Now is the ideal time to add Burt Munro to my story. Burt has long been a hero and inspiration. The common ground here is age and the art of motorcycling. At age sixty-eight, Burt set a new land speed record at the Bonneville Salt Flats in Utah. He traveled all the way from New Zealand with his 1920 Indian Scout. What started as a 600 cc motorcycle was fine-tuned for twenty years before he went to Bonneville. So, what began as a 600 cc bike ended up much larger, but still inside the 1000 cc class and below.

All of the workmanship was a credit to the owner, not some fancy racing team. While the bike was actually forty-seven years old at the time of the world record, it had undergone many changes which were behind its ability to set a land speed mark of one-hundred-eighty-four miles per hour. Someone once said that there was a common factor between the owner and the motorcycle, "rough on the edges, but purpose-built."

What I like about Burt is his overriding philosophy that a person does not have to slow down due to old age. Some of you may remember this story because it became a movie by the name of the *World's Fastest Indian*, starring Anthony Hopkins. If you did see the film, you couldn't help but fall in love with the main character.

Similar to Burt, I had a passion for motorbikes. I spent around twenty years racing dirt bikes in what was called the Enduro (Endurance) Event, a long-distance race over rough terrain going fast and nearly beating yourself to death. I never set any speed records, but I did have lots of good clean fun racing in the dirt. This is where my friend Steve Hyde and I met.

The most important factor in my life at age fifty-nine is the fact that for the first time in my life, I have an opportunity to do what I want rather than worry about working to make a living. In the back of my mind, I always thought that I exemplified the image of a conforming and hard-working government worker. Deep down inside, I knew that I was actually a free-spirited devil, with a personality and style somewhere between Jimmy Buffett and Ernest Hemingway. Now perhaps in this new setting, my hidden nature will have a chance to come to the fore. Maybe this book project will also help with self-analysis.

As part of this free-spirited philosophy, I did find some connection to a sign that I noticed at the annual Burning Man Festival. The sign said the following:

Life's journey is not to arrive at the grave safely in a well-preserved body, but rather to skid in sideways, totally worn out, shouting "Holy shit, what a ride."

What one would hope for is the luck and opportunity to live a long healthy, and productive life. The key here is living a life with quality-of-life components. In my mind, this project and the ability to work this project is now the key quality-of-life indicator for me.

Recently, while visiting the local saloon, I chatted with two older residents, and they asked about my age and background. Both seemed to think that fifty-nine was pretty damn young to be retired. That perspective helped my psyche a bit. These two gentlemen had between ten and twenty years on me, and they looked like they were going strong. There is hope here.

The phase of life that comes to mind here might be called "turning the corner." I do consider that there is a normal psychological transition period as a person moves from a working routine to a retirement routine. In my case, developing a ranch from scratch should not be confused with retirement. There are financial factors and other matters that need to be adjusted before this corner is completely turned. I am still making that turn, and I hope to finish turning this corner over the next year.

~~~ ~~~ ~~~
~~~ ~~~ ~~~

While I turn this corner, with a thousand things on my mind, I also contemplate a decision on a job offer from DynCorp International. They are running a program where they match recent law enforcement personnel with police training in Iraq and Afghanistan. The program is designed to aid in the rebuilding process for those countries that were ripped apart with recent warfare and internal strife. Now, with all the other things on my plate, I need to resolve this decision. At a time like this, I wonder what Wendell Berry would do?

I have long admired this gentleman for his works and his philosophy. Berry is an American novelist, poet, essayist, and farmer—emphasis on the farmer. In 1965 Berry, his wife, and two children moved to a farm they had just purchased in Arkansas. My property is on the west bank of Martin Creek. His property is on the western bank of the Kentucky River. Their, Lane's Landing, is one-hundred-seventeen acres. In addition to raising some grain crops, he also raises Border Cheviot sheep. Since that farming start, he resided at that location and wrote extensively. He produced twenty-five books of poems and eleven novels. He was once asked if his farm was a full-time endeavor, he replied, "No, but it is a full-time concern." I trust his judgment. Given my current situation, I am confident he would tell me to stay focused on what I have started and not start chasing some crazy idea that may have an unknown outcome.

~~~ ~~~ ~~~
~~~ ~~~ ~~~

This chapter on getting started has a family parallel. I think back to my Norwegian grandfather and how he started his North Dakota homestead from scratch. He began on a piece of prairie with limited resources. I spent time on this homestead, so I know how it ended up, but I have no idea of the tasks involved in turning that prairie into a functional farm.

Recently a wise man explained to me that our brains were capable of remembering one hundred trillion things, ranging from trivial details to major events. Thinking back to my childhood living on a subsistence homestead, I have three distinct memories, even though I was very young. The first one was that my tough grandmother was capable of the loudest burps I have ever heard. She seemed proud to make so much noise with a bodily function. She never excused herself after a loud burp because I think she was proud of the sound she made.

Second, my grandfather took a nap after each midday meal—called dinner at the time. When he woke up, he would sit on the edge of his bed and rub his temples, which seemed to be his way of rousing himself to a fully awake state.

Third, my grand-parents enjoyed a loving and peaceful marriage. I only saw them argue once every four years. This argument would start when my grandfather would tease his wife that he had just canceled out her vote on election day. He was a Republican, and she was a Democrat. This taunting made her angry, and they'd clash for most of the day. The next day, everything was back to normal.

These memories were part of that one hundred trillion capacity—many other things I have long forgotten.

~~~ ~~~ ~~~
~~~ ~~~ ~~~

The big change that needs to be dealt with is the one of personal freedom; to simply do today what I want to do rather than what I need to do. Clearly, quality of life has an influence here. As one example, I used to be in a position where I would have to budget time to allow for a daytime jog. Now today, I can jog any time I want to. Working on the ranch, I find that I do more than enough physical activity, so there is little need for a daily jog. I will strive to do whatever is required to maintain this lean and mean one-hundred-seventy-five-pound body. I have here-to-fore put in too many miles and hours of exercise to let conditioning slip away now.

Soaring Bird

Personal habits are another example of freedom and discretion. I have long appreciated a good beer, but my work routine made sure that this pleasure was reserved for later in the evening. Now that I live a new life, I have no qualms about opening a beer with my lunch if the urge is there—beer, life's little reward.

Living to age fifty-nine has taken a toll on my body. Following some hard physical training on the heavy punching bag, the tendons in my left shoulder became sore; this caused some range of motion problems and loss of strength needed in those times when I must lift something over my head. Also, I must rely on my daily thyroid medication to make up for the fact that my thyroid was removed over a year ago. Everything else seems to be in good working order.

Relative to the age issue, Thoreau started his time at Walden when he was just under twenty-eight years of age. Perhaps more important in this comparison, Thoreau made his move partially in response to the early and unexpected death of his brother. He felt that the time in the woods would be good for his mental healing. My comparison point is that we are all healing from something.

Further, Thoreau complained that in his thirty-some years on the planet, he had yet to hear the first syllable of valuable or even earnest advice from his seniors.[1] While there is some merit in this broad statement, I must admit that there have been a handful of wise, mentor-like figures in my life that have offered valuable advice.

In most cases, this was career advice and applied more to the work-life than personal life. I agree that it is difficult to find quality mentors in today's world; mentors in the sense of a senior learned person taking another younger person under his wing for teaching and coaching. I always thought that mentoring was underrated.

Even in my own family, my children had no great-grandparents to coach them through life lessons or common-sense approaches to the world. My grandparents were long gone before my first kid was a twinkle in my eye.

Age also affects how one person judges the location where someone lives. In the case of my creekside property, my children seem to indicate that the tedium (boredom) and ennui (discontent due to lack of activity) of this lifestyle are not appealing to them—I've had this property for nearly a year, and the first visit is still pending. However, as I later found out, it is best not to make judgments regarding how others might think. Over time, all my kids took a liking to this ranch.

So unlike Henry Beston, who was thirty-six when he wrote his story, or Sue Hubble, who was in her early fifties, a period that she described as the "afternoon of her life," I, in comparison, am older than those authors of similar accounts.

2: ELEMENTS OF NATURE

THE SUN

The sun is not only the center of the universe as we know it, but it serves as the center of the natural cycle, this ritual of natural events happening over and over again. These things happened even before a mining camp turned into the mining town of Queen City. In the 1880s, in the foothills immediately north of my place, sat a mining operation. This man-made operation was big enough and prosperous enough to justify the creation of a small city. As quickly as it began, the gold and silver ore ran out, and the town of Queen City disappeared.

What did not disappear is the "China Wall," also known as China Grade. The China Wall is a rock reinforced road, turned jeep trail, which runs along the foothills of what the map calls the Red Hills. The Chinese laborers that worked the mines also had time to put down rock retaining walls that marked the down-slope side of the road. This was well-engineered, as those reinforcements have held up for well over one hundred years. These roads provide one more avenue for me as I transition from my property up into the foothills of the national forest. At some point, I hope to have luck finding Spring City, another abandoned mining camp hidden back into the rocky foothills.

The sun provides the color palette to paint these foothills. Red becomes more apparent and richer as spring turns to summer. This color splash deepens with the sunset sun angle. The volcanic rock reflecting the sun's rays provides the very color of its formal geographic name.

As I write in mid-July, my reverence for the sun seems to change. In the winter, I tend to appreciate every small ray of sunshine, yet now that summer is upon me, the opposite is true. During the longest days of the year, I spend time looking for shelter from the sun. As I write this on July 18th, 2006, Reno set an all-time heat record of 104 degrees. While it is not that hot here, it has become a reality that I work around the heat of the day and run for shelter during the hottest hours.

WATER

Water is the earth's most essential element. Mark Twain once said, "whiskey is for drinking; water is for fighting." The value of water was established early on with the first white settlers.

According to local legend, the earliest settlers in this region were generally Basque sheepherders. They often took control of the valued water sources, and many of the claims established then are still in place today. A review of the thriving ranches in this valley will find that most are situated along the dominant creeks—Martin, Cottonwood, Hanson, and Singus.

If a newcomer showed up in this valley and tried to acquire water rights, he would be well over a hundred years too late. These days, when a property sells—which is rare—water rights come with the land purchase. The irrigation canal running through my property is a good example. This water is not available to me, but instead is headed downhill to one of the early established ranches, closer to town. Conventional wisdom agrees that the value of water will only increase over time.

While this locale has sufficient water, there seems to be a constant quest for a water grab. For example, cities like

Las Vegas want to export our rural water to their urban setting. There is an old saying that water will run uphill or downhill if there is enough money at the other end.

Except for the remnants of a rock dam, upstream on Martin Creek, it appears this valley has had little traffic save for the cattle drives up and down this canyon area. The local saloon has a framed photo on its wall showing the people and setting of old Queen City, kind of like a proof positive that it actually did exist once upon a time. I believe the Queen City photo was taken around 1879.

So, while this mining town disappeared, the beauty that surrounded it remains. The sharp rocky cliffs on this section of the creek look like a scene pulled out of the adventures of John Wesley Powell on the Colorado River. The terrain is rough and imposing; the first time Becky and I tried to explore upstream to the north, we ran out of trail. At this point, the only things left were the tall rocky walls with the stream running through.

Not willing to give up easily, I decided to explore further upstream. My only avenue forward was to enter the stream that was three- to four-feet deep and progress up-canyon. This is where I first encountered what is left of the mining camp rock dam. My neighbor John has an out-of-print history book with an artist sketch of this same dam. Given its remote location and difficult terrain, this dam structure was quite an accomplishment. It should also be a credit to the hard-working Chinese mine workers at the time.

The miners knew then what most Nevadans now know today that water is valuable. This story is about to play out as water-thirsty Las Vegas tries to find a way to export or steal water from Northern Nevada—White Pine County and even Humboldt County. This fight has yet to be fully fought; the battle may continue until Las Vegas wins, but many believe that it is not a foregone conclusion.

Local "water masters" hold great power as they control water rights and regulate gauging stations to determine who gets what water and when. My property is intersected by an old water canal that belongs to my neighbors, the Buckingham's.

Nevada First also controls a large number of water rights. Nevada First is a large corporate ranch consisting of many smaller ranches now under one umbrella. My neighbor, who works for this large corporation, described their holdings as ranging from lumber in Oregon to feedlots in the midwest. So, while the nearby creek is full and flowing fast, the canal has but a trickle. Neighbors explain that later in the season, the water master will open the locks and the canal will start to fill up, and water will be shared with points further south in this fertile valley.

Not only is water the earth's essential element, but water is also the most vital natural element in this valley. For here, the value of your ranch or business is linked to your water rights as water is required for crop growth or whatever else you produce.

The water demand is seasonal. In the spring, when the creeks are brimming, the ranches may take as much water as they need; however, later, when the supply of water diminishes, a priority system kicks in. This priority system is based on water rights granted when ranch properties were established. The value of land is related to these water rights, and therefore, water rights are generally sold as part of the land purchase.

This system of water rights is based on the old system of first-come, first-served established in Spanish California in the colonial period and later placed into law in the State of Nevada.[1] This system of creeks, canals, and underground wells makes up for the fact that the average seasonal rainfall here is only seven inches. The local water table seems to be at a depth between two-hundred and three-hundred feet; my well is two-hundred-forty-five feet deep.

By May 11th, I noticed that the water flow in the canal receded to its normal flow. Thanks to this water source, running right through the middle of my property, I observe many birds as they enjoy the canal. This season I've seen mallard ducks, one wild turkey hen, and a large grouse on May 13th.

My neighbor Joe Sicking describes his second hay cutting, which usually happens in early July, as an indicator for the last of the creek and canal water. From this point on, he and others must rely on deep wells to irrigate the hay fields for a third and possible fourth cutting. These thirsty irrigation wells use a lot of water and run up hefty electric bills.

I've noticed that locals don't play in the water much. First, even though ranches often establish small ponds, we have few local lakes. Second, many consider that water is simply too precious to play in. Third, the heavy summertime workload doesn't leave much time to play in the water.

WIND

On the weather scale of one to ten, with ten being perfect weather, the two ingredients that generally determine what kind of day we'll have include sun and wind. If and when these two factors agree, we find many days at or approaching a ten.

Typically in the late afternoon, the wind blows up Martin Creek canyon, from south to north, creating what is known locally as the canyon breeze effect. In short, hot air is pushed up the canyon; it ends up at the top of the mountain range, and there it cools. Around dinner time, the wind is usually calm. After dark, around 9:00 p.m., the wind changes direction and blows cool air down canyon from north to south. This breeze often lasts until dawn.

As I plan out the details and function of my ranch house, I count on this breeze pattern to help naturally cool my home in the evenings. I have designed the extended roof overhangs, the awning-type windows, as well as the openable skylights as architectural features that might capture the cool evening air current.

EARTH

When this natural year story started, April 2006, the soil here was so saturated that it was hard to walk without gathering ever-increasing amounts of mud on your shoes. Now about a month later, May 13th, the earth has lost most of its topsoil moisture.

Except for the brief moisture from a few summer thunderstorms, the earth's crust will stay dry until the first snow of the winter season.

The ground here offers a wide variety as far as geography is concerned. I'm surrounded by mountains, rolling hills, high rock canyons, and meadows. The contrasts stagger the imagination. My house location, on the upper end of my property, sits on a rocky knoll, nearly surrounded by solid rock. Only in a few select locations can I find something close to ordinary clay soil.

Of particular interest is the local prominent geographic feature called Sugarloaf. It is positioned just past the high rock canyon where the creek transitions from the mountains to the meadow floor. Sugarloaf is even featured on most all of the geo-maps.

At first, I did not understand the significance of the name, but thanks to the new book edited by Barry Lopez and Debra Gwartney, *Home Ground: Language for an American Landscape*, I've learned the namesake dates back to the seventeenth century when American settlers purchased their sugar in the form of a rounded cake that rose to a point at the top.

Sugarloaf is an apt description of this rock formation that looks to me like a rough-edged chocolate Hershey Kiss.

Sugarloaf

VEGETATION: Holding It All Together

Three native plants characterize the natural vegetation in my front yard. They include sagebrush, bitterbrush, and rabbitbrush. These native shrubs are mixed together and have adapted very well to the local arid conditions. The most spectacular is the rabbitbrush when it produces stark yellow flowers.

This vegetation is prevalent throughout the valley and the foothills leading to the mountains. The only break in this pattern is when farming or ranching has cleared the brush for grass or irrigated fields. The native brush seems to have different descriptive words depending upon English words versus Spanish words. Bosk (English) describes small woods or thickets characterized by brushes or shrubbery. Bosque (Spanish) describes forest, specifically trees, "In the Southwest, the term refers to a riparian forest situated along a river."[2]

This brush pattern even exists in large parts of the National Forest. However, I suspect to find considerably more grass in the higher forest elevations due to the cooler temperature and the moisture from the snowmelt, the natural springs, and higher rainfall; mountain conditions produce more rain than what we find on the valley floor. The mountain grass is prominent enough to support cattle grazing all summer long.

When visiting the national forest, outsiders often ask, "Where are all the trees?" They are abundant in specific locations; however, it is clear that this is a forest essential for watershed and not for producing forest products. It is especially critical for local ranchers who rely on the U.S. Forest Service grazing allotments, so their cattle herds can thrive during the summer months.

The trees that do exist in the forest proper are mainly aspen and mahogany. The number of pine trees could probably be counted on two hands. The aspens favor the riparian areas where year-round springs, more common than one would think for arid Nevada, water them. The mahogany trees seem hardy and often prefer dryer ridgelines and rough terrain—the abundance of trees at the higher altitudes provide summer shade and fall colors.

The mountain conditions also favor a vast selection of native spring flowers. Purples and yellows seem to be the dominant colors during the wetter season. Most of these flowers are present until the summer heat knocks them down. The one exception to the purple and yellow would be the Indian paintbrush, which has a subtle red color that stands out amid the common sagebrush.

Whether it is the spring bloom or the fall colors, the wildflowers are spectacular enough that many people stop their cars so they can get out and enjoy them up close. I feel fortunate to have this spectacle right in my backyard.

As I have come to learn, the unique vegetation in this region is generally associated with riparian conditions. These are the select areas that provide the green in our terrain. Every valley or ravine has its own version of vegetation, probably dependent upon the amount of water flow in a given valley.

SOUND: An Often Overlooked Element of Nature

I find that one of my favorite aspects of nature is sound or the absence of it. My life experiences have shown me that sound illustrates one of the stark differences between city life and rural life. City life rarely offers that special reward of no sound. Inevitably one hears street traffic, air traffic—including local police helicopters—police and fire sirens, dogs barking, people noise, and the like.

These noises are worse in some spots. One of my good friends was recently featured on the front page of the Reno paper as some neighbors and he sought noise relief from city officials. This friend lives on the edge of the University system with its spread-out housing. They were concerned about college parties going late into the night, keeping them awake.

I could not help but reflect on the fact that I have noises to contend with also, but mine are good sounds like turkeys gobbling, coyotes howling, frogs croaking, water falling, and birds singing. I decided it would not be in good taste to tease my friend about the disparity we now experience.

By contrast, the rural sounds here are dominated by the sound of the wind, the roar of the waterfall below the property, and the song of birds. But the most apparent audio sensation happens when things are perfectly still, and there is no sound at all. I associate this sensation most often with early morning and after sunset. The sunset experience seems best of all as this is a favorite time to start a fire in the outdoor pit and listen to the crackle of fire embers.

Last evening, May 26th, I started a pit fire to get rid of some junk paper and cardboard items. These items included the latest mouse that I caught in a trap, some animal parts that my dogs drug home, paper products from the kitchen, and scraps of dead sagebrush that got pushed aside when I used the bulldozer to clean up my driveway. These materials provided a steady burn for over two hours. When I went to bed, I had a perfect circle of red-hot coals crackling in the quiet evening. The only competing sounds at that time came from the light canyon wind.

At this time of year, any light wind is a blessing as the mosquitoes can't navigate in those conditions and therefore do not bother me. I'm happy to report that the few mosquitoes from the spring did not last long, and thus caused only a brief annoyance.

Another unique feature of country life is the fact that sound can travel much further, perhaps due to less noise competition. Sometimes I hear motors starting up and even people conversing at the Old Mill Ranch, which is over a half-mile away. I can hear car traffic approaching from a long distance on the dirt road below my property. My dogs also follow this sound, and if the car starts to approach my driveway, they will bark to announce the arrival—this is about the only time my cattle dogs will bark.

Morning is a favorite time for reading and writing. The head is clear, the pace is slow, the coffee is kicking in, and things are generally peaceful. There is no urge to even turn on the radio until later in the day. Again, the beauty here is the sound of silence. Speaking about the "Sound of Silence," I see that tickets for the upcoming Paul Simon appearance in South Lake Tahoe can be purchased for as little as $57.75 or choice seats for $89.29. While being a lifelong fan of Rhyming Simon, my retirement income can no longer afford these modern-day prices for entertainment. I will just have to listen to the other sound of silence.

The first sound at dawn on May 27th was of light rain on the roof. The music at this very moment is a songbird—sounds like a meadowlark—to my right. The western meadowlark has a different sound than the eastern meadowlark. I cannot spot this particular bird, but I sure enjoy his song.

One other sound experience comes to mind. It is not uncommon to hear rifle shots, either during hunting season or as local ranchers practice their marksmanship. When that rifle sound is down in the slough bottom of Martin Creek, the echo effect, especially up the creek into the rock canyon, is quite interesting, for you will hear the shot approximately four to five times before the echo dissipates.

Also, the early spring brings the distant lowing of the cows in the green slough bottom. While these cows stay close to their home, other larger ranches have no choice but to push their cattle to higher elevations for mountain grazing. It appears that this move takes place around mid-May each year.

Yet I must confess that my above description of sound cannot match that of Thoreau:

> All sound heard at the greatest distance produces one and the same effect, a vibration of the universal lyre, just as the intervening atmosphere makes a distant ridge of earth interesting to our eyes by the azure tint it imparts to it.[3]

By June 6th, the night time sounds are a blend of waterfall noise—but less than last month—and the sound of the crickets and frogs from the creek bottom. These sounds are in perfect pitch and harmony as one does not drown out the other. Last night this sound combo was briefly interrupted by the distant sound of an overhead jet. Beyond that soft background of natural sounds is the perfect peaceful sensation of blissful silence.

As time has moved from early April to early June, I listen for and hear more songbirds.

Throughout the summer, the early evening sound comes off the creek bottom. Even though the water flow has diminished as summer unfolds, the sound of moving water is heard in the early evening. Cricket sounds continue to dominate throughout the summer.

About once a week, the primary sound in the morning is the coyote call. Sometimes this comes from the foothills to the northwest, and other times it comes from the creek bottom to the east. When the sound comes from the creek bottom, one bark call will sound like two calls because of the echo up the rock canyon. When my wife visited in early September, she told me that there were two coyotes out there. In fact, there was one call and a subsequent echo. In the case of this September experience, I used the binoculars to find the coyote in the meadow. It seemed rare to find him calling in the open. Most of the time, I can hear him but not see him.

These same coyotes like to visit the north side of my ranch property. I think they are looking for easy prey like a stray cat. As the coyotes wander the property, my cattle dogs are alerted and often go out to challenge them.

My first instinct was not to include any reference to sound as an element that I wanted to describe. I recently read an article by Bill Donahue in the AAA Traveler's Companion entitled "Stop, Look and Listen: Thrilled by Sights in the Natural World? To Double Your Pleasure, Focus on the Sounds Too."

This article described the naturalist by the name of Bernie Krause, who is noted as the foremost recorder of natural sounds. For four decades, he traveled the globe making tapes and CDs of songbirds and other sounds of nature. This effort includes over 3500 hours of natural sounds resulting in more than two million CDs sold.

As a related anecdote, in 2002, he was asked to weigh in on a Congressional consideration issue about allowing snowmobiles additional access to the Yellowstone National Park. Rather than talk to the subject, he simply played a recording of a ninety-five-decibel snowmobile followed by another recording of Yellowstone wolves, ravens, and winter wrens. Following that move, he asked the Congressional team, "Which do you prefer?"

It is estimated that more than thirty million Americans now suffer irreversible hearing loss, and the culprit for a third of these cases is noise. The magazine article mentioned above shared ten websites that offer up recordings of natural sounds from places like Glacier Point in Yosemite, Lamoille Canyon in Nevada, and the Main Trail at Muir Woods National Monument near San Francisco.

For the most part, this valley offers similar beauty with its natural soundtrack, with a possible exception of the sound of gunshots during the peak of hunting season.

WILDLIFE: The Real Element of Nature

On May 7th, I decided to take note of the birds along the dirt road to town. Just south of my property, I noticed one male mallard duck in the Sicking Pond. Across the road, sitting on the barb wire fence were three mourning doves. Two posts down was a single magpie, the black-billed version, not to be confused with the yellow-billed version. I once heard an interview with the singer-songwriter, Ian Tyson, who noted that Magpies mate for life.

As I turned the corner to the west, I observed a red-tailed hawk sitting on a post, and I, fortunately, took a photo before he flew off. A half-mile further, I spotted a large turkey vulture, similarly perched on a fence post. He also allowed me to snap a photo from a close range. In fact, this somewhat disheveled looking fowl refused to fly off, no matter how much commotion I made from the car window.

Unknown Hawk

I appreciated the contrast in style and grandeur between the hawk and the vulture. Along the way, I viewed numerous common birds such as the blackbird, another mourning dove, the common crow, and more ever-present black and white magpies. In the subsequent weeks, the birds and I have repeated the staring contest many times, and consistently, the vultures prefer to stare me down rather than fly from their perch.

On my return trip home, I spotted additional hawks perched on the fence lines, and as I got closer to home, I noticed a large nest in the tree that overhung the county road. I thought that I spotted a head in the nest, so I stopped the car and backed up for a better angle. Sure enough, that activity on my part prompted the hawk to leave the nest for a safer sounding.

Finally, as I drove into my driveway, a single female California quail scampered across the road. A grumpy fellow from the nearby town of Paradise liked to complain that the quail had all left town. If that is true, they simply changed their location to my ranch; they seem to love rarely traveled Martin Creek Road below my property.

On May 24th, I first noticed the red-winged blackbirds. I spotted a group of about ten in my favorite bird area along the country road on the way to town. They commonly feed in the fields, pastures, and marshes from early fall to spring. These are helpful birds as they consume harmful insects during the nesting season. The *National Audubon Society Field Guide to Birds in the Western Region* list two types of red-winged blackbirds, and the one to which I refer wears the bright red color on each wing. The male's distinctive markings made them easy to spot and confirm who they were.

In this favorite bird area, I often see large size birds like the hawks and vultures, medium size birds like the doves and magpies, but to a lesser extent, the small birds, especially the songbirds.

As the spring season comes to an end, it is marked with the variegations of evening light before the cloudless sky of summer changes this pattern. The longer days and disappearance of the morning and evening chill also bring the extreme change of wet conditions to dry conditions. The wind and spring showers will soon be replaced with high-pressure systems that will keep the sky clear for days on end. The larger birds may now give way to the color and trills of the songbirds. The brilliant greens of the meadow to the east will start to yield to more summer-like yellow tones. I have spent my spring afternoons walking and observing the many wonders of my property as well as the neighboring properties.

I look forward to observing the elements and the change of the season, eagerly anticipating the wonders that will unfold.

3: GETTING ACQUAINTED

THOREAU'S ESSENTIALS

According to author and Thoreau scholar, Jeffrey Cramer, the account at Walden Pond began on the 4th of July with a journal quote, "Yesterday, I came here to live." Friday, July 4th, 1845, was a day of fair weather. The sun rose at 4:29 a.m. and set at 8 p.m. Thoreau mentioned that his house, not being finished for winter, was merely a defense against the rain. Another reference has Thoreau at his Walden location by March of 1845 so he can cut down trees for his house construction.

I intend to start my ranch house somewhere between summer and fall. Ideally, it would be nice to have the shell complete before the winter weather arrives, but this may prove to be a dream. My hand-drawn plans have progressed to approved blueprints, and soon it will be time to watch all of this go from paper to concrete and wood, or brick and mortar as they say.

I will forego Thoreau's long and philosophical first chapter. His reference to the cost of land and food a century-and-a-half ago would offer value little as the comparisons to the current day would be extreme.

Thoreau's philosophy seemed to focus on the four essentials or "necessaries" of life required in that New England climate. These four items included: food, shelter, clothing, and fuel.

The rest of his first chapter is a disjointed account of how he approached these subjects in his self-deprivation style of living. While his theory that "simple is best" makes perfect sense, I see no advantage in replicating his deprivation approach. Perhaps my age is a factor, as I'm approximately twice his age at the same point of reference, or perhaps different times have different values. In short, I have no intention of depriving myself.

However, I do find value in comparing topic matter, and I will add perspectives on these same four essentials as described by Thoreau.

Thoreau said an advantage would be found in living a primitive and frontier life, even if that advantage was only to get in touch with the gross necessaries of life and what methods have been taken to obtain them. His perspective, while focusing on the four topics mentioned above, gives evidence to his objective of experimenting with life. After all, he was still a young man.

The broader perspective on what I desired to accomplish can be summed up with the quest to answer the question of how to live in both nature and society while leading a moral life. The perception that Thoreau was just a hermit, living in a tiny cabin and subsisting off of berries and such seems to be off the mark. Direct accounts indicate that he was a social person.

He was also a poet before the fame of Walden. His first compilation of poems was published in 1943. He was also part of the transcendentalist movement in the nineteenth century. His journey and stay at Walden was an effort to go beyond the usual human knowledge or experience and to connect with the basic elements of nature and humanity. These constants are still relevant today.

As but one brief example of his poetic side, I found this sample poem:[1]

> It is no dream of mine,
> To ornament a line;
> I cannot come nearer to God and Heaven

Than I live to Walden even.
I am its stony shore,
And the breeze that passes o'er;
In the hollow of my hand
Are its water and its sand,
And its deepest resort
Lies high in my thought.

My only alteration above would be to replace the word/place of Walden with Martin Creek.

In contrast to this above poem, I have one that is much shorter. Envision a scene in rural England many years ago. The main character is the wife and mother of the Lamb family. At one point, without any explanation, she up and left the family farm. She was gone for many years. Then, all of a sudden, she reappeared at her previous home, again without any explanation.

The nearby neighbor was so disgusted with this story that he wrote the following poem. By many accounts, this may be the shortest poem ever written in England.

Doris Lamb
God Damn

Others may argue that the shortest poem in America, written by Strickland Gillian in the early twentieth century, for which I have no background, is called "Fleas."

Adam
Had 'em

FOOD
I attribute my slender build to both good genes and personal practice of eating when I get hungry as opposed

to a set routine of three meals a day. Additionally, I don't snack. When my regular working days came to an end, the first change was to hold back on breakfast to a point about mid-morning when I was most hungry.

Having never been a good cook, I find that my personal menu choices are minimal. Much of my diet is considered to be life-threatening by today's cholesterol standards. As I approach sixty years of age, I have little intent to give up my regular beer, my M&M candies, my cheeseburgers, and the assortment of grilled meats. I am eating to live rather than living to eat. As an example, I am working on a three-course meal as this chapter is being typed. This dinner consists of left-over meatloaf, baked beans, and a Budweiser, a perfect ranch meal in my book.

SHELTER

I sincerely envy every male brave enough and talented enough to build his own house. I do not have that skill and do not intend to learn now. Instead, I have worked hard to find likable contractors who can reasonably work with me to build everything from large sheds to my ranch house. I understand contractors add to the expense, but for me, it's all relative, just as Thoreau described his self-labor and his minimal cost to construct his one-room house.

On different occasions, Thoreau referred to his house as a cabin. Perhaps our experiences are parallel, as the design of my ranch house will be small and simple.

One aspect of Thoreau's that I intend to copy is the commitment to not posting a No Admittance sign at my property entrance. My new home is in a pleasant rural setting; good people will be welcome, and bad people will be shot.

Thoreau suggests that our homes should not provide an obstruction between ourselves and the celestial bodies. The house should provide shelter, but not to the point that we forget to sit out under the stars as much as possible.

Unlike Thoreau, I do intend to pay my taxes so that I do not end up in the local jail as he did, during July 1846, a year after his natural year started. My first full year tax bill before construction was $215.66, or less than $18 per month. However, my tax bill would soon change.

CLOTHING

I have built a wardrobe around typical blue jeans and boots. I have a weakness for Patagonia work shirts. This has as much to do with the company philosophy of Yvon Chouinard, the businessman that started Patagonia, as it does with the long-wearing nature of these shirts. This unusual business philosophy has been described in his book, *Let My People Go Surfing: The Education of a Reluctant Businessman.*

Whatever my attire, it never takes long for these work clothes to get dusty and dirty.

Thoreau made the argument that if a person was dedicated to hard labor, then he was forced to spend money on heavy-duty clothing. This extra expense then contributed to the cycle wherein the cost required even more work to pay for this additional expense. I am not sure how much logic there is in this line of thinking. For some, much work is required. For others, less work is required. For all, there is some requirement to get your hands dirty and your muscles sore.

I have reached a point in life where less work may be necessary. The trick now is to mentally accept this fact so that I do not feel guilty for those rare days when I purposely do very little physical labor.

I have one more lesson to share about clothing here. If and when a person works directly in the sun, it is more practical to wear a long sleeve shirt to protect the arms from too much sun. I've had success with lightweight blue denim shirts that breathe well, thus allowing the air to pass through the fabric.

FUEL

Fuel seems like a dirty word at present. Much of our country is up in arms about the recent increase in gasoline prices. This past week, the Reno newspaper recorded the average fuel price at $3.29.

Tree-huggers have an interesting perspective that the sooner these prices go higher, the better. Their theory is that escalating gas prices may speed up the priority development of alternative fuels. A recent CNN special, *We Were Warned: Tomorrow's Oil Crisis* paired two potential scenarios that might cause a drastic cut in the average production and refinement of gasoline.

The consequence of this combination—one a natural God-made disaster and the other a man-made act of terrorism—set the U.S. economy and the world economy back on its heels as $10.00 price per gallon of gas became responsible for a host of serious problems.

My first reaction to this T.V. show was one of discomfort and worry. My second reaction was that it might be good timing for a move to the country.

On a related note, my second closest neighbor, John, makes a point of telling and retelling the fact that he bought his piece of land immediately following the terrorist attacks of September 11th, 2001. Survival instincts remain strong in many of us.

This reference does not imply that I am a survivalist or doomsday prognosticator. It does mean that I feel a wee bit smug about the timing of world events and my move to the country.

Back to fuel, initially, I planned to maximize the solar features of my new home. However, in response to this plan, the alternative energy company threw a price tag of nearly $71,000 at me. This shock and surprise quickly killed this green idea. Once again, it looks like it takes money to save money.

The one idea that did survive the early planning scrutiny was the idea of a wood-burning stove. I lived in New England a while back, and since that time, I've been a fan of the New England stove company called Vermont Casting. I plan to purchase one of these expensive wood stoves as soon as the house is ready.

As mentioned above, I have every intention to use wood fuel to heat my house and keep my toes comfortable. However, later in the summer, I learned that I lost my woodcutting source, and this news prompted a switch from the planned wood stove to a pellet stove.

I had one additional thought regarding the parallels between Thoreau and myself. When Thoreau moved to Walden Pond, he was a relatively young man. Much of what he set out to do was part of a personal experiment in living style. In my case, there is an age difference compared to Thoreau, and I have no time for experiments, this is the real thing for me. I plan to stay at this location regardless of the good or bad things that might come of the next natural year.

CONSTRUCTION DELAYS

I learned long ago when I built my first house that the owner may have the best possible construction plan and timetable, but this does not provide much assurance that the weather will cooperate or that the subcontractors' help will be available when promised.

In the case of this first major project on Martin Creek, building my shop, the work started on June 9th.

After a full day of dirt moving progress, I encountered rain and mud. As that mess dried, my dirt-moving help evaporated with it, for even though he worked through his foot injury, his other ranch job beckoned him away.

Later, after finding that my site preparation did not meet muster, I consulted with neighbor Joe. He took a second turn at operating the bulldozer to better the building site and made wavy ground level again. My job during this first weekend in May was to finesse the final dirt-work steps—which mainly included watering and soil compaction—and most of one workday was spent on these two steps.

I am sorry to report that the only soil compaction tool at my disposal was my 2000 V.W. Jetta. While this may sound deficient, it did a good job as I drove mile after mile in small circles until the soil was as hard as pavement.

~~~ ~~~ ~~~
~~~ ~~~ ~~~

At this point in my stay here, I still struggle with a means of reliable communication. I have wireless internet access that beams my signal forty miles south so that I can connect with the rest of the world. I am out of cell phone range as the terrain is not friendly to cell signals. A phone service box sits at the edge of my property, but I have not yet had time to pursue that landline option. After the ranch house is finished, I will tend to this matter.

Over time, the communications did improve. I changed providers on my internet connection, and for some reason, the cell phone signal came in better at my ranch location. When I first arrived, you had to stand in one specific spot if you wanted reception.

When I do have an internet connection, I make an effort to check Elko Fire Weather to view the local weather forecast. Lately, the reports are about the same, partly-cloudy, chance of showers, cool at night (30s and 40s) comfortable during the day (60s and 70s). With weather patterns moving from west to east, we often have wind. Additionally, there is a wind pattern up or down Martin Creek depending upon the time of day. I am still trying to figure that pattern out. The canyon wind effect is perpendicular to the prevailing winds; thus, the most common wind pattern runs on a northeast to southwest line.

〜〜〜 〜〜〜 〜〜〜
〜〜〜 〜〜〜 〜〜〜

Finishing the site preparation is taking longer than expected, and therefore I may lose my place in line for the contractor who busily jumps from project to project. He has at least five shop or shed projects in this immediate neighborhood. As of May 12th, we still need to have the final leveling of dirt followed by spreading the rough gravel that has been trucked into my site.

Thus, the start of my first ranch structure continues to get delayed. As of May 23rd, I was still waiting for the contractor to bring his tractor tool to fine-tune the site work.

On May 24th, I found Dale, the contractor, and asked for an update. Due to add-ons to another shed project, he now expects a one-week delay to the end of May before he can start.

On this same date, while in town, I accepted an offer from Andy to tour his shed. His shed was the first one of five that Dale constructed. Also, on this date, another neighbor, Casey, told me that he expects Dale to build a covered hay shed on his place close to the Chevron station.

While all of this is going on, I learn that we have our first sales offer on the cottage home in old Reno. If this sells quickly, it will speed up the process of getting the ranch developed, especially the ranch house.

As I continue to wait for the building project to start, we have had mixed weather. This third week in May has been cooler than normal. On May 27th, nearby Winnemucca reported 38 degrees at 7:07 a.m. Snow is forecast, but as I look up towards the Santa Rosa range, I see no evidence of that yet. At this point in the year, our sunrise is at 5:23, and our sunset is 8:13. For those of us with mountains to the west, the actual sunset is a few minutes earlier. The morning temperature was cool enough to justify starting the heater. My dogs, cold and wet, looked relatively miserable this morning as they emerged from their large kennel.

CUTTING AND SPLITTING WOOD

Today was the first opportunity to cut firewood. First, I need to get permission and an access key to the property in Cottonwood Creek. My goal was to try to cut as much wood as possible before the summer heat made this too difficult.

Today, the temperature in the valley floor was around 83 degrees. The woodcutting site is at a higher altitude, and consequently, the temperature was closer to the mid-70s. In the shade of the mature aspens, this was perfect weather for cutting wood.

For nearly five hours, I switched back and forth from cutting wood to hauling it from the canyon floor to the side hill where the pickup and trailer were parked. Most of the work was associated with the wood hauling as opposed to the woodcutting. It took nearly five hours to cut and move enough wood to fill the trailer and the new wood hauling rack that has been installed since I did this chore last year.

I found a new woodcutting location that will produce more than enough wood for the next winter season. The excess firewood came from a dryki, an area where trees have been killed by flooding. This dryki resulted from the same flood sequence that damaged the Reno area in 1997.

The attraction of a tall dead aspen is that it has hardly any branches on the stem. It is similar to a new wood telephone pole, except for branches on the upper five to ten percent of the tree growth.

On the way to the creek bottom, I attempted to follow the existing brecha, the natural walking trail made by cattle, deer, or other animals. But often, these natural paths were blocked by fallen trees. It became impossible to drive more than ten yards without a roadblock. In today's cutting location, three large trees fell crisscross on top of each other.

By the end of the workday, I made many cuts in the larger downed trees so that in the future, I might be able to navigate my quad down into this deep creek canyon. Being able to bring the quad and quad trailer down to the valley floor will speed up the movement of the fresh-cut wood.

This entire upper creek section, closest to the mountain runoff, is a true bosque—a riparian forest adjacent to a body of water. Trying to determine which trunks are dry and which are wet makes for creative woodcutting. Wet wood binds the blade on the chainsaw.

My Stihl chainsaw continues to work wonderfully. The chain blade is sharp and speeds through even the thickest dry logs, some of which are almost two feet in diameter. These large segments create rounds so big that I could only carry one at a time to the trailer.

The road conditions to this site were terrible. Usually, the dirt and gravel roads into this Cottonwood property are in good shape, but this wet spring season changed things, leaving deep ruts in the road as well as strewing rocks and large boulders across the path.

I did not bring enough drinking water to keep up with my sweating. After running out of water by mid-afternoon, I decided to fill up my jugs with the natural waters of Cottonwood Creek, which tasted good and should be pure unless a dead cow lays upstream.

With the new side racks for hauling firewood, I could tell that this trailer load was hefty. To make matters worse, I threw in about two dozen pieces of smooth black slate. I am sure I will find a place for these slate pieces later on.

My youngest cattle dog, eleven months old, got lost because she didn't know how to navigate the fast-moving stream crossing. I drove ahead, thinking that all the dogs were close behind. However, I ended up going back to the stream crossing to encourage Rocky to make it across. In the meantime, the middle-age dog, Gruden, got lost at the Lodge turn around. By late afternoon, I managed to have all three dogs back safely under my control, along with my trailer full of wood.

The drive from my property to the Cottonwood Creek property is only 16 miles, but the rough roads turn this into a trip that takes 45 minutes to cover the distance.

On the drive home, I watched and photographed a cock and a hen pheasant. The male had a brilliant red crest that glowed every time the sun illuminated his head. As he walked into and out of the sage shade, the color contrast was striking. My camera was always one step behind when this bright, vibrant red flashed. By the time the shutter clicked, he was back into the shade of the sagebrush.

By the time I got home, my feet were sore and freshly blistered, and I was hungry. I skipped lunch for the sake of work progress, and dinner time did not come around until 8:30 p.m. Nothing is better than good food and drink following a day of hard labor.

Since I am hungry and the sun is setting, I offload this fresh-cut wood for tomorrow.

～～～
～～～

On June 6th, I offloaded the wood from yesterday. I was now on my second consecutive day of woodcutting. I learned a few lessons from yesterday. First, bring more water than you could possibly think you'd drink. Second, wear comfortable footwear suited for all of the hiking required. And third, just cut and stack the wood on site. Later I can figure out a plan for getting the quad and the new quad trailer down into the deepest part of the creek bottom that supports the dense growth of mature aspens.

The only wildlife that I scared up while cutting wood in the creek bottom was one female deer that heard me searching for fresh wood. She jumped the creek and headed south along the steep creek bank.

It is tough to call this work as the shady aspen site is as pretty as any place in Nevada. For some reason, I found no mosquitoes in the north and west end of the valley. Davy, another neighbor, confirmed this as he said his nearby ranch hardly ever has mosquitoes. I asked him if there was any explanation for this, and he did not know of any. Just lucky, I guess.

As mentioned, the conditions are near perfect. The temperature is in the 70s. The tall aspens shade the creek bottom. The three dogs are my constant companions. I work, and they watch. Today I had company as a neighbor, Davy, stopped by on his quad. We ended up with a real dog gathering. I had three cattle dogs, and he had seven long hair ranch dogs.

Davy took the time to explain the local procedures for dealing with Mormon crickets, a local pest. Not only do these crickets devastate crops, but they also make the roads slick when too many of them get squished in one area. Apparently, the county sets out poison bait that kills them off. I'll talk more about these pests later.

When I got home around 6:30, my body was tired and sore, the good kind of sore body after an honest day of hard labor. This condition called for a shower in my new outdoor shower stall. There is something special to shower outdoors.

ᴍᴍ ᴍᴍ ᴍᴍ
ᴍᴍ ᴍᴍ ᴍᴍ

Based on two days of woodcutting, I decided that I need to place an order on the internet for the heavy-duty trailer to tow behind my quad. The one I have picked out should be ideal for moving the wood from the cutting site to the road on the top of the creek embankment. I hope this will save many hours of humping two rounds at a time up the steep bank to the awaiting trailer.

On the third day of dedicated woodcutting work, I took advantage of the high cloud cover to use that as shade to split the 206 wood rounds that were cut and hauled two days earlier, and I put to use a new hydraulic log splitter. The tool proved to be easy to use and efficient. Twenty-seven tons of hydraulic pressure takes care of the most stubborn aspen round. On the first afternoon, I enjoyed the novelty of the work and managed to split my way through nearly half of the three cords.

Log Splitter

Though I was used to working alone—my wife spent her time in Reno working on her business startup—

splitting would go even faster if I had two sets of hands, one moving the wood and one at the hydraulic controls of the splitter. However, the splitting of wood rounds was totally on me.

The woodcutting for 2006 took place on June 5th and 6th, and round splitting took place on the 7th and 8th. I ended up with a row of stacked wood four feet eight inches high, eighteen feet long, and eighteen inches wide, the width of a single log.

Yet I am motivated to have more than enough wood ready for winter wood-burning, and so I will return to Cottonwood Creek this fall to cut more rounds.

ᗰᗰ ᗰᗰ ᗰᗰ

On June 9th, I returned to the woodcutting site. Today was another cut and stack day of work. I continue to work my way deeper into the creek bottom, where the best deadwood is located. Because of the density of the aspen growth, both dead and alive, it is necessary to cut through large logs on the ground so that the quad can move around for wood collecting. As of today, I have cut my way through a couple of hundred yards of heavy timber. This advance puts me at the creek crossing. Right now, the creek flow is subsiding from the heavy spring flow; however, the creek is still about fifteen yards across.

The motivation to continue clearing this new quad trail is the fact that there are dozens of downed trees on the other side. It is expected that in seven to ten days, the quad trailer should be delivered. When it does arrive, I should have at least two trailer loads of firewood to move. I believe that I should have up to four loads of wood on hand before this cutting season ends.

I concur with the sentiments of Thoreau when he said, "Every man looks at his wood-pile with a kind of affection. I love to have mine before my window, and the more chips, the better to remind me of my pleasing work."[2]

Although I only worked four hours today, this kind of labor does take its toll on this old body. It is both the task and the sore muscles that help make this a rewarding chore.

The lesson learned here is this; cutting wood is a lot of work; buying pellets is less work. Eventually, my source of ranch house heat would be pellet stoves and gas logs. I still had the wood-burning stove in my shop, so all of my hard labor wood was put to use.

Before I set out on the woodcutting today, I walked my property and tried to be creative in how to water the few surviving trees left behind by the prior property owner. I have located two lilacs and one peach tree that survived with no care and little water. Rather than drag a five-gallon water bucket over distance, I strapped a fifty-five-gallon plastic water jug on the front rack of the quad. Not sure about supporting that much weight—up to 413 pounds with a full barrel—I decided to start with a half barrel.

Despite our wet winters and the spring runoff, I do not understand how any tree can survive on this west bank during the dry season of summer and fall. Between two and three times per week, I water these few survivors. According to the family that previously owned this property, these few surviving shrubs and trees actually lasted five years with no care or water outside rainfall.

OIL RESERVES

On June 8th, 2006, the first oil revenue check arrived by mail. Oil revenue is unanticipated money from my father's farm, where he retained the mineral rights after he sold the land. This decision paid off as a wild cat oil company did an exploratory well during this past winter. This first well was located on the farm where I grew up and used the very site where we had a water dam built, my childhood summer swimming hole.

Because these exploratory wells cost around $3.5 million, it is safe to assume that their seismic efforts are well-calculated risks. As of March 7th, 2006, we knew that this well was a good producer with one-hundred-fifty barrels per day output. Due to oil well protocols, a few months passed before the monthly checks arrived.

When the first revenue projection came in by phone, the international price of oil was just over $50 per barrel. The last time I checked, this price had increased to $72.29 per barrel. While this sounds good, the reality is that oil is a commodity, and commodities fluctuate vastly in price.

This revenue example is just one in a series of pleasant surprises in my life. When I considered going to Iraq as a police advisor, the tax-free income was advertised at $127,600 per year. Yes, it will take sixty-five or sixty-six monthly payments to make up for this lost salary, but my life expectancy will be greater. This new oil news made the decision much easier to say thanks, but no thanks to DynCorp International.

I calculate that this monthly surprise oil income may help cover the new ranch house mortgage, kind of like someone up there is looking after me.

Eventually, the horizontal (straight down) system of drilling will be replaced with the new style of drilling, where they drill down two miles, then branch out horizontally for another couple of miles. While this improves the volume of oil drawn from the ground, it also increases the cost to drill a well by three-fold. This newer system is called fracking.

CONSTRUCTION BEGINS

As of June 9th, 2006, my wait for the first day of construction is over. Around 9:30 a.m., I heard my dogs signal the arrival of company. Three vehicles approached, carrying the construction team. Dale was accompanied by a work crew of two other fellows.

On this first construction day, they leveled the gravel, dug the post holes, and received delivery of materials. The original projection was that this construction project should take around three weeks for completion, with a target date at the end of June.

Dale indicated that the building site was not level because the southeast corner of the building site displayed a sixteen-inch drop from the opposite corner. He dragged extra gravel to that corner to help level it. He said that he might have to order additional gravel from Dennis Heitman, the go-to-guy when it comes to delivering gravel or other dirt material.

Flattening the Building Site

With the help of the post hole digger on the back of his orange Kubota tractor, they dug eighteen post holes, each sixteen inches wide and around two to three feet deep. Scanning these new holes, I begin to envision the size and shape of the future structure.

It is clear in my mind that this modest beginning is a reason for joy because this marks the real beginning of my ranch infrastructure. The delay of five weeks only makes this new start date more special. Upon going to bed this evening, my thoughts were on this progress step and the joy that goes with this humble beginning.

As darkness starts to set in tonight, a storm cloud moves from west to east over the Santa Rosa range. This cloud does not take up the entire sky but leaves a low sun angle so that the low light creates a beautiful rainbow, in fact, a complete double rainbow. The law of physics dictates that the rainbow angle must be opposite the sun at forty-two degrees from the observer. This rainbow was set on the east bank canyon rocks and the adjacent foothills. Its glorious color display marked the end of the day.

⁓⁓⁓ ⁓⁓⁓ ⁓⁓⁓
⁓⁓⁓ ⁓⁓⁓ ⁓⁓⁓

On Saturday morning, June 10th, the sky was clear, and the air was moist from last evening's two rain showers. While I type, I wait for the sun to warm up the east windows. On my left, a medium-size young jackrabbit explores my driveway. He seems nervous and fidgety as he paces back and forth. By this point, he is aware that my three dogs are close by somewhere. What Mr. Rabbit does not know is that these dogs are fond of sleeping in on chilly mornings.

Looking past the rabbit to the southwest, I see the snow-capped mountain range. The snow cap is slowly melting off, but the top one thousand feet of elevation is still about half white, especially on the north-facing angles where the shade helps protect the snowpack.

I did some casual chores around the property for most of the morning. Later I re-marked the footprint layout of the ranch house and the bathhouse. I want to have this ready for when the contractor, Roy, comes out for his first look. I also have indicated locations for the septic system and the L.P. gas tank.

Yesterday I picked up one free tomato seedling from the post office. Today, I planted it in the vicinity of the beach located along-side the canal in a rich flat spot. I picked this location because it is next to the canal water, and afternoon shade protects it from the hottest part of the day. I configured a wire cage to protect it and used some nice topsoil I found close by. It will be interesting to see if this tomato reaches maturity before the completion of the R.V. shop. If this spot works out, I will plant more tomatoes there next spring.

By mid-afternoon, I decided that I had done enough work for a Saturday. It has been a couple of days since I took the time to give the dogs a good run. With this in mind, I jumped on the quad, gave the signal for the dogs to head in the right direction, and we were off. I drove fast to the point where Martin Creek is compressed between the two rock canyon walls.

I decided to try my first creek crossing of the season. I could see the bottom and calculated that today was a good day to give it a try. The current was still strong, as it started to sweep my quad sideways. The water depth was between two and three feet deep. I got separated from my dogs at this point. It took fifteen minutes before we all found one another.

On the drive back, I noticed a bird that warranted closer attention, perched on a fence post. I did not know the name of the bird, so I took mental notes and researched my Audubon reference book as soon as I returned home.

I am quite sure that this bird was the western kingbird. Its two dominant features were the soft grayish/brown colors on the top and chest and a soft and subtle yellow on the lower breast. The reference book description seemed to match on all counts to include the olive-brown above and the yellow below. The voice is described as a loud and sharp "kit." They like open country, ranches, roadsides, streams, and ponds with trees. Martin Creek offers all of this.

Western kingbirds are found on nearly every ranch in the West, where alfalfa and livestock pastures provide many of the flying insects that make up the bulk of its diet.

WILDLIFE WHILE WOODCUTTING

By late morning on 11 June, I decided to continue my woodcutting, my fourth day of dedicated cutting. So far, I have worn out three chainsaw blades.

On the way to Cottonwood Creek, I stopped to observe the large number of birds hunting in and around the irrigated sweet clover field southwest of the Sicking Ranch. Included in the group was one large, totally white, and very impressive great egret sitting in the sprinkler path. This bird looked like he was in heaven with this location and water source. I also saw six red-tail hawks sitting on the irrigation lines and a single turkey vulture. A bit further on, I found mature wild turkeys sitting in a close-by field.

Closer to the woodcutting area, I noticed a bird new to me, and I was able to observe it up close. Since I was not sure what I was looking at, I took field notes and later confirmed in the Audubon Field Guide that this was a male chucker. I have noticed female chukars before, but not the colorful male. All of the locals in the valley recognize the chukar without the help of a guide book, but I am new here and still learning.

The chukar that I observed had remarkable coloration. The first striking feature was the red bill and the same color across both eyes. He also wore a Zorro-like black mask across the eyes, which blended into the body. The rest of the feather colors were a muted olive-brown. The next distinguishing feature became apparent with his side profile. He had prominent black and chestnut stripes on the wings.

According to the Audubon source, this bird is best known for its loud call. The chukar has been successfully introduced to the West from the dry Mediterranean area of southern Europe. He is a hardy bird and able to outrun most natural hunters. Outside the breeding season, they move about in coveys of up to forty birds. In this instance, I spotted a male bird, and no females were visible. This bird seemed larger than the standard thirteen- to fifteen-inch size. The chukar favors the rocky, arid hillsides and canyons; the geography in this valley is a perfect match. When you hear locals talk about bird hunting, they're most often referring to chukar season, which runs from fall until the end of January.

Eleven days remain until the official start of summer. It looks like I can be assured of some visible construction progress by that turning point.

CONSTRUCTION RESUMES

On June 12th, the construction work crew returned for day number two. Today's crew consisted of three. Most of their effort was spent breaking through rocks in the post holes to ensure the holes would attain a depth of three feet. They also set string-markers to layout the post lines. The crew chief pulled the lumber from the bound pallets and stacked it in neat piles. The lumber consists mainly of two-by-six planks, pressure-treated six-by-six support posts, and a couple of pallets of OSB plywood boards. At mid-morning, a flat-bed trailer dropped off the larger forklift.

After a brief trip to Reno for supplies, I returned home to find good progress on the R.V. shop; progress included eighteen six-by-six pressure-treated poles planted in the ground. Now for the first time, the size and shape of the large building become apparent.

Hand made trusses are constructed on the ground so that they can be placed across the four-center post supports. Different types of trusses will be saved for the two ends. A total of six post spans make up this structure. These six spans cover the fifty-foot length of the building. These are heavy-duty trusses with two-by-six framing on both sides, and OSB board glued and nailed into the center. Each truss has been pre-engineered. The crew has a forklift to put these heavy pieces into place.

I continue to order more loads of pit run gravel at the cost of $80 per delivery. So far, five loads have been delivered. This gravel not only provides the correct base for the cement slab but has also elevated the floor of the barn to the point that it sits up above the grade. I reckon this will be my protection from any water runoff or flooding potential.

As the final day of spring comes to an end, this project is nearly one-third complete. Today the crew size grew to four men, compared to the standard crew of three. A crusty crew chief oversees the work, and the hard work is saved for the younger guys who look to be in their twenties.

With colorful language and years of work experience, the crew boss barks commands to the younger workers. He also manages to mix in a good dose of humor and ridicule as the workday progresses. Working conditions have been ideal with sunny days and comfortable temperatures.

According to the Reno newspaper, the local Winnemucca temperature range for this last day of spring is a high of 85 degrees and a low of 50. Per the Fox News Internet, the conditions here in Paradise Valley are slightly cooler with a forecast high of 84 and a low of 47. The relative humidity is higher than the average at fifty-nine percent, and the early morning temperature for this location was listed at 40 degrees.

∼∼ ∼∼∼ ∼∼
∼∼ ∼∼∼ ∼∼

This chapter ends with a memorable event that happened on the morning of June 20th. I had ordered a third delivery of gravel from a source I had not yet met, and by 9:00 a.m. I noticed a huge gravel truck enter the neighbor's property. It was the semi-tractor pulling a large center dump gravel trailer.

I was surprised when I saw this truck come across the by-pass trail towards my property. My first impression was that my property is not large enough to handle that size truck. Little did I know.

Dennis, the driver, came busting down my dirt driveway. His truck occupied about a lane and a half of my narrow drive. Most of the time, either the tractor or the trailer had wheels up into the sagebrush. Both my work crew and I quickly started moving our pickups and other vehicles that obstructed his entrance. He proudly pulled into the middle plot and backed his load right to the front entrance of the R.V. shop. In no time, he pulled forward and dumped his load from the center hatch. This gravel drop extended out about forty to fifty yards.

When Dennis got out of the tractor cab, I noticed that I had a colorful character on my hands. He puffed on the last portion of a cigar. He had a straw cowboy hat and a good size belly, indicating that he had not missed too many meals in his fifty-nine-year lifetime.

The mudflaps on this trailer advertised for a whore house called Donna's Ranch, Battle Mountain, Nevada. The mudflap also offered an internet address of www.donnasranch.net and a slogan, "Where the Wild West Still Lives." It seems Donna's Ranch is the wild west and more.

Before I stray too far from the subject of Donna's Ranch, an internet search shows over ten websites offering different information on this establishment. Donna's is but one of twenty legal brothels in the state. It has been in operation for over one-hundred-thirty years and was once owned by Maxine and Jack Dempsey, the famous world heavyweight boxing champ. One web site indicated that this business is up for sale.

Dennis and I introduced ourselves and chatted while I wrote the check to pay for my last two loads. Dennis explained that during his previous three truck runs to California, he received three tickets.

The first was for doing fifty-six miles per hour in a fifty-five zone. The second was for being two-thousand-six-hundred pounds over the weight limit on his load of cattle—the rancher produced more head than he had expected. The third ticket was for indecent exposure—this one seems to push the limit as his offense was taking a leak on the side of the road. The latter offense was reduced to urinating in public so he would not have to register as a California sex offender. Somehow this is not what the advocates and legislators had in mind when the sex offender laws were put together.

Needless to say, Dennis is not fond of California's ways, at least in the way that the enforcement of California law is administered. I would have to say that law enforcement had it out for Dennis during these tickets.

I paid Dennis $560 for gravel deliveries, and I was about to get my money's worth in entertainment value, watching him try to get off my property back to the county road.

He first attempted to go down my circular driveway across the canal bridge. As he pulled his tractor onto the bridge, his trailer wheels nearly entered the deep canal. As I frantically tried to give hand signals to say that this exit wouldn't work, Dennis crept along, and his wheels were within inches of the drop-off.

Ultimately Dennis agreed that this exit would not work, and he backed off the bridge. I suggested that he try the circular driveway to the top step, even though this section of the driveway was rough and full of large rocks. Most of these rocks were half-buried and left-over from my attempt to improve this section with Joe's caterpillar. Dennis took a run at this steep incline and made good progress until halfway. As he hit the rough ground, he had to slow down. When he slowed down, he lost traction. At two-thirds of the way up, he realized that plan-B was not going to work either.

He had no choice now but to back his big rig down the circular driveway. This decision worked reasonably well until he entered the area next to the canal bridge.

To keep his trailer in the driveway path, he had to turn his rig so that it was hanging over the cliff edge, overlooking a dry stream gully. I tried to signal that this track was not safe, because I could tell that his front right tire was giving way and starting to slide down into the gully. At this point, he was pretty well screwed. His trailer had backed into the wall from which the driveway had been cut, and his tractor was sliding down the gully. He could not go forward, and he could not go backward.

As luck would have it, the construction crew had a heavy-duty forklift on the job site. The crew chief agreed to try to lift the back end of the gravel trailer, so it was not hitting the wall.

After multiple tries and different angles, we brought the tail end of the trailer back to the center of the drive. Now the only problem was that the cab was still fixing to roll down the gully on the north side of the drive.

The next step was to take a tow chain and pull the rig backward towards the site where Dennis first dropped his gravel load. At first, the forklift and tractor were not powering at the same time, so it turned into an ugly heavyweight tug-a-war. Finally, we agreed that I would signal when the truck tires were spinning, and then the fork driver could power up. This coordinated effort paid off, and we pulled the rig backward to where the gravel was dumped.

Dennis and the Forklift

The crew boss, with his tractor, knocked down the gravel pile so the rig could back over this spot. He angled his way across my building site and started to back up the driveway section to the south, from the direction he first entered.

Despite my hand signals, Dennis still managed to bounce off my metal dog kennel that we put up just a couple of days ago. Once he was back up a distance of fifty yards, he pulled his rig into the sagebrush and made a u-turn back to the drive. The rig crushed a couple of dozen four-foot-tall sagebrush plants. He also managed to bounce off some rocks that I did not think he would clear, but he did.

Before he drove off to retrace his entry steps, he stopped and said maybe he could have waited for the smaller gravel truck to become available. After his dramatic departure, I compared notes with the crew boss, and we both agreed that this event was very nerve-wracking. We both were quite sure that his rig was going to roll down the gully after he dropped his front right wheel off the ledge.

As I discovered later, most people in this community have similar stories to tell about Dennis getting his equipment either stuck or in an unfortunate predicament. One thing that I did notice was that during all of the stress of the above scene, Dennis never seemed to be phased. Everyone else seemed to be having a heart attack.

That evening at the bar, I spent a typical social evening. The bar had a full house with lots of good people willing to visit and be friendly. I made an effort to introduce myself to the new neighbor who has a camping trailer and a new fence at his property on Martin Creek Road. We had an enjoyable visit as we watched the De La Hoya boxing match. We compared notes on everything, from buying gravel to building plans for future homes.

4: THE SPRING SEASON

In any clime where four seasons abound, spring marks the season of rebirth. Things become alive; the color green appears again, more birds appear, and, in my case, the nearby Red Hills show off their reddish tint again.

Rebirth has another meaning of discovery or re-discovery, perhaps a way of seeing things again as if for the first time, with a better appreciation of beauty and harmony. Some of this self-discovery is most easily accessed when one has solitude and time to think.

While spring is special, some naturalists say that their favorite season is the one they are in at the moment. That would appear to be the approach of the optimist.

Many authors acknowledge that you can see things better and more clearly if you are alone. Author Clay Jenkinson made this point in his 2002 book, *Message of the Wind*, a spiritual odyssey on the northern plains. Clay Jenkinson grew up in North Dakota, the centerpiece of this story, and beautifully describes the spirit of place.

I, too, grew up in North Dakota. Illustrating the smallness of our world, Jenkinson pays tribute to his great mentor, Mike Jacobs. It turns out that Mike Jabobs was a high school classmate of mine in Stanley, North Dakota. Jacobs has achieved considerable notoriety as a community activist and newspaper editor, ranging from Dickinson to Grand Forks, N.D.

Jacobs influenced much of the book and life of Jenkinson. Jacobs is given credit for proclaiming that the Jeffersonian agrarian dream is dying on the Great Plains during this decade. This point is shared because it relates to the lifestyle and character of my new home location.

I have to admit that when I was in high school, I did not see the full potential of my classmate Mike Jacobs. Perhaps he was a late bloomer, or maybe I failed to see the future potential in this young man.

Another author influencing my book draft is Sue Hubbel. She pointed out in her forward that her husband had come and gone several times, but now it appeared he was gone for good. She lived in the Ozark Mountains for twelve years and spent most of that time alone. The final line in her forward is that there are more questions than answers. It seems that insight comes later in life. Certain stories and accounts are better presented by adults in the second half of life. And here I am in my second half.

The Hubbel book offered quaint accounts of living a simple life, while she managed her property and made a living all by herself. By her winter chapter, she proclaimed that country-living required cooperation. In the same chapter, she explained that winter was not an enemy, but rather a time of less going about, bringing quiet and peace.

Of course, the author, Thoreau, was the picture of solitude in his year at Walden. While Thoreau and I differ on the issue of self-deprivation, I do find common ground on his theory that simple is better; he whose needs are simplest lives best. Regarding self-deprivation, I see no practical value to do without the basic comforts of life. I have spent too much of my life in areas where life was sparse and frills nonexistent.

Just one example that comes to mind includes too many months in the remote mountain valleys of South Korea living off the land and whatever handouts the local farmers were willing to share. At this point, I see no advantage to replicate these past hard times.

Thoreau was a learned man; however, parts of his book seemed to be an unrelated rant.

Author Henry Beston was alone for most of his natural year, although his supportive partner encouraged him to finish his book before their wedding in 1929. Beston did not experience full-time solitude thanks to the surfmen and coast guard workers who patrolled the shore. Yet the fact remains that he lived alone in his small two-room house and spent more time by himself than he did with any companionship.

In my temporary solitude, there is a need for explanation. I do have a wife, Becky, and the marriage is alive. Becky is but four hours away, slaving at her own business, a mom-and-pop business, without the pop. She does it so well that I would only screw things up; therefore, I try to keep out of her way. While I am alone in my writing and observations, I am happy to say that I don't think that I am alone permanently.

The first striking elemental contrast in spring is that the evenings are either cold or cool, while the days are warm and comfortable. I have long found that temperatures in the 60s and 70s are ideal, especially when it comes time to cut and split wood.

∿∿ ∿∿ ∿∿
∿∿ ∿∿ ∿∿

The most evident feature of spring is when I look to the west and see the snow-capped range running north to south. The range is the highest geographic feature, protecting this valley to the north and west. The white of the snow seems even brighter when it contrasts the soft blue sky.

This mountain range has grown and nurtured the tree stands that provide the firewood I will cut and split. The majority of this wood supply comes from the downed mature aspens in the riparian sections of Cottonwood

Creek, generally in the six-thousand to eight-thousand-foot elevation. The flood of 1997 managed to put down a lifetime supply of suitable firewood.

The second reminder of spring is below and to my east, where Martin Creek flows from the mountains to the Humboldt River to the south. As the creek breaks through the sharp rock cliff walls, it opens to a green grass meadow. By April, this meadow is the same sort of green found in Ireland. The lush green is accentuated by the black or brown colored livestock grazing the open fields.

This northeast to southwest water flow of Martin Creek is one of many feeder sources for the Humboldt River, which generally runs east to west. The Humboldt River is named after the famous explorer and statesman who never set foot anywhere close to this river. On the other hand, Alexander Von Humboldt, 1769-1859, did have a significant influence on the physical interpretation of this region. The flow of this and other nearby creeks provide water resources to many ranches before it ever sees the flow of the Humboldt.

The pervasive sage shows early new growth as it enjoys a current abundance of water that will be absent in just a few months. Sage is what distinguishes the Great Basin topography. My good friend Mike J. is well-read and is an experienced geologist; he tells me that there are twenty-six species of sage, most coming from the steppes of Asia. He should know.

The Great Plains, where I grew up, reflected their beauty through vast waving wheat fields. In contrast, here, the beauty of the land arises from its awe-inspiring natural geography and topography rather than from fields of production crops. However, potatoes do flourish further south in this valley floor. My place is well north, where only irrigated alfalfa fields interrupt the sagebrush.

But, for me, what really signals spring is that comforting feeling that only comes when the warm sun shines down your neck; the type of sunshine that provides healthy skin color when you forget to throw on a hat or cap; the healthy skin tone that quickly turns your face to leather. This color was absent as my father was dying of cancer. I often wished that I could have shared some of my color and, in the same instant, find a way to rid his body of the killer cancer. I did not have such power, quickly nature took its course, and he was gone.

He often reminded me of two things. He told me to be observant—to see things—and to be aware. He also told me to slow down and find time to think things over. He explained how his father had a favorite large rock west of the homestead, where he went to find solitude and think things through. Perhaps this large rock was his personal therapist. Those two points serve as philosophical bookends to my attempt to frame this story.

Spring marks the rapid flow of water down the nearby creek. The water level and speed of the rapids is such that neither dog nor quad dares to cross. By mid-summer, this creek flow invites crossings to the other side.

Locals expressed the observation that with the extended wet winters of recent years, the spring season is unusually short. The months of March and April have been cool and cloudy. By May, the temperature starts to climb up to the low 80s, and the sun has prolonged periods of clear exposure.

Between the two extremes of cold and hot, we generally find the best hiking conditions, but we have to wait long enough for the snow to clear from the mountain trails. As this moisture changes from snow to runoff, we see different arrays of natural flowers. The best descriptions about Nevada's wildflowers are found in Mike White's book, *50 Classic Hikes in Nevada*. White points out that approximately seventy-five percent of the plant species in this state depends upon the riparian zones for their survival, even though only one percent of the state's lands are classified as riparian.

A favorite hike of mine that White recommends is the Singas Creek hike; it is the only hike listed on the eastern side of the Santa Rosa range. Springtime is my favorite season for hiking. Both the temperature and the abundance of wildflowers make this an easy choice. The Singas Creek Hike starts at a trailhead five and a half miles in from the main road. As warned in the book, access to the trailhead requires an appropriate four-wheel-drive vehicle because the road is rough, and center clearance is required. What's more, is the fact that there is one good-sized stream crossing that no standard sedan should dare attempt.

One advantage of starting the hike before the trailhead is the ability to immerse oneself in the riparian zone leading into the alpine zone. Walking this last section of access road offers views of snakes, lizards, birds, and rock formations that would otherwise be lost if one was confined to a car.

My hunch that the Singas Creek trail would be available by early May was wrong. The snow line was just a short distance above the trailhead. Further, the spring season is not yet ready for full bloom because it is simply too early. Time permitting, I will try this again later.

〜〜〜
〜〜〜

Approximately four major creeks flow from the Santa Rosa range downhill to the east and eventually into the valley floor. The volume of each of these creeks—Singas, Abel, Cottonwood, and Provo—seems to peak during the May timeframe, explaining the commonly found standing water on the valley floor as you drive to and from the valley ranches.

Based upon this close up viewing of Singas Creek, I have decided not even to try to get into Cottonwood Creek yet for my next attempt at cutting firewood. It is tempting to get started early because of the ideal temperature in the months of April and May.

~~~ ~~~ ~~~

On May 27th, a cold Saturday night, I spotted a hawk soaring high above. Temperatures in town dropped to 33 degrees overnight. This unseasonably cold wet weather also scattered fresh snow on the mountain ridge connected with Hinkey Summit.

The amazing thing about northern Nevada weather is that temperatures approach 90 degrees one week, and then a few days later, drop to the low 30s. It makes life interesting. I did ranch chores this morning for about four hours until the temperature reached a point that the long sleeve pullover no longer kept me warm.

As the spring season ends, temperatures have become warm and stable during the daytime. As I compare the effects of this temperature change, I can see the snowcaps on the Santa Rosa range starting to disappear. On this the last day of spring, the highest peaks still have a few streaks of white snow left. While midday temperatures start to get hot, viewing a snow-capped mountain range seems to make the sensation cooler.

This change of season has signaled the start of the dry season. The sagebrush ranges have lost their topsoil moisture. The only wet areas left at the end of spring are the riparian stream areas and those fields, especially alfalfa, that are under irrigation. The typical irrigation system dispenses sixteen-hundred gallons of water per minute on a standard two-hundred-acre circle of greenery. These circles are called pivots. Despite the changes associated with the seasons, the birds can find comfort and good feeding in and around these irrigation lines. During one drive by in early June, I counted seventeen red tail hawks sitting on the fence posts around the Sicking pivot.

〜〜 〜〜 〜〜
〜〜 〜〜 〜〜

Another feature of the changing season is the arrival of the Mormon crickets, as described throughout this book. This cricket problem only comes around every few years. When they arrive, they come hard.

The surviving trees or shrubs that I inherited now demand regular watering. I still need to invent a watering system that will make this watering chore easier. That will have to wait for the summer season. My one and only tomato plant is still trying to establish itself.

The Martin Creek basin remains fresh and green as the water flow is still impressive. Most of the local cattle have been moved to higher ground grazing in the mountains or foothills.

At the end of the workday, I made a courtesy call to neighbor Joe K. We briefly discussed the cricket population. He offered to let me use his quad and poison sprayer to put down an application for the Mormon crickets. This poison is not available to average citizens. It is restricted so that only state and local officials can disburse it. I felt fortunate to have access via Joe, and I put down one application around my property.

〜〜 〜〜 〜〜
〜〜 〜〜 〜〜

On the last day of Spring, I drove to town to watch a playoff game on TV. This evening, the most abundant wildlife was the magpie. I saw scores of these birds along the drive to town. The jackrabbits were the next most abundant wildlife along the way. I saw one deer grazing in the sage past the Sicking place. One female pheasant flew in front of my vehicle as she moved from the south side of the road to the north side.

Once in town, I pulled up a stool to the bar and visited with Rick and Andy. We discussed the recent fireman's BBQ fundraiser. Later, neighbor Graydon and his wife and son joined the crowd for the basketball game. I got to tell the story of Dennis making his gravel delivery a couple of times. Most of the locals already knew how this Dennis story would end.

5: THE WILD THINGS HELPED

On the first page of Sue Hubbel's book, there is a nearly blank page with only four words: "The Wild Things Helped."

In the case of my new home in Paradise Valley, this line could not be more true. For those avid hunters out of Reno, the hunting area in and around Paradise Valley has long been one of the most valued areas when you happen to draw a tag.

From my first visit to this region, I have been struck by the number of bird species. The first time I saw the property that I now call home, I was distracted by the flock of wild turkeys. Competing for attention were the sage grouse close to my ranch entrance. Many hawk species circle overhead, either enjoying the art of soaring or searching for dinner, whichever comes first.

Often as I drive to town, I need to slow down or even stop while the cock pheasants take their time crossing the road.

Pheasant on the Road

I have never figured out their habit of crossing the road so slowly; either they are a bit dumb, or they think they rule the road. With time, I promise to get better acquainted with the proper names of each and every local bird.

One thing over which I have no control in this setting is the fact that my three cattle dogs enjoy chasing anything that will give them chase. The birds provide this opportunity as they scoff at the fact that these four-legged creatures are stuck to the land.

HAWKS

By the third week of living on my new property, I started to pay more attention to the hawks hanging out near the meadow on the way to town. I first spotted three or four hunting the pastures and sweet clover fields. Next, I spotted the same bird sitting a nest in a cottonwood tree overhanging the road to town.

Red Tail Hawk

At first glance, I thought I was viewing the northern harrier (marsh hawk). Upon review of a book dedicated to hawks, I realized that I was actually dealing with the red tail hawk. This bird is the most common of the American member of the genus Buteo. Like other hawks in this group, it soars over open country in search of its prey.

Still, it just as often perches in a tree at the edge of a meadow, watching for the slightest movement in the grass below. Approximately ninety percent of their diet is composed of small rodents, and they generally do not hunt poultry. This food source is plentiful as I often see over a dozen gophers running across the road as I drive to town, and field mice are abundant here as well.

Some of the western birds with grayish, faintly streaked or mottled tails were formerly considered a separate species called Harlan's hawk. The coloration of these birds varies; some have lighter, dirty colored chests, and others have darker brown fronts, yet the rust color in the tail is consistent.

These hawks perch and hunt side by side with the turkey vultures; however, they are less likely to hold their perch position when I drive by with my camera at the ready.

This is the same family that has a large nest overlooking the dirt road to town. If I could have looked inside that nest during April, I probably would have seen two to three white eggs with brown spots. I have yet to see any evidence of young hawks from that particular nest.

Later, during early summer, I had a red tail fly overhead, with the sun shining through his wing and tail feathers. For the first time, it was abundantly clear why they acquired this red tail name.

As mentioned briefly in the second chapter, it has become common to see the red tail hawks sitting on the fence posts along the roadside as I drive to and from the village. They are perched in a prime hunting spot with green vegetation and a wild assortment of birdlife. This prime location was more popular during the spring months than the hot summer months.

The hawk is, of course, a raptor with a respectable size. Their bodies can measure nearly two feet long, and their wingspan can reach fifty-six inches. The female body size is larger than the male, and at times can be as much as one-third larger.

Unlike certain birds such as the magpie, the red tail hawk has a range of colorations and plumage, which ranges from light brown to dark brown on their backs. The adult birds generally have a cinnamon color on their necks and chests. Their underside is most often a light color with some darker bands. While in flight, the rust color tail is a useful identifier.

On my drive to the ranch in late May, one such hawk flew off his perch as I drove by. For some reason, he decided to pace my car for an extended duration. This bird flew just outside my driver's side window for the longest time. This extended flight period allowed me to check my speedometer. While the reference material does not consider this a fast bird, I was impressed to see a sustained thirty-five miles per hour. No wonder they make good birds of prey.

Their life span ranges from ten to over twenty years. Though it is an adaptable bird as its presence can be found across varied terrain in this state, their preferred habitat is a perfect match for this valley floor, which offers sagebrush, grasslands, and rich riparian features.

Accordingly, this hawk is the most widespread and familiar of the soaring hawks. They nest in early spring, generally by March. I was able to photo a larger hawk nesting in a large tree immediately over the county road.

The egg incubation period is one month, plus or minus a couple of days. The chore of sitting on the eggs rests primarily with the female, but not exclusively. The general gender role calls for the male to find food for the young birds. These youngsters usually stay in the nest for about forty-eight days.

According to the Nevada Department of Wildlife, this hawk population is between one-hundred and one-hundred-fifty during the Nevada winters. Also, this particular hawk is the most common member of the buzzard hawk family and has raptor eyesight that is eight times more powerful than us humans.

I recall from the Sue Hubbell book that she too recognized this bird at her location. I have also read that you should be able to find the red tail hawk in every state.

These hawks were scattered in with a couple of ferruginous hawks, which are similar in appearance and favorite habitat. The ferruginous hawk prefers prairie dogs and ground squirrels; though prairie dogs are present, ground squirrels are plentiful in the bird zone between my property and the town.

WILD TURKEYS

One of the dogs wore a look of confusion, perhaps surprise, when he flushed out a large hen turkey. For the first time, my thirty-five-pound dog encountered a fowl that was larger in weight and girth.

Since I can both see and hear the wild turkey flock below my property, I will start with this wild animal. Some bird species take an effort to identify, not so with the wild turkey, because they are too large and distinct to be confused with any other bird.

There may be four million in the U.S., yet I never thought of them as plentiful in Nevada. A check of the Bird Breeding Survey (BBS) and Christmas Bird Count (CBC) maps reflect turkey spottings are not found in this region. This is also the case in the *Sibley Field Guide to Birds of Western North America*, which does not identify any turkey activity in the northern half of the state.

But, they are here for sure, and their numbers seem plentiful. Could it be that the bird book has it wrong? Or, maybe Paradise Valley is special.

Springtime, specifically the end of March to the end of April, is also hunting season. I have heard talk of turkey hunting at the local saloon; however, I have no evidence of any active hunting going on here.

These birds are omnivorous, living primarily on vegetation, and about ten percent of their diet includes ground-dwelling insects. Their diet preference helps explain why they generally favor a combination of tree cover and open meadows. Because they take some time and effort to take flight, they do not prefer woodlands that are too thick.

Wild turkeys generally travel in flocks during the day looking for food. I did notice that the hen that my dogs chased out was solo at the canal on my property. I have read that after breeding season, males tend to hang only with males and females with females, but I cannot say that I've personally observed this point.

Springtime is their breeding season when you will see the males—gobblers—strutting as part of the mating ritual; one male will mate with several females in the flock. The gobbler ritual also includes the gobble sound and the wide fanning of his tail, and the pecking order among turkeys is based upon age and size. The gobbler will not offer any parental help after the breeding season concludes.

The hen, who lays ten to fifteen eggs, will sit the ground nest for twenty-seven to twenty-eight days. During this month-long period, the hen is vulnerable to predators such as raccoons, red foxes, striped skunks, crows, and snakes. Except for this incubation period, wild turkeys would prefer to spend the night in a tree for better protection.

From a distance, it is hard to distinguish between the gobbler and the hen. As you get closer, the distinction becomes more apparent. The gobbler is about one foot longer, and the male has a larger head with two obvious features, including the wattle at the throat and the caruncle, a wart-like projection of skin attached to the upper part of the forehead. Males have black-tipped breast feathers, while the hen has brown tips on her breast feathers.

Finally, the male and female have a different voice. The female gives a loud, sharp, iike, iike, iike. The male offers the familiar descending gobble.

This spring season will deliver newborn turkeys called poults, which mature quickly and can eat on their own within a day or two. They are also mature enough for breeding at ten months.

I will be on the lookout for the little poults as I dedicate personal time to hiking and exploring. I fear that this division of time will take some effort as I expect the month of May to be primarily spent on building my large shop. Early on, I called this structure a shed, but my cousin Chris reminded me that a shed defines a smaller, lesser structure than what I have planned. While he is right, I have grown more comfortable with the shop term, and hereafter will strive to discipline my choice of words for the rest of this story.

It was not until mid-July that I spotted the first three poults. They were already a good size, approximately at large as a mature chukar. These birds, probably just under four months old, were located near the thick underbrush further up the creek canyon. When I did scare them out, the adult turkeys flew away while the three young ones simply ran into thicker brush for cover.

During late July, I noticed increased activity and feeding in the creek meadow below my property. Since the meadow hay was recently cut, activity is present in and around the hay bales as well.

SAGE GROUSE

On May 26th, I drove to town with a keen eye out for birds in my favorite zone—by the way, today is an important date because it is the birthday of "Duke," otherwise known as John Wayne; every Marine I know adores Duke.

For some reason, today's observation found little bird activity except for a solo sage grouse. This bird should be in habitat heaven as they are dependent on sagebrush. By fall and winter, sage is essential to their limited food supply. I later learned that this bird prefers the sage-covered foothills where they mark out their breeding leks.

The bird I spotted was a female with a luxurious brownish coat and lighter color trim throughout most of her body. From my angle, I was not able to see the black belly. A longer neck seemed to be a distinguishing feature of this grouse. This bird seemed unafraid as she sat on a roadside fence post, staring me down.

In the springtime courting season, males gather on a traditional display ground, called a lek, to attack the female. This courting ritual is as unique as it is colorful. It is the chance of the male to dance and display his best plumage for the female audience.

Once mating is completed, the female goes off by herself to raise her family. The female lays from six to nine olive-green eggs, lightly spotted with brown. These nests are well-concealed ground depressions.

Over time, I have learned more about the mating ritual of the sage grouse. The protection of sage grouse habitat is becoming more apparent, and it has gained significance in wildlife circles. Protection of this habitat is also in evidence when you look at state or federal funding for this specific bird and habitat.

The status of sage grouse is also a matter of ongoing legal battles—this topic is briefly covered at the end of this chapter. *The Birder's Handbook* addresses their population problem. They were officially Blue Listed from 1972 to 1981. In 1971, the National Audubon Society ornithological field journal, *American Birds*, began publishing a list, the Blue List, to provide early warning of those North American species undergoing population or range reduction.

The Blue List was designed to identify patterns of impending or ongoing critical losses in regional bird populations, not to duplicate the function of the U.S. Fish and Wildlife's Service's Threatened and Endangered Species. "The effectiveness of the Blue List depends on the accuracy of the data supplied by regional compilers and the responsiveness of government agencies accountable for species conservation."[1]

In 1981 sage grouse moved off the Blue List and onto the Special Concern list from 1982 to 1986. I am not aware of its status since 1986.

One common feature for the wild turkey, the pheasant, and the sage grouse is that all of these birds will generally be found on or near the ground, as opposed to the smaller birds who favor flight through sunshine and banking off into far distances.

MORMON CRICKETS

While not part of the traditional wildlife, I did observe something today that was rather impressive. I took my quad further up Martin Creek past the steep rocky gorge. This was new country for me as the trail access gets very tight and technical as you move up canyon.

Approximately five miles from my property, on a rough trail, I encountered massive numbers of Mormon crickets. I was under the impression that they would make their appearance later in the season, but today's spotting came on May 26th. Previously I'd heard them being described as being as thick as carpet; this was true today. They seemed to be marching or hopping south towards the valley floor. I tend to revisit this topic at various times in this book.

As one begins to research these crickets, it quickly becomes apparent that they are not crickets, but rather a shield-backed katydid. They are common to many of the western states, especially those states inside the Great Basin. These katydids will thrive in rangeland dominated by sagebrush and forbs—milk vetches, penstemon, arrowleaf balsamroot, dandelion, and several mustards. They also relish cultivated plants such as wheat, barley, alfalfa, and sweet clover.

Because of their limited migratory habit, they may be present in a particular site for no more than three to four days. Their hopping and walking mode of travel can cover from a half-mile to a full mile each day.

At higher altitudes, their embryonic development may be delayed. The logic here is that egg hatching does not start until the ground temperature reaches 40 degrees. Once hatched, it only takes sixty to ninety days to reach the adult stage. This 40 degree hatching point is much lower than for grasshoppers. Research out of Utah indicates that the Mormon crickets do not do well in temperatures below 40 degrees nor in extremely high temperatures.

My first observation found them nearly as thick and plentiful as I could imagine, and their high density can reach one-hundred crickets per square yard.

Natural predators include California gulls, hawks, crows, rodents, and the digger wasp. Many of these predators are present locally. The reality of this spring and summer season is that neither natural predators nor man-made efforts did much of any good.

In 2002 Jeff DeLong wrote an article for the Reno-Gazette Journal that focused the Mormon crickets in the Winnemucca area. During a drought, a decade prior, over one million acres were overrun in the worst infestation since the 1930s. The insects damaged crops, briefly shut down Interstate 80, and nearly invaded downtown Winnemucca.

In early June, I had a roadside visit with Davy, who ranches at the site of the old army fort called Fort Scott. We covered many topics, one of which was control of these Mormon crickets. He indicated that the county has a good cricket management program so that if a rancher feels that these critters are becoming a nuisance, he can call for control measures. The control measure includes a poison that kills the first crickets to eat it. As is often the case, the live crickets will eat the dead ones, which means that the poison has a second chance to kill. According to Davy, this poison will work through three cycles before it loses its effectiveness. Unfortunately, the best poison is limited due to state restrictions.

During the last week in June, I made a trip to Reno. When I left, the population was very heavy, despite the personal and county efforts to poison them. When I returned home, less than a week later, I found that these critters were all but gone.

As it turned out, this observation was short-lived. I enjoyed nearly a week with almost no crickets. Then as quickly as they had disappeared, they returned. Perhaps a second wave came through as opposed to the first wave turning back north. The second wave has now continued into July 9th.

During this past weekend, Becky and I spent time relaxing on the canyon portion of Martin Creek. While sitting quietly and with time to observe, we watched in amazement as one willow tree on the west side of the creek was so laden with crickets that the branches turned brown and became alive with movement. The volume of crickets on the tree was so dense that one or two would drop into the creek every couple of seconds.

When they entered the water, they kicked their six legs and propelled themselves to either side of the stream. At certain points, when the sand bar or rocks would allow them a foothold, they would rest for a moment then slowly but surely make progress across the creek.

During the weekly cookout at the saloon, on July 8th, conversation focused on these crickets, and many points of view were shared. One old guy got a chuckle when he described his new version of the cricket dance; he described his footwork as he attempted to step on as many as possible.

By July 27th, I spotted only a single cricket on my property. When I took the dogs to the creek for shade and cooling, I noticed only a few crickets around the water. Hopefully, this signals the end of their adult life cycle. Based upon a life cycle of sixty to ninety days, we should be at the end of that cycle. I hope we won't see any more unwelcome visitors for at least two full months.

In fairness, the cricket problem turned out to occur only in my first year on the property. As time passed, I discovered that the following summer had no Mormon crickets in my area and limited sightings in this county.

RING-NECK PHEASANTS

In late July, after a day of woodcutting along Cottonwood Creek, I followed and photographed a pair of ring-necked pheasants, one male and one female. As they walked parallel to the dirt trail, I tried to get a photo from the perspective where the sun was striking the red color of the male's head.

The feature that first caught my eye was the brilliant flash of color from the head of the pheasant, illuminated by the setting sun. When the bird ducked under the shade of the sagebrush, the color returned to a more subdued tone. At this point, the pheasant and I played a game of hide-and-seek. The female that followed along was not the subject of my camera lens because her colors were typically duller. The female color is a mottled sandy brown with a shorter tail.

As is the case with the chukar, ring-necked pheasants descended from stock brought over from the Old World, and thus they are somewhat variable. These birds are most plentiful in the central plains; however, this region has a reputation for good hunting of several game birds. During hunting season, many Reno hunters drive their pickups and trailers three-hours to Paradise Valley. These rigs dot the landscape, and many of the hunters frequent the local saloon in the evenings with wondrous tales of conquest.

CALIFORNIA QUAIL

One common Nevada bird is the California quail, which appears on the ranch as often as it appears in urban Reno.

Here, on the ranch, I have not seen them in as large numbers, as I did in a pine tree near a previous home in northwest Reno.

These are stocky, gray birds with a distinctive plume on the top of their heads. The plume is a dark black and is larger on the male than the female. As with many birds, the female has less distinctive body markings than the male. They prefer roosting in trees in large family numbers, which provides them a degree of safety.

GREAT EGRETS

On May 14th, as I drove the country road into town, I shifted from viewing the commonly seen quail to spotting my first rarely seen egret. This road section winds through several irrigated alfalfa fields. This regular water source not only changes what grows in the ground but influences what feeds in these lush green settings. For example, the deer love the alfalfa fields. It seems to me that the deer are smart enough to find sanctuary in these private fields to get away from the deer hunters.

After a brief visit to the local saloon on a Saturday night, I saw four great egrets in the alfalfa field south of the county road; they stood under the spray of the extensive irrigation system.

At first glance, these tall birds appear to be white cranes; however, research and closer observation indicate that these birds are actually from the egret family. This tall bird can reach forty inches in height.

Many names describe this species. Wildlife watchers gathering at the Spring Wings Bird Festival in Fallon, Nevada, indicate the correct name is the great egret. Previously, this bird was known as the American egret, common egret, great white heron, or large egret. No matter its name, this truly is a graceful and magnificent large bird.

Their diet consists of water-related creatures usually found in shallow waters, including fish, frogs, and snakes. The great egret is common to the Stillwater National Wildlife Refuge in Fallon. The Fallon region has become one of Nevada's birding hot spots. The routine annual number of visitors, around five-hundred, is expected to increase as this birding location now has exposure in the *Audubon* Magazine. The flight distance from the Stillwater Refuge to my valley is relatively close.

Besides being attracted to the irrigation water source, the entire valley floor is now a springtime marsh as multiple creeks and streams flow out of the mountains. By April and May, this creates a beautiful wetland for these and other birds to feed and flourish.

The graceful neck and elongated beak are noticeable features for the egret and the heron family. You can see the elegant neck change its position to a long up and down trumpet when they make their croaking squawking sound. When they fly, two prominent features become apparent. First is the long and crooked neck. Second is the dragging of the hind legs. When they take flight, their long legs remind me of black landing gears folding back to a sleek flight position.

Even later, when summer arrived, I saw a solo egret fly up and down the creek bottom as it connects between the rock canyon walls and the green fields below. This solo flight repeated itself off and on during July, always with just one low flying egret. Later I realized at least two egrets were patrolling.

The egret is an example of a species once approaching extinction thanks to plume hunters. Further, the reduction of wetlands, especially in the western half of the country, have hurt their survival. Despite these two factors, it does appear that their numbers are recovering.

TURKEY VULTURES

On the drive to Singas Canyon, I observed numerous large and small birds along the country road. The sizable bird that caught my attention was a turkey vulture. On the first impression, this appeared to be an ugly bird sitting on a wooden fence post next to the road. Despite stopping next to him and taking a photo, he was in no hurry to fly off.

The first visual impression of the turkey vulture is the bare-skinned red head, an ugly looking feature. Even the rest of the feathered appearance seems to be one of disarray. The surface feathers seemed to be ruffled and unkempt.

They use their keen sense of smell to locate carrion, and they are capable of feeding off small mammals to dead cows. Often, they search for dead birds, and you will generally see them flying close to the ground. They like the meadows and adjoining farmland for the best feeding.

Despite being related to the black vulture, the turkey vulture is not as social and likes to hunt solo, which sometimes poses a problem when they find a carcass. Since the turkey vulture is larger, it can ward off another single black vulture. However, black vultures often travel and feed in groups and can overpower a turkey vulture at any given carcass site.

Another distinguishing feature is that the black vulture has a white patch at the end of their wings. They also have shorter wings and do not soar with the same ease as the turkey vulture. The big difference is a black head versus the red head on the turkey vulture.

Turkey Vulture

Oddly, a turkey vulture will defecate on its leg as a means of cooling down as evaporation transpires. This habit, similar to behaviors exhibited by its stork relatives, is a reminder about certain egotistical and self-destructive bosses that I knew in state government.

A week later, I found the same vulture with a partner. The first sighting was the large male sitting on a medium-sized tree.

Just up the road, I found the partner lunching on roadkill. I had my camera at the ready and got multiple shots of both partners. Seeing these two together provides some contradiction to the theory that they hunt and fly alone.

Again, I was struck by the contrasting appearance. Sitting on a perch, they appear disheveled with their bare-skin head and ruffled feathers, yet when airborne, they become beautiful flying specimens. Turkey vultures are large and graceful soaring birds. When cruising around, looking for food, they seldom flap their wings. When in groups, they hunt in a methodical formation, and a good portion of their systematic patrol was down just above ground level.

Author Henry Beston shared the same point that no one really knows a bird until he has seen it in flight. He said, "The difference between the bird on the wing and the bird at rest is so great that one might be watching two different creatures."

Perhaps there is a lesson here for the egotistical fighter pilots that I have mingled with in my earlier years.

PRONGHORN ANTELOPE

A common sight in local meadows is pronghorn antelope. These big game animals, whose life spans five to ten years, range in size from one-hundred-twenty-five pounds for the male and ninety-five pounds for the female.

Their bodies are distinctly marked with white on the underside and the rump, and their backs are brown with shades of cinnamon. They also have a black cheek patch, muzzle, and forehead. This dark mask is more pronounced on the male.

Their usual territory is the valleys between mountain ranges in both central and northern Nevada, and they seem particularly attached to the irrigated alfalfa fields in this corner of Paradise Valley. As I would come to learn, the antelope prefer the wide-open spaces where they can have broad vistas of vision for protection.

Their numbers are much more plentiful in the higher reaches of the national forest because the trees offer better protection than the fields.

From a natural history perspective, pronghorn antelope were probably first observed in North America by European explorers in Mexico in the mid-sixteenth century. Lewis and Clark collected the first specimen for science in 1804, and Peter Skeen Ogden, who has Paradise Valley connections, reported the first antelope in Nevada in 1829. The Nevada population improved with the establishment of the Charles Sheldon Antelope Refuge west of my ranch location.

From a breeding perspective, pronghorns have a two to four week mating period in early fall. Bucks will fight for harems of up to fifteen does. After a gestation period of about two-hundred-fifty days, the does give birth, in solitude, to one fawn at the first birth and twins thereafter.

This animal is the fastest running hoofed example in North America. Speed is their only defense. They have been clocked at fifty-five miles per hour and may reach sixty miles per hour for short periods. To put this speed in perspective, it is twice the sprint speed of my fastest cattle dog. I have often tracked Gruden at speeds of thirty miles per hour while we chase each other on the county road—Gruden readily accepts the challenge to race my quad. Needless to say, my fastest dog would pose little threat to catching the speedy antelope.

On one notable day, I saw approximately fifty antelope walking in a row along my fence line. I had never seen this sight before, and I haven't witnessed it since. It appeared they were headed up canyon to find drinking water.

DEER

Another common sight in the meadow and at the edges of the roads on the way to town is deer. During the first half of July, it was common to see either single or a pair of deer in the nearby alfalfa fields. They do not seem startled by cars, even when they are within forty feet of the dirt road.

The deer presence has become so prevalent in select areas that local drivers instinctively slow down to avoid hitting them with their cars. Not long after I moved here, I heard the local wisdom that we do not need police patrols to enforce reasonable road speeds because the deer population does it in their stead. Chit-chat at the saloon suggests two groups of local drivers, those who have hit deer in the past and those who will hit deer sometime in the future.

My neighbor John once told me a story of when he saw over one-hundred deer gathered in the meadow below his place; unfortunately, I have not seen deer gather in numbers nearly that large on my property. When I see deer, they are generally around the lush alfalfa fields along the road to town.

On these occasions, I often view around a half dozen deer at a time, eating up the farmer's profit. My other neighbor, Joe, has reported seeing over sixty deer at one time in his irrigated fields. Though I haven't seen large numbers gathered together, I commonly flush out a few deer when I drive my quad into the foothills behind my house or during the outings that take me into the mountain streams and ravines.

MAGPIES

Recent trips to town confirm an ever-increasing number of black-billed magpies. I now count their numbers by the scores. They prefer open woodlands, brush-covered country, and growth along streams and creeks. They are also fond of the irrigated alfalfa fields, where so many birds flourish. Magpies generally nest individually but can sometimes be found in loose colonies. They are social birds during feeding and after breeding season.

Throughout the summer, the number of magpies and the size of the flocks seem to increase. If there is roadkill around, they are the most likely birds on the scene doing nature's clean up.

By July 13th, I noticed that the magpies are spending more time in and around my RV shop. They have also roosted on the RV and seem to take joy in bugging my dogs. The dogs think that their bark should scare them off their high perch, but it does not work.

During July, I have observed that magpies are the most frequent birds in and around my ranch. They seem to enjoy tormenting my cattle dogs, flying low to encourage a dog to chase and then stay just out of reach of the dogs, for they know the dogs cannot catch or reach them.

JACKRABBITS

As the magpie seems to dominate the bird population, the most dominant land animal is the jackrabbit. As best I can determine, the local rabbits are black-tailed jackrabbits.

This type of rabbit is characterized by the buffy gray body color and very long ears. Originally the large ears helped to give this rabbit the name, jackass rabbit. Like other jackrabbits, this animal is a hare rather than a rabbit. This distinction is based on the fact that newborns start with their eyes open and a ready coat of fur.

While the vast majority of the local rabbit spottings are the black-tail version, I do have a couple of white-tail rabbits living across from my driveway entrance.

One reason that their numbers are so plentiful is the well-known fact that they reproduce often. In the case of the rabbit, they have from one to four litters per year, and each litter produces between one and eight young with a typical litter size between two and four. The mother has numerous tricks for protecting her young as she must care for her newborns for around a month before they can fend for themselves.

We generally see them as they sprint across the county road in front of car tires, and they usually give little notice to the drivers. On one particular July Sunday morning, I noticed four of them became roadkill in the six-mile stretch of road between my property to town. Nighttime driving is particularly affected by these rabbits; frequently, the rabbits dart into the dark road without warning and get hit by my car.

Their habitat seems connected to the green slough bottoms and the irrigated alfalfa fields, and their activity increases during the later part of the afternoon. While their diet may vary as a species, it is clear they favor the local green alfalfa.

While the rabbits have numerous local predators—such as coyotes, hawks, owls, and snakes—their current numbers indicate good survival traits. As part of their survival, they apply an exceptionally high leap about every fourth or fifth hop. This technique of employing a random extra-high hop allows them a better view of the predator pursuing them as well as the surroundings to which they may want to flee. They can only use this technique when they are running at a moderate speed.

Around July 10th, my neighbor, who manages irrigated alfalfa fields and cuts hay for the Nevada First Corporation, apparently got fed up with all of the rabbit traffic and their consumption of high volumes of fresh alfalfa. He pointed out to me the damage that these animals can do to an alfalfa field. As a result, he sought out the young bar-tender, who enjoys hunting, and invited him to shoot some of the surplus.

It seems that our afternoon temperature broke into the 90-degree range today. It was 94 in Reno, and I do not yet have my own temperature gauge. In contrast to the day's heat, it is pleasant in the outside shade by 7:00 p.m. While enjoying the current outdoor conditions, I spent time surveying the meadow floor with my binoculars, and there I found six to eight wild turkeys feeding in the grass.

BREWER'S BLACKBIRDS

While observing these large birds, I noticed a smaller bird land on a post support for my new RV shop. With the binoculars in one hand and the Sibley field guide in the other, I determined that I was looking at a Brewer's blackbird.

These birds are a drab one-color olive-brown with no distinguishing features. Today they are around in large numbers, flying in flocks of twenty to thirty, spending time between my property and the creek bottom.

According to the field guide, this bird is common year-round in this upper half of Nevada. They like agriculture fields as it gives them easy access to plant seeds and insects on open ground.

On July 27th, I spent over an hour sitting on the edge of Martin Creek. I noticed four of these blackbirds, walking and feeding their way upstream. They hopped from stream rock to stream rock, feeding as they moved north. Again, I noticed that this bird has one solid brown color. Only when the sun hit the feathers in a specific way could I see a very subtle bluish tint color on the back-wing section.

While watching this bird, I heard the peaceful sound of the mourning dove to my west, near the top step site where the ranch house will soon be built.

BOBCATS

On the first day of Autumn, on our way to town, I saw my first bobcat crossing the road. It appeared to be a well-fed cat that stood about two feet tall, approximately twice the size of a domestic cat. A bobcat's weight generally ranges from around eighteen pounds for a female to twenty-six pounds for a male cat.

It is plain to see that this animal could give most local dogs a rough time in a fight. These animals are digitigrade, meaning that they walk on their toes, and they have sharp retractable claws.

Their habitat varies widely, ranging from swamps to deserts to mountain ranges. In Nevada, their habitat choice is dominated by weather protection, an abundance of available prey, avoidance of human traffic, and terrain and vegetation that provides cover. They often prefer rocky areas near the mouths of canyons, which is precisely what exists outside my front door.

Their home range covers a span of approximately thirty-seven miles. They do not like to compete with other bobcats for terrain, especially cats of the same sex. Bobcats tend to be nocturnal or crepuscular—active at twilight—however, in the winter, they may change their activity to daylight hours.

Bobcats and coyotes compete for food sources such as rabbits; however, generally, the cats prefer to hunt in rockier terrain, which is not suitable for the coyotes. These cats breed from February through July, and the female typically produces six to eight kittens.

OWLS

I know that owls are out there because while driving at night, I see their large mass fly past the front windshield. The night time impression is one of a large wing mass, without much other detail visible.

All that I know about the night owl is that their nocturnal hunting is based on sound. My initial understanding also indicates that they have two built-in audio advantages. First, they can find their prey with their acute sense of hearing. Second, they can swoop in on their prey without much, if any, sound.

Despite the large wing mass, they have special wing design features that mean there is no wind or disturbed air sound when they approach their dinner on the run. Owls would be the bird version of a stealth bomber.

The Sibley Field Guide for Western North America lists nineteen different types of owls. Ten of the nineteen are indigenous to northern Nevada.

Thanks to the precise details of *The Birder's Handbook: A Field Guide to the Natural History of North American Birds*— my essential companion and identification guide—my curiosity was satisfied regarding the question of how owls hunt at night. I specifically wondered whether their successful night hunting was based on exceptional sight, keen hearing, or both.

The *Birder's Handbook* indicates that the owl is a formidable, silent hunter. The reason that they can move in on their prey is due to the unique structural modification of the first primary feather on each wing. While this feature is unique to the owl, it is a common trait with all owls. The forward edge of the feather is serrated rather than smooth, which disrupts the flow of air over the wing surface. This feature eliminates the vortex noise created by airflow over the smooth surface. Thanks to this feature, the owl can swoop down on its prey without a sound.

This reference also confirmed my hunch that the owl has an uncanny ability to locate even the slightest sound. Studies by neurobiologists Marc Konishi and Eric Knudsen confirmed that a barn owl is capable of finding and capturing prey by sound alone.

In the case of the barn owl, the ear is specially designed so that they have a concave surface of stiff dark-tipped feathers around its facial ruff. This ruff serves as a deflector, channeling sound into the ears.

Further, the hearing acuity of each ear can measure the difference in the time it takes for a sound to reach each ear. When there is no difference from right to left, then their target is straight ahead. The owl's ears are linked to a specialized cell contained within a discreet region of the midbrain. At least in the case of the barn owl, their brain contains a neural map of auditory space.

Perhaps this one evolutionary trait helps to explain why the barn owl has become the most widespread bird species on Earth.

The final feature that compliments the owls hunting prowess is their familiarity with their hunting environment—especially such things as the heights of favorite perches above the ground—which seems to be essential to the owls' ability to pounce on prey. Hearing helps replace the absence of sight, but intimate knowledge of their habitat completes the job.

Since owls are nighttime hunters, they must enjoy the extra-long nights associated with the fall and winter. As evidenced by my observation times just after sunset at twilight or early in the dawn light, this leaves fourteen hours of dark before they go back to rest.

I wonder how these winged creatures endure the sometimes cruel winter nighttime low temperatures. Never have any of the local fowls appeared to be in discomfort.

One time I was driving westbound past the Sicking property just before sunrise, and I spotted a solo owl flying southbound.

It was soon apparent that we were on a direct collision course as if a mid-air crash was developing. It appeared to me that the owl was either playing chicken with my car or oblivious to my approach—this would be hard to believe given the accounts of superior eyesight for owl hunting. In any case, I was sure that the owl was going to fly directly into my car windshield.

When we were about five feet apart, he did a right snap roll and avoided the impact by less than two feet. This close encounter seems hard to explain.

GREAT HORNED OWL

On the way to town on July 17th, around 5:30 p.m., I spotted my first owl. Mike, the local expert birder, tells me that it was the great horned owl, the king of the owl pecking order, and the largest and best known of the owl family. It wasn't until December 17th that I saw another one at twilight as I drove home from church; it sat in a tree next to the road near the alfalfa fields below the Sicking property.

Besides being a tall and broad bird, the most noticeable feature was the horns that prompt the name great horned owl. It had long been my hunch that this was the kind of owl that I had seen quite often in the dark.

According to the *Sibley Field Guide* and the *Audubon Guide*, the great horned owl is common across all of North America.

They are similar in size and coloring to the nearby red-tail hawk, and during the day, they roost in trees, in this case, the thick underbrush and small trees associated with the creek run bottoms. For food, they forage for medium size mammals such as rabbits, rodents, skunks, and occasionally smaller owls. If so inclined, they may also feed off the abundant field mice, perhaps for appetizers. He should be in predator heaven with all of the rabbits in this neighborhood.

Great Horned Owl

This is a large bird with a forty-four-inch wingspan and a body length of twenty-two inches. Despite this large mass, their weight is listed at just over three pounds. It is the largest and best known of the common owls. They usually lay two to three white eggs, generally on the open ground or near cliffs and caves.

Their color varies from dark, most common in the Pacific Northwest, to the paler shade associated with west taiga. The owls of the southwest tend to be grayish overall. They have a cat-like face with the widely spaced ear tufts.

Weeks later, my car hit a rabbit sprinting across the dirt road while I was going to visit a neighbor. When I returned home after dark, that same rabbit was being consumed by a very large owl. Based on the large wingspan, I assume this was the great horned owl.

I can say without qualification that the local great horned owl is by far the most intriguing bird in Paradise Valley.

BARN OWL

Later in December, I had a strange encounter with an owl. This is only the second time that I have spotted an owl close up. The previous observation was at the same time of day in the same location, and the earlier spotting was a great horned owl.

Today the owl observed was a barn owl, which would be appropriate in that the Sicking barn was less than a hundred yards from the fence post where this owl was perched. Joe S. indicated earlier that this owl has resided in his barn for years. One day, I stopped by to check, and sure enough, there he was trying to get some sleep.

I was driving as I spotted this owl, and as I drove past, I noticed that the owl did not flinch, so I backed up the car for a closer look. I observed this beautiful bird from less than ten feet. When it became clear the owl was not frightened, I got out of my car and walked closer to the post perch.

From this perspective, I could clearly see the heart-shaped, white face and the dark eyes. While on the perch, the white face contrasted with the dark hood and coat. The barn owl is considerably smaller than the great horned owl.

The dusk lighting did not permit an ideal observation, but it did appear that the dark color was a light to medium brown. Tawny is the color used to describe this type of owl in the Sibley Field Guide. Buff brown was the descriptive color from the Audubon Field Guide.

Barn Owl

Eventually, I convinced this owl to fly so that I could observe the flying profile and the body colors; it was a treat. When the owl did fly to the next post over, I noticed that the shade under the wings and part of the body was light-colored, but not quite white.

GOLDEN EAGLE
During my first fall here, I failed to see the golden eagle in this valley; however, during my second October, I saw one. It was perched atop a telephone pole alongside my neighbor's alfalfa fields in the spot where I normally saw turkey vultures.

The turkey vultures have moved south at this point in the season, and I trust that this golden eagle will soon do the same since their normal winter range extends to the northern portion of Mexico.

This eagle is truly a large and majestic bird. My first impression was that this golden eagle was anything but golden. Its color is somewhere between a dark brown and slate grey. The bird books reference the pale golden nape on this bird, but I wasn't able to get close enough to identify that feature.

This bird is majestic in both the perched position as well as in flight. It has a wingspan just over six feet long, and it feeds off the large rabbit population in and around the irrigated alfalfa fields.

The golden eagle tends to be a solitary bird and is more common in the mountains than in the grasslands. Paradise Valley manages to provide both. Some of the birder books mention that this bird may be mistaken for a turkey vulture; however, that makes little sense when you consider the great difference in head appearance and the perching posture.

Considering that this is a migratory bird, I was surprised to see this solo bird still hanging around by the end of November. Seeing it this late in the season means this bird has been around for two months.

Normally this bird's territory covers roughly thirty-five square miles. Yet, this eagle seems to prefer one particular power pole overlooking a target-rich environment of blacktail rabbits.

Golden eagles have been protected since 1962 after approximately twenty-thousand were destroyed over ten years by sheep ranchers despite little evidence of sheep depredation. Their numbers are now stable to increasing.

I have reported on many bird sightings, but finding this eagle may be the most impressive find. First, their numbers are few. Second, when you see one close up, you realize how large they are. And third, to have at least one pair living permanently in this valley is extra special.

Golden Eagle

To share a perspective on size, I noticed a dead eagle spread out between two power lines. From the ground, the spread-eagle wing span looked to be a least six feet across. Power pole electrocution is listed as one of the causes of death, but it is not common because the local power company installed bird protectors on their lines to prevent this, but a power line is still a power line.

RAVENS
As opposed to those wimpy birds that fly south each winter, I tip my hat to the rough and ready raven. As I have learned, the common raven is a year-round resident.

This seemingly nondescript ebony bird has sparked my interest since my first reading of the Edgar Allen Poe poem named after the bird. And, my appreciation and curiosity about the common raven were enhanced when I read Bernd Heindrich's book, *A Year in the Maine Woods*, and the associated detail on his personal relationship with a young raven.

As described by the above author, the raven is fond of diving and erratic flight, which is reportedly a form play, and pairs often soar together with their wingtips touching.

The raven is versatile and is capable of thriving in either forest or brushland terrain, and is well established across all of Canada to the western third of the United States.

It has a reputation as an intelligent bird, as evidenced by the interaction described by Heindrich. As a member of the crow family, it also is capable as a predator and an opportunistic feeder.

In "The Raven," by Poe, is a line near the end that reads, "...desert land enchanted." Deserty land is a close enough connection to the terrain in which I see the local ravens. As the poet considers the bird "sitting lonely," I too have taken better notice of the perch from which this ebony bird presents itself.

So now this coming winter, after the turkey vulture is gone, followed by the golden eagle; I will think better of the black companion whose habit it is to share the winter elements with me.

I am also reminded of the John Prine song line, "the raven at my window was only a crow." At least now, I know the difference. I do enjoy the twists and turns from poetry, to nature, to the experiences in my own backyard.

BIGHORN SHEEP

During a visit with Max W, I was told that the Fish and Game Department released twenty-one bighorn sheep near my property; I suspect this is because their transport trailers could not get further up Martin Creek Road. The release point also made sense because the sheep are within a half-mile of finding their way to higher ground up inside the national forest.

As described on the eNature web page, the bighorn sheep, a medium-sized bovid, is a prized and interesting animal. Their winter coat sheds in patches beginning in June and continuing into July.

The hallmark of this species is the massive brown horns on the ram, which curve up and back over their ears. This horn spread can reach thirty-three inches in length. The ewe also has horns; however, their horns are short and slender, and they never form more than half of a curl.

The male weighs between one-hundred-twenty and three-hundred-fifteen pounds. A different source indicates that the weight range is between one-hundred-forty and one-hundred-eighty pounds. According to one source, the female weight range is between seventy-four and two-hundred pounds, and another source indicates the female range is normally between ninety and one-hundred-fifty pounds. When my cousin was at his lodge in Upper Cottonwood Creek, he reported that he occasionally viewed a bighorn with his spotting scope.

This animal is on the U.S. Endangered Species List. Their population decline dates back to the mid-1800s as settlers moved west in large numbers. This decline has an assortment of causes, including disease, sometimes related to domestic sheep. Predators also affect their population; in this local area, the mountain lion is the dominant predator.

However, local hunters report several mountain lions killed this winter. Notably, early this winter, a large mountain lion, a one-hundred-eighty-pound male, was shot and killed on the opposite side of the Santa Rosa range, near the Upper Willow Creek Ranch.

In this case, the animal showed evidence of some tough battles with facial scars and a broken right-side canine tooth. The hunt in which this lion was killed was a commercial hunt where an outsider paid a local guide to get them into position for a particular kill. The local guides get paid for twelve to fifteen hunts per year.

For perspective, it is estimated that the State of Nevada has a current mountain lion population of around two-thousand. This particular hunt included dogs that started in upper Willow Creek and moved north to Flat Creek Canyon.

Locally there was massive outrage when the story got out that someone had shot a Bighorn near Hinkey Summit. Anger was sparked because the shooter removed the head and left the body fairly close to the main dirt road. This behavior is not the normal action of hunters in this region. By contrast, my friend Eddie shot and killed a trophy ram this season during the regular season. This hunt was a long process by an experienced and considerate hunter.

Bighorn sheep breeding season is fall and early winter, depending upon geographic latitude. The normal gestation is approximately six months, meaning a single lamb will be born in the April to June time frame.

The breeding ritual is one of interest. The dominant ewe is the herd leader, and when the smaller herds come together for winter join up, each herd is led by the dominant ewe.

As the fall rutting season arrives, the rams begin to have butting contests. These contests progress and increase as the mating season gets into full swing. The butting contests are classic events as the rams charge each other at speeds over twenty miles per hour, sometimes reaching speeds of thirty miles per hour.

Interestingly enough, these contests are between males with similar size horns, and the contests can last twenty hours. The sound of two heads crashing is loud and can be heard a mile away, and the sound of the battle will prompt other males to follow suit.

The rut begins with the ram elevating his nose, cocking his head to one side, and curling his upper lip. The rutting male will follow any female that is in heat. If more than one male follows a female in heat, there will be butting jousts along the way.

The dominant male moves between herds seeking those females in heat. If one ram tires of mating, another will take his place. The breeding season runs from July through September. There is no computer dating here; they still do it the old fashion way.

When it is time for lambing, the mother will find secluded safe spots on the cliffs. During the early months, the lambs are vulnerable to predators such as the golden eagle. Within a day or two, the new lamb is capable of climbing nearly as well as the mother.

The newborn lamb remains hidden only for the first week; after that, they will graze with the mother. The weaning period takes place between five and six months.

The normal life span ranges from six to eight years, although an exceptional life span reaches eighteen or nineteen years. If they are fortunate enough to escape their predators, it is not uncommon to find bighorns living for about fifteen years.

Normally the gregarious animal will gather in herds ranging in size from five to fifteen. These herds will include all the mothering ewes, their lambs, yearlings, and two-year-olds. Again, these herds are led by the dominant ewe.

Meanwhile, the rams gather in smaller herd sizes of two to five. When winter arrives, these smaller herds group together. The combined group size may be up to one-hundred. From spring until fall rutting season, the males will separate and graze in the higher ranges.

The bighorns feed on grasses and sedges during the summer. Regarding water, the ram may go three days without water, while the ewes and lambs come to water holes during the hot and dry summer months. In the winter, they feed off woody plants such as willow, sage, and rabbitbrush.

They have a home range, but not a territory. They have evolved to rocky, high altitude terrain so that they can be free from human traffic and safer from predators such as the previously mentioned mountain lions and golden eagles. They also have to deal with other predators such as wolves, coyotes, bears, bobcats. Their rocky terrain provides good protection from most of these predators.

By next spring, it would be good news to verify that the herd of twenty-one, recently planted near my property, had produced some healthy young lambs who will now call the Humboldt National Forest their new home.

While visiting Max's shop, I noticed his spotting scope. It was pointed towards Hinkey Summit. From his property, I could see the road winding to the summit, probably eight or nine miles north. Max suggested that I shop for a more expensive model. On my next trip to Reno, I found these scopes in a price range from $130 to $2500. I found one I liked priced at $500; however, this can wait until I recover from the cost of building my ranch house.

HUMAN PERSPECTIVES

As a final point on wild things, I want to highlight a troublesome matter. After being in this community for a while, I have learned a battle is brewing between traditional grazing and the advocacy for certain wildlife.

Two birds that seem to be at the heart of this matter are the sage grouse and the yellow warbler—the yellow warbler population covers most of Canada and all of the U.S., except for the southeast edge of our country.

The advocacy groups that have taken legal action are the Western Watersheds Project and Forest Guardians. These two particular groups have forced the U.S. Forest Service to reconsider their grazing management plan around Mineral and Lyon Counties in western Nevada.

Closer to home, there is a push from the Idaho based Western Watershed Project to protect the sage grouse. A well-known activist speaks for the Western Watershed. Although their web material does not outwardly advocate extreme positions, it does seem that the comments and intentions of this activist are extreme.

Her remarks to Forest Service employees indicate that her goal is to curtail the long-standing cattle grazing in the higher-altitude Forest Service grazing allotments in order to protect the sage grouse. I am not privy to goals and objectives, but her comments indicate that she does not care if ranchers are forced out of business.

Published media reports suggest that she is trying to get the sage grouse listed as one of the endangered species. It appears that the current management plan to handle local grazing allotments is simply not acceptable to her way of thinking.

It does seem scary to me that any advocacy group could take such a harsh stance that would force local ranchers out of business. As I learned later, the land management specialists that work for the Forest Service have conscientiously endeavored to find a workable balance between wildlife interests and traditional cattle grazing interests. I have much more to learn about this person and her group, but at this point, I find their direction is disconcerting as it seems she is trying to put my friends and neighbors out of business.

I have come to realize that many advocacy groups take a much more reasonable approach to finding solutions to grazing controversies and land management. One such group is the Quivira Coalition.

A few years ago, I attended a grazing seminar that gave credit to the Quivira Coalition, and I liked the theme that I heard, moving towards the radical center.

At the current time, the two opposing perspectives are extremely far apart. Their membership support comes from over 1000 diversified members that include ranchers, land managers/owners, federal/state employees, tribal entities, the general public, and conservationists. I know that they are diversified because now, I am even a member. Seemingly more centered around New Mexico than Nevada, The Quivira Coalition's motto is: "Education, Innovation, Restoration: One Acre at a Time." This sounds much more reasonable than "Saving the Sage Grouse: One Law Suit at a Time."

While on the subject of "good guy" advocates, I should mention C.J. Hadley, Publisher and Editor of *Range* magazine. I've heard her speak, and I believe she is a true advocate for the rural and ranching interests of this state and region. Her magazine is devoted to the issues that threaten the West, its people, lifestyle, lands, and wildlife. C.J. Hadley is dedicated to the search for solutions that will halt the depletion of a national resource—The American Cowboy. More power to her.

The local ranchers who rely on summer grazing, via the Forest Service allotments, could use a few more C.J. Hadley's and a few less lawsuits challenging their right to graze cattle

6: LOCAL HISTORY & FOLKLORE

The eighth chapter of Walden Pond is one of the shortest sections by Thoreau; it chronicled his local village. Thoreau described that he did most of his work and reading in the morning, thus leaving his afternoons absolutely free. Every day or two, he would stroll to the village to hear some of the gossip.

I feel some parallels here. I try to get to town every couple of days. I need to check my post office box for new mail, and a visit to the local saloon has become the norm. I feel that this visit is one of the best ways for me to meet local people. Unlike Thoreau, I have little interest in or appetite for local gossip. Actually, I find there is little to gossip about, or else people here have different manners and priorities.

As I do not yet have TV service, it is good for me to check out some baseball scores and see what is happening to this crazy world of ours.

In the middle of his chapter on "The Village," Thoreau interestingly observes that he is checking on matters of war and peace, and he ponders if the "world was likely to hold together much longer." Despite the 161 years separating the start of Thoreau's stay and today, the concerns have not changed much.

At the time of this writing, our country is struggling with the War in Iraq. The point here is that it is easy to get into a war but much harder to get out. While I understand and support the rationale for this war, I see public support eroding week by week and month by month. Our country does not have much of a stomach for conflicts that last longer than a year or two.

Regarding the topic of war and peace, the news on June 8th, 2006, indicated that the number one terrorist in Iraq, Zarqawi, had been killed. While this is good news, it is incredible that this notable killer eluded U.S. forces for so many years.

QUEEN CITY & NINETY-SIX RANCH

My property marks the southern edge of the mining camp town, called Queen City, and my neighbor John's property marks the northern boundary of this old mining town. This site was not for pulling ore out of the mountain but rather in processing the ore.

This mining town seems to have flourished for approximately twenty years, from 1865—twenty years after Thoreau started his stay at Walden Pond—to 1885, and was active approximately six years after the discovery of gold and silver in the Comstock Lode.

The location of this mining town seems to be set at the point where Martin Creek busts out of the mountain rock gap. This source of steady water was instrumental in the operation of gold and silver miners. According to my neighbor, John, this mining town reached a population of one-hundred residents, and business boomed enough to justify a daily stagecoach run to Winnemucca, forty miles away. The deeply cut ruts of the stage wagons are still visible in the terrain north of my property. I often use these same ruts as the trail for my new quad.

A framed photo of Queen City hung on the wall of the town saloon portrays a full-blown mining operation with many miners who migrated West after the Civil War for a get-rich-quick opportunity.

The story, according to John, tells of a severe food shortage near the second half of the camp's twenty-year run. In response, a wheat mill was developed nearby. This location, now called the Mill Ranch, is now owned and operated by the Cassinelli family. My seventeen-acre property exists thanks to a sub-division from the Cassinelli owners.

John is fond of sharing his 1861 local history reference books, which includes an artist's sketch of the mining camp dam further upstream. Though eighty percent of the old structure is gone, remnants can still be seen. The location and scale of this dam are well portrayed in this sketch.

Ninety-Six Ranch

The oldest established ranch in this valley is the Ninety-Six Ranch, owned by the Stewart family. The front entrance to the ranch is a historical marker that celebrates the date of 1846 as the beginning of that ranch operation. For perspective, this was but one year after Thoreau moved to Walden Pond.

INDEPENDENT THINKING NEVADANS

The Ninety-Six Ranch also holds a place in modern folklore. When I first arrived here, I was surprised to hear the locals share favorable opinions about a local hunter and trapper who later was convicted of killing two federal agents—the actual conviction was for manslaughter.

This story is portrayed in the book *Outlaw: The True Story of Claude Dallas,* written by Jeff Long, as well as Jack Olson's book, *Give a Boy a Gun.*

The Ninety-Six Ranch was one of the first ranches that Claude Dallas worked on when he moved to this valley. Local lore says he learned basic cowboy or buckaroo skills at this ranch, and to use cowboy terms, the Ninety-Six Ranch is where he learned to sit a horse.

The independent thinking of old Nevadans helps explain this sort of silent support for Claude, a local "bad guy." This independent thought shows up again in 1979 during the Sagebrush Rebellion. At that time, Assemblyman Dean Rhoads, representing Elko County, introduced the so-called Sagebrush Rebellion bill.

This bill attempted to reclaim forty-nine million acres of public land from federal control and offer it for state control. This concept not only had strong local support, but at one point, President Reagan declared himself a Sagebrush Rebel, too.

Assemblyman Rhoads proposed this bill during a period when local ranchers were reeling under the pressure of new laws and new agencies, including BLM, EPA, OSHA, NRDC, and NEPA. In an effort to fight back, some locals started their own group called League for the Advancement of Equal Rights (LASER).

Again, independent thought showed up more recently in another locals versus government conflict. This rebellion played out approximately ten years ago in the town of Jarbidge, which is located in the northeast corner of Nevada.

Government officials took a position on river and road access that differed from what local residents thought made sense. A shovel brigade began as locals decided to rebuild a section of road that the feds deemed too sensitive. The town population swelled when regional sympathizers showed up—with shovels in hand—to help the well-organized road repair rallies. The government could not muster any local support for their position.

CLAUDE DALLAS

I'd like to talk a bit more about Claude Dallas. At first, I wasn't sure if I wanted to include his story in this book, but by the end of the first chapter in *Outlaw*, I recognized why many of the locals have come to support the Claude Dallas' version of killing two federal game wardens.

Because of the aggressive manner in which the game wardens presented themselves, Dallas calculated that he was either going to jail or was going to be gunned down on the spot. He acted first and shot both federal agents. As it turned out, he may have gotten off with justifiable homicide except he followed the first wounding shots with fatal headshots, much like you would for a wounded animal.

According to local accounts, the prosecution never bothered to go after the local guy, Craig Carver, who aided Claude Dallas because they knew that they would not be able to get a conviction from a local jury. Craig is well-known and well-liked in this community. He is the guy who later hauls my hay.

It appears to be a classic story of a young guy completely satisfied to lead a quiet life living off nature in the rough country called the Owyhee Desert—the word desert does not do justice to this vast and fertile area.

Dallas was reported for hunting or trapping out of season, and two game wardens from Idaho made an aggressive move on his camp. The lead warden was extremely badge-heavy and repeated multiple times that he would have to take Dallas in. He made sure Dallas knew the arrest could either be the hard way or the easy way.

The nature of this contact was not unlike the FBI fiascos at both Ruby Ridge and the Waco (Davidian) Compound. By most objective law enforcement accounts, these actions were beyond the scope of good police work and thus dark accounts of how not to enforce the law.

This Claude Dallas story tells me two things. First, the rough terrain of this locale—especially north into the national forest and northeast to the Owyhee Desert—is capable of sustaining a mountain man with food for long periods. Second, that common sense folks will generally sympathize with any person victimized by overly aggressive law enforcement.

I did not have to spend many months living here before several local stories were shared about the incompetence of certain government employees and the abuse of power of others. It is easy to see a common thread here on how some government employees deal with local residents.

Rather than attempting a fair and objective account of this shooting incident, I thought it would be better to simply share the words of the ballad, "Claude Dallas," co-written by Tom Russell and Ian Tyson.

> In a land the Spanish once had called the
> Northern Mystery,
> Where rivers run and disappear, the mustang
> still is free.
> By the Devil's wash and coyote hole in the wild
> Owyhee Range

Somewhere in the sage tonight the wind calls
out his name.
Aye, aye, aye.

Come gather 'round me buckaroos and a story I
will tell
Of the fugitive Claude Dallas who just broke out
of jail.
You might think this tale is history from before
the West was won,
But the events that I'll describe took place in
nineteen eighty-one.
He was born out in Virginia, left home when
school was through;
In the deserts of Nevada he became a buckaroo,
And he learned the ways of cattle, and he
learned to sit a horse,
And he always packed a pistol, and he practiced
deadly force.
Then Claude he became a trapper, and he
dreamed of the bygone days,
And he studied bobcat logic and their wild and
silent ways
In the bloody runs near Paradise, in monitors
down south
Trapping cats and coyotes, living hand to mouth.
Aye, aye, aye.

Then Claude took to livin' all alone out many
miles from town,
A friend—Jim Stevens—brought supplies and he
stayed to hang around.

That day two wardens—Pogue and Elms—rode
into check Claude out,
They were seeking violations and to see what
Claude's about.
Now Claude had hung some venison, he had a
bobcat pelt or two,
Pogue claimed they were out of season, he said:
"Dallas, you're all through."
But Dallas would not leave his camp. He refused
to go to town.
As the wind howled thought the bull-camp, they
stared each other down.
It's hard to say what happened next; perhaps
we'll never know,
They were gonna take Claude in to jail, and he
vowed he'd never go.
Jim Stevens heard the gunfire, and when he
turned around
Bill Pogue was falling backwards, Conley Elms he
fell facedown.
Aye, aye, aye.

Jim Stevens walked on over; there was a gun
near Bill Pogue's hand.
It was hard to say who drawn his first, but
Claude had made his stand.
Claude said "I am justified Jim, they were gonna
cut me down,
And a man's got a right to hang some meat
When he's livin' this far from town."
It took eighteen men and fifteen months to
finally run Claude down.

In the sage outside of Paradise, they drove him
to the ground.
Convicted up in Idaho—manslaughter by
decree—
Thirty years at maximum, but soon Claude
would break free.
There's two sides two this story; there may be
no right or wrong,
The lawman and the renegade have graced a
thousand songs.
The story is an old one. Conclusion's hard to
draw,
But Claude's out in the sage tonight he may be
the last outlaw.
Aye, aye, aye.

In a land the Spanish once had called the
Northern Mystery,
Where rivers run and disappear, the mustang
still is free.
By the Devil's wash and the coyote hole in the
wild Owyhee Range
Somewhere in the sage tonight the wind calls
out his name.
Aye, aye, aye

I am not sure how to provide a more succinct account
than via the words of this song. The only mystery
associated with this song and the guy who co-wrote it has
to do with a comment during a November 2006 live
performance. Tom Russell, one of the co-authors,
acknowledged this particular song but said he couldn't
play it and moved on. He never explained why. At other
times, I have heard Tom Russell sing this song.

During one of the workshops at the Elko Cowboy Poetry Gathering, there was a songwriters workshop featuring both Tom Russell and Ian Tyson. During that session, Russell explained that it was a challenge to write the "Claude Dallas" ballad without taking one side or the other. I think you will see by the words and the story that he achieved this goal.

One local rancher observed that in one of the books about the Dallas story, a comment was made that when a person turned east on Highway 290, they were going back one-hundred years in time. Many locals feel this is a positive observation rather than a negative one.

To this day, there is a kind of mystique associated with the Claude Dallas story. The reaction runs the gamut from disdain to outright support. Those in favor seem to live closest to this valley community. To this date, some people, who wish to remain anonymous, still report Dallas sightings.

Finally, an interesting side note to the Dallas story was the fact that during his murder trial in Idaho, a group of loyal females from that community gathered in support of Claude. This group of supportive women quickly received the nickname the Dallas Cheerleaders.

COWBOY STORIES & WISDOM

On May 25th, I spent the morning doing hard labor, such as moving rocks, raking, cutting sagebrush. By early afternoon, I decided that I had put in enough hours for a legitimate workday. Consequently, I took a couple of hours off to read and write.

By happy-hour, I decided to make a quick drive to the local saloon for a couple of beers and some socializing. Upon arrival, I found Davy Kern at the bar, along with some of his cowboy friends Joe and Jerry.

Davy Kern

Joe had just spent the day on top of a Caterpillar bulldozer clearing brush. He told some wild tales of rolling a 40,000 pound Cat off the top of a flatbed trailer, and in another account, he told of a Cat doing a front-end wheelie and rolling over backward. These stories would be wild enough if they were quads or tractors, but the sheer weight and volume of a Cat is something to behold.

Joe also explained the economics of clearing brush. In the past, he used to pay state inmates to do this job, but now the cost of labor for one inmate is $10.00 per hour. Based on this labor cost increase, he no longer hires this work out.

As part of the cowboy advice session, I was told that if I wanted to explore the Owyhee desert region, I should bring extra spare tires—yes, more than one—along with spare food and water. I should also inform someone where I plan to explore because that region is infamous for swallowing up people that are never seen again.

Jerry told a story about the guy who stopped to look over a ledge. He even left his truck running. Two years later, they found some of his bones scattered at the bottom of the ledge. Since he failed to tell anyone where he was headed, search and rescue personnel searched other states and other counties before someone else found his remains in the Owyhee.

This whole region bears the name Owyhee as a memorial for three Hawaiian trapper-explorers who departed from the main body of Donald McKenzie's fur trapping expedition in 1819 and vanished.

~~~ ~~~ ~~~
~~~ ~~~ ~~~

The Paradise Valley seems to attract a diverse array of free-thinking and free-spirited cowboys. On August 12th, I met Monty at the local saloon.

Monty was from Alberta, Canada. He was well-traveled and very savvy to the world, especially the cowboy lifestyle. He was fascinating to visit with because his philosophy seemed so basic and solid, for it was based on good common sense.

We managed to have a five-way conversation for a couple of hours without wasting any time on social problems, terrorism, or other stuff that clobbers our bigger news picture. Monty has many projects going on with cowboy culture, media, and enjoyable things to do.

COWBOY HANDS

After some small talk, I couldn't help but notice the difference between the hands of a working cowboy and mine.

This book started with the sentence, "With my own two hands..." My hands are relatively soft and unbeaten. I still have some splinters and barbs under my thumb skin. But I have smooth hands in comparison to these working guys. Their hands are average-sized, but their fingers are large and beat up. Dirt and grease stains are the norm, paired with blood blisters and damage marks on the fingernails. These hand traits were in evidence from Davy, to Joe, to Jerry, to Jerry's sons Joe and Sam.

These hands are nothing to be ashamed of as they symbolize the hard work ethic that makes up the working class from this community. My hands may get there someday, but they'll have to endure a lot of abuse before I reach that level.

Over time this summer, I found myself dissatisfied with the twenty-dollar cloth and hide fancy gloves. They look good on the shelf, and they wear well for the first few workdays. However, after a couple of days of real work, these gloves come apart. I have tried numerous different types, and the end result is always the same. Consequently, I find myself doing most of the tough chores—hauling rocks, cutting and hauling sage—in my bare hands. Time will tell if I join the rough hands club.

By November 2006, I started to notice the beat-up fingernails, the dry skin around my nails, and how the skin was prone to cracking open. These and other signs tell me that my office hands are a thing of the past. By the middle of February, the tile mortar and the hammer abuse from installing wood floors had changed the appearance of these hands even further.

PARADISE VALLEY

The town of Paradise is located right in the middle of the valley called Paradise Valley, and the town and valley are not on the way to anywhere. To get to town, you have to turn off the main highway for Highway-290, and the only thing at the end of this road is the town.

This location may help keep out some of the curious, though many hunters know of this area as a prime spot to hunt.

Cottonwood Creek works its way east out of the Santa Rosa Range. It snakes east, then turns south as it runs through town and on towards the Humboldt River. This creek generally has flowing water, but occasionally runs dry.

This valley is approximately forty miles long and twelve miles wide. The altitude in the valley-bottom center is 4,500 feet. The Santa Rosa Mountains surround the valley on two sides. The high point on the mountain range is Santa Rosa peak at approximately 9,700 feet. In a way, this valley is shaped like a horseshoe opening to the south towards Winnemucca.

〰〰〰
〰〰〰

According to the 2000 census, Paradise Valley, the town and surrounding area, has one-hundred-thirteen people in the 98426 zip code. The community has two-hundred-eleven housing units, and of this, eighty-three are family households. Demographics reflect eighty-eight percent white and fifteen percent Hispanic. My guess is that the Hispanic numbers are undercounted due to the problem of legal status; they stay below the radar.

The town of Paradise has a population of around a hundred, with a mix of full-time residents and many weekend residents from Winnemucca or Reno. Town proper is centered around the post office and the old saloon. Two nice churches seem only to get Sunday use. The town still has a small but active elementary school as well as a grave-yard just west of town. A Forest Service office is on Main Street, which is fitting since they are the largest property owner/manager in the region.

The houses are a mix of handsome newer homes and a like number of older abandoned homes. On the east end of town is a small ranch-type complex with barns, cattle trucks, and farm machinery that is owned by Kenny

Buckingham. This ranch hosts several cattle, a few horses, and one white goat.

The last operating hotel in town was the Micca House. During the peak years, this small town had three thriving hotels. Today the only place to stay commercially is the lovely bed and breakfast, the Stone House B&B, owned by Steve Lucas, which is located south of town. I stayed there during 2005 when I was property hunting in this valley.

Paradise town is easy to see from any of the high ground surrounding the valley. It is full of mature trees that provide an invitation for a closer look.

≈≈≈
≈≈≈

On June 22nd, I had the unusual experience of spending extra time in Paradise town because I was expecting a UPS delivery—my new quad trailer for hauling wood out of Cottonwood Creek. UPS could give me a delivery day, but not a delivery time; therefore, I went to town early in the morning and decided to wait it out.

I arrived two-and-a-half hours before the saloon opened, so I brought a book and my youngest dog, and we parked ourselves in the shade of the saloon. This spot gave me a clear view of Main Street and any incoming traffic. Almost all of the traffic included pickup trucks; some were old, and some were new. Many pulled horse-trailers. My friend Casey drove through town with his new pickup, pulling his horse trailer full of horses. I recognized about a third of the folks driving past.

My year-old dog was exceptionally well mannered while other dogs barked out greetings as they passed by in pickup beds. We walked to the post office to collect the mail. As we entered, the dogs on both sides of the door got loud and excited, but Rocky remained calm. She is better mannered when she is away from the older, more aggressive dogs.

Approximately one block south of the saloon, on Main Street, is a historical marker that tells a brief history of this town. It reads as follows:

Hudson Bay Company's Peter Skene Ogden traversed Paradise Valley November 1828. Settled in 1863. Indian trouble started the next year, causing the establishment of Camp Winfield Scott (1866-70) four miles from here. Paradise Valley was the produce center for nearby Nevada and Idaho Territory Mines." "In the original town of Scottsdale (1866), John C. Kemler built the first hotel. Now used as a residence. Renamed Paradise City (1869). The town was a mining supply center: 1878-1920. Later, when livestock raising dominated, the town was again renamed. This time "Paradise Valley.
—State Historical Marker No. 89, Nevada State Park System.

The only other activity on Main Street, while I killed two-plus hours, was a young girl doing laps on her bicycle and a family of three that departed the RV park across the street on their two quads.

The atmosphere of this time and place was one of an ideal little town. The near-perfect morning temperature, coupled with clear and sunny skies and large trees on Main Street, which offered comforting shade, made for a pleasant spot to wait.

At 10:30 a.m., Kristi, the saloon manager, drove up in her pickup truck to open the bar. She offered me entrance even though the official opening time was still half an hour away. My dog joined me in the bar, which seems to be an accepted practice here. In the months since I've moved here, I have gotten to know Kristi better; she is a lovely young lady and has an ideal personality for tending bar and serving people. This bar's interior organization includes two sofas and one easy-chair along the north wall. This living room type atmosphere also includes a coffee table with interesting books on display, including *Paradise Valley, Nevada, The People and Buildings of An American Place*, written by Howard Wright Marshall. I shall try to purchase this book someday. The black and white photo on the cover is that of my neighbor's ranch, The Old Mill Ranch, and is the same ranch that my future house will look down on.

On the cover flap, the author argues that a "society's material culture is one of the most expressive clues to its character: the handsomely constructed buildings of Paradise Valley are symbolic of its distinctive aesthetic system, its folk traditions and culture, its ethnicity and shared vision." This statement says a lot about this place.

In Paradise Valley's case, that industry was exemplified by its settlers—Italians, White Americans, Hispanics, Germans, Basques, and Chinese. This diverse group of people all left their imprint on the community. It was a close-knit group of skilled stonemasons from the Alpine valleys of the Piedmont region northwestern Italy, who most clearly shaped the valley's architectural face.

～～～
～～～

While different stories and legends abound on how this place was first located, it seems that the hard rock miners first entered this valley in May of 1863. As the white settlers started to replace the native Paiute Indians, trouble followed.

With the death of several European American settlers in 1865, the U.S. Army followed with a location at Camp Winfield Scott—also known as Camp Scott—which is now under the ranch ownership of Davy Kern. As the Indian threat was neutralized by 1871, the troops moved north to Camp McDermitt.

What I find odd about Camp Scott is that it is located on the creek bottom in a low spot. Typically, military camps liked higher ground for tactical reasons; however, the lower location did provide a good source of water.

The village of Paradise City grew up around the Nichols family ranch in about 1866. The name of the town changed ever so slightly over the years. At first, it was called Paradise City. Later it was shortened to simply Paradise. Finally, the name Paradise Valley came when the government mapmakers provided that name.

The town was in its prime from the 1870s to the 1920s. This run of fifty years saw the usual mix of shops and businesses of that era, which included blacksmith shops, general stores, livery stables, hotels, and saloons. Currently, locals report an increase in population as smaller properties become available for sale.

I currently sit and write in a building built by Steve Boggio, an Italian immigrant stonemason. It still stands because of the granite blocks and skilled craftsmanship of the builder. It is still a comfortable building, warm in the winter, and cool in the summer.

RANCH HISTORY

Both the pace and activity of a farm and ranch community is dictated by the season. In the spring, the cattle move from the home ranches to the mountains for grazing. Around April is the time for branding the calves, although fall branding is also required for any late cattle births during the summer.

By the summer, the emphasis shifts to haying, with multiple crops for those lucky enough to have irrigation systems. Normally this second hay harvest is around forty days after the first.

By fall, it is time to bring the herds down from the mountains in cattle drives that even include city-slickers coming out to help.

Winters are a time of idleness or resting. While less may be going on during the winter, cattle still demand to be fed daily.

As I take a closer look at the long-term ranch history in this valley, I quickly learned that an effort to capture local history was made in earnest during 1980 when the Paradise Valley Folklife Project was conducted by the American Folklife Center in the Library of Congress. Also, the Smithsonian Institution was a party to this study. This effort was called "Buckaroos in Paradise." The end product of this two-year study was both a book and a web page, both by the same name.

While this effort looked at over one dozen local ranches, the detailed focus was directed at the oldest ranch, the Ninety-Six Ranch. Today this large ranch is still in the same family, with the current owner-operators being fifth generation locals. Marie Stewart, whose smiling photo is recorded on page xii of *Buckaroos in Paradise: Cowboy Life in Northern Nevada*, is still healthy and active in the community.

Another featured ranch was the Old Mill Ranch. Robert Cassinelli, pictured on page xiii, has passed on leaving the Old Mill Ranch in the capable hands of his son, Dan. The Mill Ranch is photographed on page 2 and 44 of the *Buckaroo* book. This meadow ranch location is still beautiful, and it is the first sight I see every morning when I get up and look southward out my window.

In the twenty-seven years since the above effort, it would appear that the established local ranches remain alive and well. In a few cases, ranches listed in the 1980 study have changed hands, but for the most part, the old family names in this valley are still working the ranches described in Buckaroos in Paradise. Often accounts describing this region will describe the neighboring Owyhee Desert as a harsh and barren expanse of land—the book *Buckaroos in Paradise* held this view. A description such as this implies that no one can eke out a living in these parts. However, proof to the contrary is evident with a visit to the Harper Ranch, whose proper name is Little Humboldt Ranch, located around forty miles east of Paradise Valley town. On the Little Humboldt Ranch is a thriving family with husband and wife as well as two remarkable sons.

I had the pleasure of watching Joe, the oldest, and Sam, the youngest, work cattle, while at the same time, they demonstrated rancher neighborliness. During the spring branding at the Ninety-Six Ranch, the two sons and their father, Jerry—from Little Humbolt Ranch—did all of the rope work to bring in the calves for branding. The young sons prided themselves in being able to rope both hind legs for a clean delivery of the calf for branding. There were a few exceptions when only one rear leg made it into the lasso. In these instances, a healthy round of badgering and good-natured ridicule cropped up.

THE HARPER BOYS

Shortly after moving to this valley, I heard local talk about the publication called "Desert Trails," a monthly newsletter, crafted by Joe and Sam Harper—both of these boys became world-class saddle bronc riders on the national rodeo circuit.

The newsletter tells down-home stories of various events in the lives of these Harper boys. Their subject matter runs the gamut from hunting and trapping accounts to their impressions of attending a local funeral. These newsletters are complete with related photos, taken by their talented mother, Nancy. It was not until the end of my first year here that I got copies of back issues.

The origins of this newsletter, or as they call it, newspaper, date back to when Joe was entering the second grade in September 1999. Rather than writing sentences that his mother put on the board for him to correct, he wrote down stories of the interesting things he did every day.

For me, the important thing here is the heartfelt communication from these boys to the local community, and the distribution of this newsletter is quite widespread throughout the greater community.

The boys also developed a popular local cookbook called the *Desert Trails Cookbook*. The cookbook includes more than cowboy recipes; it offers tributes, bible verses, stories, photos, and sketches. The cookbook sections are divided into clever categories, such as soup in the cow tracks, salad in the sagebrush, around the campfire feeding the crew, buckaroo breads, main bites, taters 'n beans, and so on. When the Harper boys first published their cookbook, they had a distribution of three-hundred-twenty-one, and I am trying to increase this by one more.

Both the newsletters and the cookbook are engaging and well produced. Both boys are clearly exceptional young fellows, and any time spent around them would quickly prove my point.

I had the good fortune a few months ago, to watch a local rancher present one of the boys with a special gift pocket knife. The joy and appreciation for this special gift went well beyond ordinary descriptive words. Months later, the recipient of this gift was roping calves during the spring branding for the person who made the gift.

Out here, this proves again that what goes around, comes around for both goodwill and giving.

CHIMNEY DAM

On July 3rd, I drove twenty miles east of the valley to explore a local water spot called Chimney Dam, which consists of two reservoirs, perfectly situated in the middle of the open Owyhee high desert. The dirt road heading to this spot crosses two small streams and connects a couple of ranches.

This regional terrain is remarkable because no trees grow here, except for at ranch sites and along some of the waterways. Before leaving the valley floor, you drive past the historic Stewart property—Ninety-Six Ranch. Further east, you drive nearby the Bull Head Ranch, a part of the Nevada First Corp.

The reservoir behind the dam provides recreational relief during hot temperatures. On the day I visited, I saw approximately five active campsites and a couple of inner-tube floaters on the water. The only signs of wildlife included two pelicans and a number of killdeer.

∼∼∼ ∼∼∼ ∼∼∼
∼∼∼ ∼∼∼ ∼∼∼

The pelican was the American white pelican, a relatively large bird with an average weight of just over sixteen pounds. The dominant features of this bird include the pure white color and the large yellowish bill and pouch.

Upper Nevada marks the southern extreme of their summer location. Although I did not see these birds in flight, the Sibley reference book indicates that they have a black secondary, trailing edge, wing color.

These birds typically roost on sandbars and small low islands, and they forage in shallow sheltered waters of lakes, marshes, and lagoons, feeding on small fish. They usually gather in groups up to ten.

The two birds that I followed did not like my presence, and they continued to move further from shore every time

I changed my location while trying to get a suitable photograph.

The killdeer is a common bird widely spread across America. They are visible in the Nevada area year-round, though they tend to move further north into Canada for summer periods. They are generally seen on any open ground, though not always near water, and are often in small groups that pipe with a loud, persistent high pitch. They nest and forage on gravel parking lots, shortgrass fields, and similar open areas.

Unlike the pelicans, the birds I saw were not afraid of humans and scampered in front of me as I walked the sandy beach of the reservoir.

∽∽ ∽∽ ∽∽
∽∽ ∽∽ ∽∽

Following my trip to Chimney Dam, I paid a short visit to the local saloon and learned that the locals were headed back to Martin Creek for some socializing. I drove back towards my property and paid a visit to the shaded section of the creek where the water holes are suitable for swimming.

When I arrived, I found different groups on different sections of the creek. After a couple of stops, I approached a white pickup truck that pulled over when I came in with my quad. Junior drove this pickup with Jon as the passenger. They explained that the party was further upstream, where the trail crosses the water. We gathered at a campsite where an older Class-C camper was parked.

After pulling in, I was introduced to Craig, the adult in charge of this campsite. Craig is the son of Stan, whom I recently met from Paradise Town. Craig managed a bunch of kids moving between swimming and setting up a tent. Junior, Jon, Craig, and I started a hardy conversation, supplemented with some beers.

Other groups soon followed suit and joined the party. We spent about three hours visiting and drinking in the best possible social setting. Constructive conversation came forth on topics ranging from the war in Iraq, to the quality of life in this community, to raising kids. I valued this excellent chit-chat, which covered an impressive cross-section of local society. This conversation gave me even more reason to be thankful for residing in this community.

While adults talked about adult things, the kids were happy-go-lucky playing in the creek. The kids occasionally intermingled with the adults to create an all-American family setting. Before the party scaled-down, the kids, the younger adults, and the older adults were all mixed into one big social circle.

7: SUMMER SEASON

My second season of local observation starts on the summer solstice. I acknowledge that an inevitable psychological letdown happens knowing that tomorrow the days start getting shorter as we inch towards winter. In the meantime, I will enjoy these long days and warm temperatures.

Summer is the season for getting work done, and my neighbor, Joe, just told me that the summer season means working twenty-four hours a day, seven days a week. I guess this implies that the winter season is more kicked-back. We will see.

MORMON CRICKETS REVISITED

The first observation for this summer season is the fact that the Mormon crickets are still around. From what I can tell, they move southward when they are not feeding. The Reno paper just updated an article on this topic.

They referred to the infamous start of the Mormon cricket story in 1848 when they overwhelmed the settlers' crops. Unlike that early account, I do not see any seagulls on the horizon, ready to neutralize the threat.

The article points out that the state spends increasingly more time and money on this infestation. Over four-hundred-thousand acres have now been sprayed across the state; pesticide spray comes at the cost of $1.5 million per year.

According to Jeff Knight, state entomologist, we are now seven years into this cricket spread. By the end of the summer, it is expected that the crickets will cover between ten and twelve million acres. The newspaper map indicates that twelve states are affected, and they are capable of covering a total of fifty miles in a single season. As I observed yesterday, when the large gravel rig crushed many of these crickets on the road, the other crickets will often cannibalize the dead.

Later, a grey pickup truck drove down the county road with a red sprayer pumping. If I had to guess, this spray application might have had something to do with the cricket population. In a subsequent conversation with my neighbor Joe, he suggested that the only use for an airborne spray would be to control mosquitoes.

As of July 22nd, I sensed the cricket population seemed to drop off. Joe agreed with this observation.

Where do these crickets come from, and why are they front and center of local conversation? The first evidence of baby crickets came in spring. The first report came in mid-March from the Willow Creek Ranch on the opposite side of the Santa Rosa mountains. The first little critters were spotted clinging to the sunny side of the house.

My first spotting came during mid-April when I found a few of the same small crickets on my wall. From the time of the first spotting to the current spotting, we have had two cold snaps where the night time temperatures dipped below freezing.

Hopeful thinking would speculate that there was some freeze kill during this period. We will have to wait and see what the entomologists report later.

The pending population is of concern as my spring of 2007 is focused on planning and starting a garden and yard landscape that will be able to protect itself.

HARD WORK AND FREE-SPIRITEDNESS

As I continue to re-read Walden, I am struck with two references. First is his philosophical lecture to the hard-working Irishman by the name of John Field. Thoreau set out to convince him that the life of hard labor did not make sense. Hard labor caused a man to eat more; therefore, his regular living expenses, including heavy work clothing, would be higher, and thus little benefit would be accomplished.

In the meantime, the constant labor would prevent time for huckleberrying—to use Thoreau's term—in the summer for amusement. Thoreau professed that his lifestyle of working when required to support his simple means was of greater value and quality of life.

Having recently concluded thirty-six years of adult hard labor, I agree that a certain amount of balance between work and play is essential. However, I also understand that in the competitive world of merit and achievement, unless you want to remain average, the urge is always to work harder and accomplish more. To my knowledge, there are no known examples of tombstones or headstones, saying, "I wish I'd worked harder."

Second is the issue of free will or free-spirit. I find it invigorating and refreshing to see the free-spiritedness of many of the locals in this valley. Thoreau made a journal entry once that said, "*original and independent men are wild, not tamed and broken by society.*"[1]

With my many years working in government at federal, state, and county levels, I found the vast majority of my peers to be followers with few original thoughts. Most were eight-to-five workers who just wanted to get by.

The few that were creative or reform-minded appeared to have an uphill battle because the status quo seemed to be the preferred path. It was always harder and more dangerous to take on large problems because most people are not prone to change.

Consequently, many, if not most, eventually gave in to the pressure to be average and just get by. It was always refreshing to find a rare leader who wanted to take on the world and make things better. For me, those days are gone now, and my focus is on the working-class people who promote the commerce of this valley.

My experience with the gravel delivery man, Dennis, helps to define the free-spirit model. If there is any stress with Dennis, it is safe to say that it does not show. In a short amount of time, I felt confident that I had tagged Dennis as one of those wild and entertaining men who was neither tamed nor broken by society. In truth, after most of his early morning gravel deliveries to my place, he was fond of asking for a beer for the trip home, one for the road.

This community seems full of free-spirited and hard-working men. This time of year, haying is the work priority. For those farmers and ranchers who own irrigated fields, this is the season to bring in that first crop of hay, usually alfalfa. The days of hand hauled small hay bales are gone, but the process of cutting, curing, baling, and hauling hay is still hard work. It must be done quickly because, with irrigation, the next crop is waiting to get nourished to mature growth.

Last evening, June 20th, I had a beer with some of these neighbors who are in the midst of haying. They circled a huge barrel BBQ grill, cooking steaks, fresh oysters, and salmon just delivered from Alaska. While the eating was good, it goes back to the Thoreau lecture that hard work demands good eating. I am convinced that my neighbors would like it no other way. They live the motto of work hard, live hard, and play hard.

As of July 2nd, only a few Mormon crickets are to be seen. Because of the hot temperature, the few remaining hide in the shade of whatever they can find.

SAGEBRUSH

Any description of this region would be incomplete without mention of our most significant plant life here in the Great Basin, sagebrush.

The sagebrush is an ever-gray shrub, usually growing to approximately four feet tall and four feet wide. In lower-lying areas where moisture is abundant, the height can get up to ten feet.

This plant is native to the dry regions of the western U.S.; it needs full sun and is drought tolerant. This drought tolerance has been achieved through evolution so that this plant can water itself. In other words, at night, the taproot pulls moisture from deep in the soil up to shallow branching roots that grow near the surface. If you should ever need an example of a large taproot, then try to dig out sagebrush with a pickax sometime.

Sage has a characteristic sharp odor that the early pioneer travelers along the Oregon Trail described as a mixture of turpentine and camphor. This plant is important to wildlife as it provides food to sage sparrows, sage thrashers, loggerhead shrikes, and sage grouse. Additionally, sagebrush helps to protect the fragile bunchgrass, a staple for cattle grazing.

By late summer and early fall, a small golden-yellow flower blooms on the sage. The fruit of the plant is edible, and according to some sources, it aids digestion.

Most geological maps, as well as plant life maps, show this northern section of Nevada within the area known as the Great Basin. However, one internet sagebrush site indicates, based on sagebrush coverage, that northern Nevada is actually part of the Columbia Plateau, covering most of eastern Oregon and parts of Idaho. This northern tier includes the upper portions of Washoe County and encompasses High Rock Canyon, the Quinn River, the Santa Rosa Range, the Owyhee Desert, and the beautiful area of Jarbidge.

It should also be noted that sagebrush makes a quick fire for cowboys working on the range who need fire for both cooking and to heat their branding irons. This plant produces little smoke and is an ideal source of instant fuel.

EMERGING WIND PATTERNS

Since my arrival here, I have noted the wind patterns, and my attempt to understand them is still ongoing. On this first day of summer, I noticed a pattern that I think I've determined to be the norm.

By late afternoon the wind blew from south to north, which meant that the breeze was blowing up Martin Creek canyon.

Around dinner time, the winds were perfectly calm, and they remained calm for an extended period while I cooked dinner outside.

After dinner, I started a pit fire, as I often do, to burn dead sagebrush as well as scrap wood leftover from the day's construction work—not to mention getting rid of the two mice that I caught overnight. By the time the fire got roaring, and the sun started to set, the winds picked up again.

This time the wind direction was from north to south, down the creek canyon. By 10:30 p.m., the sky is dark and clear, no storm systems are in the area, and the wind continues to blow south. This observation is a continuation of what I reported in Chapter Two.

On July 2nd, we had a steady wind all day. It was around fifteen miles per hour and came out of the southwest. This wind did not calm until around 7:30 p.m. It was calm enough that I dared to start a pit fire. I had a large pile of sage pieces and scrap lumber that I needed to get rid of. By 7:50 p.m., the wind was totally calm.

Before 8:30 p.m. rolled around, the wind started up again. This time, it was coming down canyon from the north, favoring northwest. The wind was pesky enough that I had to water down the cheatgrass around the fire pit. I reluctantly let the fire burn until almost 9:15 p.m.; at that point, I flooded the fire pit with water to avoid any more fire risk.

The pattern is starting to emerge with the up canyon and down canyon breeze effect.

On July 8th, we had little in the way of late afternoon winds, and it seemed calm enough to start a pit fire. This was a good idea until it got dark, then the winds started from the north.

They were mild winds until around 10:00 p.m.; at that point, the gusts were so strong that the motorhome was rocking. For the sake of safety, I went outside and watered down the red-hot coal bed that was starting to throw sparks into the sage.

On July 13th, the winds were very mild to calm during the day. From late afternoon, they did not blow at all, so I started a pit fire around 6:30 p.m., and the wind remained calm until 9:50 p.m. when they picked up from the north—thus falling back into the regular evening pattern. By comparison, the winds tonight are mild, perhaps only ten miles per hour.

A SUMMER'S DAY OBSERVATIONS

As of June 2nd, activity has calmed down here because the construction work crew is taking a four-day holiday break. I will not see them again until the 5th.

At this time of year, the temperature is hot, and the weather is mild. During the past few days, the daytime high has been in the upper 90s. Fortunately, a slight breeze helps with the hottest part of the day.

I look forward to the stage when the RV shop is enclosed. I think this will offer my first midday shade, and it will also provide a more comfortable place to accomplish work than what I have experienced so far. I was getting used to working in the direct sun.

This afternoon, I watched some solo birds hunting east of me over Muffler Meadow—a red-tail hawk, a great white egret, and several crows and magpies.

For the first time, I witnessed the red tail on the hawk; as the hawk flew between the sun and me, the angle illuminated the red tail. The tail is the only feature of the bird that had this color, which is a washed-out rust color.

The hawk was most impressive as it soared with the winds, approximately 700 feet above the creek bottom. This bird has an impressive wingspan and seems to be at the peak of its glory while soaring in search of prey.

Earlier in the day, many ducks floated down the canal. The first one to catch my eye was mostly white. The ducks ahead of that one were standard mallard color. My dogs instinctively wanted to give chase; however, a sharp command from me helped ward them off.

Summertime seems to bring out the jackrabbits, and any time I go out, I see them by the dozen. The dogs alert on every rabbit and give chase, but I have yet to see any evidence that they are winning this race.

I cleared a large sage stump today. It is late in the season to be digging in the earth; however, I did notice that after I dug past six to eight inches, I found some subsoil moisture. This is better moisture retention that I would have expected for early July.

At 7:55 p.m., the sun dropped behind Santa Rosa peak, and the Santa Rosa range is silhouetted on the western sky. Before the sun gave way, it was apparent that the higher peaks still protected the last few snow banks. At this point in the season, probably less than two dozen snow banks are visible.

This evening's temperature is ideal, perhaps in the low 80s or high 70s, a perfect transition to cool and comfortable nights. The sleeping temperature is as good as it can get for mid-summer.

With the sun now well past sunset, the predominant sound is the waterfall in the creek, just below me. The waterfall sound has diminished as the water flow is much less than it was only one month ago.

My neighbor, Joe, has made a couple of trips to that spot with his backhoe, trying to remove obstacles, so he can regain some of the water flow that he had earlier in the spring. I can see the same trend in the canal flow through my property. It is about half the volume that I saw earlier last month. The seagrass has grown up and is now a part of the canal landscape. The willows on both sides continue to flourish and grow taller.

SUMMER WILDLIFE SIGHTINGS

July 5th was my day to drive to Winnemucca to accomplish some errands and chores. Most of these chores were related to getting construction projects underway. On the way to the big town, I saw an unusual abundance of birds and wildlife.

First was the deer, knee-deep in the fresh alfalfa below the Sicking Ranch. Next was the single hen wild turkey in the field immediately adjacent to Sicking's place. Immediately following was the sighting of two sandhill cranes.

Apparently, these were younger cranes because they had brown features as opposed to the standard grey with red forehead on the adults. This sighting is further south than usual for this breed, according to the Audubon field guide.

Next in view was a flock of five turkey vultures feasting off jackrabbit roadkill in the middle of the road; this is the largest number of turkey vultures that I have seen in one spot.

Sandhill Cranes

Later in the day, while visiting the canyon part of Martin Creek, I spotted a solo bird floating south. It was the size of a duck but with different coloration and body features. It also had a different profile from any other duck-sized birds. I was unable to find it in either of my bird field guides. I will continue to work on this mystery.

On July 27th, I noticed a different type of duck family swimming upstream. Several adults and young paddled until they swam abeam my position, and at that point, they were startled and reversed course. As best as I can determine, this family of ducks was either the common merganser or the red-breasted merganser. According to the sighting maps, the odds should favor the common merganser because my region is in their permanent range.

I suspect this breed because I could not find the white throat. As opposed to the red-breasted merganser, the female common merganser is grayish with a red-brown head shading gradually into a gray neck. The most distinguishing feature that I noticed was the plume of brownish/red feathers sticking out the back of her head, which the field guides call a shaggy crest. It was styled like a sort of punk hair cut, where the feathers were spiked to the rear.

The map range indicators show that this type of bird is located mostly along the west coast as opposed to inland areas. However, a different field guide indicates that this breed exists in my region, but is considered rare.

COOLING OFF AT THE CREEK

The July weather pattern is no surprise. We generally have bright and sunny skies during the day. The temperature has been consistently in the 90s for the first nine days of July.

To find relief from the sun and heat, the best trick is to strap a canvas sun chair on the front of the quad, add a book and a cooler to the toolbox in the rear, and head for a shady spot on the creek. It is best to drive further north into the canyon section.

Recently I've enjoyed driving the quad upstream until I find a shady spot under a cottonwood tree. I park the quad in the water near the bank, and the seat and rear toolbox offer a comfortable setup for book reading. On July 9th, my youngest dog decided to jump on top of the toolbox. She provided a new soft headrest for my reading position.

On subsequent days, I selected various shade locations, searching for the optimum spot for comfort and beauty.

My selection on July 10th was just past the second creek crossing. I found the water crossing to be much deeper than expected, and I started to drown the quad engine just as I was crawling out of hip-deep water.

Once safely on the other side, I parked facing downstream under a tall cottonwood. This day was exceptionally peaceful, inviting me to stay longer than usual.

From that vantage point, I could see a ten-inch tree stump chewed off by local beaver. This evidence is a reminder of a previous story from local neighbors who told tales of beaver damage. Beavers sometimes fall trees in locations that either flood the main dirt road or disrupt the normal flow of the stream, which, in turn, affects the critical water flow for local ranches.

On July 19th, I had the opportunity to watch a yellow butterfly land in front of my feet and display itself long enough so I could make notes and sketch its color pattern. Later, from this sketch, I was able to research this insect.

This particular butterfly turned out to be a tiger swallowtail butterfly. Swallowtails have two species; one is the eastern tiger swallowtail, and the other is the western tiger swallowtail. The color combination of these butterflies is identical to the dominant colors of yellow and black in the black-eyed Susan.

The butterfly I observed was yellow with black wing borders and had four tiger stripes running away from the leading edge of each wing. It also boasted an aqua blue detail near the trailing edge of the wings.

This insect enjoys a large variety of host plants; however, its favored habitat is broadleaf trees and shrubs, such as the willow and cottonwood, and this preference explains why they are attracted to this location. As I sat and read and enjoyed the afternoon, I found three of these butterflies enjoying the same creek-side location.

THUNDER BUMPERS AND THE MOON

Yesterday on July 8th, late afternoon thunder bumpers developed over the valley. Judging from the dark underbellies of the cumulus clouds, it appeared rain might be on the way.

However, we received no precipitation, and all that was produced was dry lighting on the west side of the Santa Rosa Range, which started a fire outside this valley towards Orovada. I watched the brown smoke rise as I entered town for the evening saloon cookout. Fortunately, the blaze seemed to burn itself out as the smoke went away after a few hours.

In more instances than not, the summer skies appear to prepare for an afternoon rain shower, and while the thunder bumpers are relatively common, it is rare to get rain out of them. When it does rain, it is scattered and only affects small areas.

However, a few lingering snow banks are still visible on the upper levels of the western Santa Rosa range. The temperature at my ranch today was over 100 degrees; clearly, it is the elevation difference that protects the remaining snow. As of July 22nd, I could still count seven snow banks on the mountain tops.

I am not much of a student of astrology; however, I heard on public radio two nights ago that the current moon path is of significance. I did notice the early rising of a full moon two nights ago. What seems to be significant is that this full moon is following the path that the sun takes during the shortest day of the year. At this point, it will be as far south in the evening sky as we will see for a couple of decades.

Another unique feature is that the moon is directly opposite the sun, so as the sun sets, the moon rises. I am not sure if I can attest to any world order significance to this sun-moon path; however, it is just another piece of trivia on the natural wonders that amaze.

MORE WILDLIFE

During my regular midday trip to the shade and comfort of the creek bottom, I found the usual solo egret and a new similar size bird from the crane family.

This new bird was similar in size and shape to the egret; however, it had a darker olive or gray color. By shape and color, this would appear to be the little blue heron; however, per the field guides, this bird should not be in northern Nevada.

Since 1979 it has become more frequent in California, but that seems to be limited to Southern California. Because the terrain here is not typical to Nevada, it might be possible that he is out of his territory.

If I needed a back-up guess here, I would select the sandhill crane as my second choice. They do have habitat in this area according to the field guides. Later, my friend Mike, the local bird expert, indicated that sandhill cranes are common here.

Today I also spotted some wild turkeys way up into the Martin Creek canyon; it's the first time I've seen them this far up canyon. The group was seven birds, which included three youngsters born this spring. I'm happy to see this population has a healthy growth. My dogs forced the adult turkeys to fly away, but I noticed that the three young ones simply ran into the thicker brush.

As of July 17th, I observed fourteen young California quail running along the road, accompanied by four adults. I suspect this signals a good crop of young from this past spring. The young can fly, but they only will get airborne when the adults take the lead; otherwise, their preference is to run.

AUGUST OBSERVATIONS

It's now August 1st, and I have a few more observations for the summer season. First, the weather has mellowed out, and we've had a break in the hot weather. The daytime high temperature is in the low 90s, and the night time temperatures drop to the wonderful 50s.

The recent high temperatures at the end of July has removed the final snow banks of the Santa Rosa Ridge. The water flow in the canal has decreased to a modest flow, yet enough water remains to keep the many ducks that frequent this protected location happy.

The Mormon crickets have completed their adult life cycle and are gone from the landscape.

By mid-August, I started to see the first hunters moving around my neighborhood. Hunting is certainly a big conversation topic in this area, as many locals have different types of hunting permits. By all accounts, this seems to be a good year for hunting upland game, which include deer and antelope. Some of the best reports come from the guys who run the hay swathers because they scare up wildlife from the green hay fields.

By mid- to late-August, the daytime temperatures settled down to very warm, but not hot days with temperatures generally ranging between the high 80s and the low 90s. These temperatures ensure that you break a sweat when you work outside; however, the heat is not as ugly and oppressive as it was in July. The temperatures after sunset are comfortable and cool, which makes for excellent sleeping conditions.

The RV shop is recently completed, and I have been extra busy working on both inside and outside projects. This activity leaves less time to get out and observe wildlife. As of August 23rd, I only have one more month of summer left to enjoy.

On August 29th, as I drove home from town, I noticed the first of two black hawks located on the fence posts alongside Joe Sicking's irrigated alfalfa fields.

Yesterday, I saw a good size flock, over a dozen, of wild turkeys feeding on the upper end of Muffler Meadow. Except for the turkeys and those two black hawks, I find that bird activity is less common now than it was in spring and early summer.

The locals are talking about hunting season and the fact that we'll soon see different types of hunters arrive in this valley. The influx of hunters is evident as you look at the number of camper trailers and tents along Hinkey Summit Road.

By late August, I started to see the change in temperature during the dark hours. By this time, the morning temperatures are cool to the point that it is common to break out the long sleeve work shirts, but by 9:00 a.m., the day warms up. After sunset, it starts to cool off nicely, and sleeping conditions are pleasant again.

One fact seems to be true when it comes to the summer season in the Great Basin; it doesn't rain in the summer. Though thunder clouds formed, they didn't produce moisture, and throughout the summer, my property had a few light sprinkles, but nothing close to a sustained soaker rain.

SEPTEMBER OBSERVATIONS
On September 1st, Becky and I transplanted a few cottonwood seedlings from the creek bottom, which was filled with thousands of eight-inch sprouts. I transplanted these into pots near the front of my RV shop.

In my brief time here, I have planted many trees and shrubs, all of which came from a Feed Store in Winnemucca. Jeff, the owner, offered excellent coaching. One day when shopping, Jeff asked me if I knew the best time to plant a tree, and I did not know the answer. He went on to say, "20 years ago."

Then he asked if I knew the second-best time to plant a tree, and again, I was not sure about the answer. So, Jeff said, "today." Twenty years ago, I was doing other stuff, so I had better get to planting right now.

During early September, I noticed that the local coyote ventured closer to the property. While taking a shower in my outdoor shower stall, I looked down at the meadow floor and saw him watching me. We had a short conversation and eye contact before he slowly ran to the cover of the shrubs along the creek. I explained to him that he was coyote ugly, but that it was nothing personal.

By the end of the first week in September, the daytime temperatures continued to break 90 degrees. I found these outside conditions uncomfortably hot for heavy work, especially when I had shop construction projects pending, such as the new workbench that I am now building.

For some folks, the end of the summer season is marked by the passing of the Labor Day weekend, which was last weekend. Locals often reference the symbolic end of the summer season as the first of the cattle drives from the upper elevation pastures down to the ranch homes on the valley floor.

September 7th marked the first of the cattle drives. Today's drive was the smaller of the two, and a larger drive is scheduled for September 16th.

The cattle drive today seems to coincide with the night time temperature change. By 9:30 p.m., last night, the temperature outside was chilly.

When I departed for town this morning, Duane Boggio guarded my entrance gate. He was on horseback and had already closed my gate so the herd would not wander onto my property.

As I drove through the gate, I heard the cattle mooing from up canyon. I also saw the start of the dust cloud that would follow the herd into the valley floor.

The weekend of September 8th and 9th is an enjoyable and busy time for our town. It marks the rib-cookoff, where the entire block around the Fireman's Park is filled with cooking grills. The cookoff provides an excellent excuse for a town party. It is one of the few times when you cannot find a parking spot near the town center. I am reminded of the big rib-cookoff in Sparks, except ours is in miniature.

As usual, the saloon is the center of the universe and provides a hub for traffic and activity. As the sun sets and darkness creeps in, the sounds of karaoke drift out of the packed bar where locals mingle with out-of-town visitors.

On September 15th, we got our first cold spell, and the overnight temperature dropped to 31 degrees. This temperature took care of the final few flies hanging around the RV shop.

The dogs are not so anxious to get out and chase around now that the temperature has cooled. The daytime temperatures in the 60s and 70s, a welcome change after many months of hot and dry conditions, and is ideal weather for physical labor.

On September 16th, the larger cattle drive from summer grazing areas to the home ranches is expected to slog by my property. Dust clouds and mooing confirm this event. I have learned that this seasonal process includes three or more different cattle drives before all of the stock is off the high grazing.

As the season ends, and the temperature changes, the first cottonwood leaves turn golden with autumn color.

8: MEANWHILE BACK AT THE RANCH

This chapter picks up where chapter three left off.

JUNE PROGRESS

The RV shop construction is now nine days along. On this first day of summer, the construction crew grew to a five-man workforce.

They're spreading the recently delivered gravel—pit run gravel from a stream bed outside of Orovada. And, they continue to add the Simpson Strong Ties to the trusses so that the two-by-six roof supports can drop into their proper places. Most of this day's work is dedicated to nailing this hardware into place, and I assume that the extra-large work crew is related to the need to move the large and heavy trusses. A forklift is handy for the positioning of the trusses, but manhandling is still a requirement here.

This particular morning has a pleasant breeze from the northwest. The breeze not only keeps the working conditions cooler, but it blows away the last few remaining mosquitoes.

I spoke with the crew boss about some of the particular details I wanted to be included in this project. We discussed the placement of the doggie door. More importantly, we determined how to best set up a line, or conduit, so that electrical wires, satellite TV cables, and other wires can easily be brought inside, without having to cut holes in the wall of this new structure.

Shop Construction

While the crew inches closer to finishing the wood framing, I have kept myself busy with the non-stop maintenance on the driveway, a large part of which is cleaning up the driveway trail, as many pieces of dead sage are buried in the berms. Also, these berms are filled with medium size rocks that need to be removed, and I have found that the best place to dispose of these excess rocks is to simply fill the other trail sections where runoff gullies cross and cut into the trails.

Once I clean up the driveway, I need to plan to bring in gravel. Without gravel, the driveway is too dusty during the dry time and too muddy during the rain time. Over time I learned you could never add enough gravel to satisfy a clay driveway, for clay seems to suck up gravel endlessly.

As of June 29th, I returned to the ranch after doing errands in Reno. Good progress had been made on the RV shop, including cement work for half of the structure. I was surprised to see the RV shop profile sticking up into the skyline as I approached the Old Mill Ranch.

While away, I received a phone call from Ken Ahorn, in Montana to see if I was still interested in buying his thirteen-by-fifteen feet log cabin. I need to rethink this offer as I continue to coordinate the two larger construction projects.

JULY PROGRESS

On July 1st, I attended the regular Saturday night feed at the local saloon. As usual, there is no shortage of conversation and good people to visit with. On this particular evening, I became better acquainted with Stan, from Paradise town, Bill, a new resident doing what I am doing, and a nearby neighbor named Bill. To yet again show what a small world this is, Bill, referred to as Uncle Bill by one of my former co-workers, has since moved from Reno to Winnemucca. Our connection includes a wonderful middle-age couple, who both work in local public safety.

As we finished the rib dinner, Kristi, the bartender, handed each of us a face-cleaning wipe packet, which was intended to help clean up any BBQ sauce smears from the ribs. Uncle Bill was not sure what had just been handed to him, and after some speculation, the waitress had to explain. We all shared a good laugh over this.

〜〜〜
〜〜〜

Because the scheduled cement delivery for July 5th failed to show, progress on the shop has slowed down. The work crew did not show up on Friday the 7th, and we now wait for the second half of the cement pour on the 10th.

Despite the lack of progress lately, this partial shelter does offer morning and evening shade protection, and I have set up a plastic chair and table to enjoy a respite from midday full sun.

The delays continue. After the unexpected delay in cement delivery, the work crew now has a conflict with a project in Jarbidge, five hours away. The boss announced that he needs to pull off for two weeks so he can finish the Jarbidge project, and he told me that I would not see them again for two weeks. Additionally, the boss explained to me that he continues to have trouble finding and keeping experienced carpenters.

One of his crew bosses has left again for greener pastures in Idaho. In the past, this fellow would depart for a year and then come back, asking if his job—safety net—is still good. I hear the same is true for other industries.

∼∼∼ ∼∼∼ ∼∼∼

At the same time that the RV shop construction is delayed, so too is the start of the ranch house construction. I asked the contractor to begin on July 1st. He has told me twice that he will come out for his first site survey, but I have yet to see him. Once again, I am learning that patience is a virtue when it comes to construction work.

I continue to plan out the location and size of the dog run—around three sides of the RV shop—placement of future trees and other landscaping features. I like to engage my mind in planning projects, and this has been the case since I was designated a planner while working at the Pentagon.

Until the RV shop is finished, I don't have many projects for me to work on. I try to create a suitable daily routine that doesn't include work, for so much work is pending.

On the 13th, I spliced together three pieces of scrap irrigation line to create enough length to reach southward to the surviving peach tree. Also, today, I started setting up the wood storage system under the RV shop lean-to.

I have lost nine days of construction progress—July 10th to July 24th. During that time, I dug an electrical trench, approximately sixteen feet long and two feet deep, from the power pole to the RV shop.

I found this task to be difficult, considering that the working temperature was generally around 100 degrees. During the 23rd and 24th, Becky and I moved the living room furniture off the slab floor to be ready for the returning work crew.

On July 23rd, neighbor Joe K. came over to replace my twenty-amp breaker with a new thirty-amp breaker. This simple project means the difference between air conditioning and no cooling. I will need to get both contractors talking to one another, so we have better coordination on future electrical upgrades on the property. For the first time during this heatwave, I can turn the motorhome into a comfortable place.

~~~ ~~~ ~~~

Also, on the 23rd, I met the family that is building a place further up the canyon. Their location is no longer in the valley but further up the high rock canyon where the terrain opens up significantly. They have had a difficult time getting building supplies across the stream crossings and over about six miles of very rough roads. The property owner is Marcus Tolitti.

Marcus shared his account of how the government has abused its power. His efforts to remove rocks from this road caused the Bureau of Land Management to close the road and initiate a formal criminal investigation. They even employed crime scene tape, clearly overkill. This investigation prompted a government employee to come down from Oregon to threaten this property owner.

The problem is that the only road to this property is the old China Road, built by Chinese immigrants over one-hundred years ago. Any modification to this road is considered a violation of a historic landmark. A government representative told Marcus that he could not build on his own private property because they did not want him to drive on the road.

This demand statement was not accurate. Marcus pointed out that this road is also the main route for the annual cattle drives where more damage is done to the way than he could possibly do.

Ultimately, this problem was resolved, but not before the government came in and threw its weight around and proved again that common sense is not a requirement for their actions. This legal issue represents the classic challenge presented by old-time laws, many of which relate to what is, or is not, considered a road and who has access and permission to make changes. This ongoing problem does not have a not cut and dried solution.

~~~ ~~~ ~~~

Also, in recent days, I built a new outdoor shower located inside the new lean-to wood storage area. It is a simple garden hose with a ceiling mount and a nozzle that provides an ideal spray, and it has an on/off valve at the overhead point.

The solar heating of the garden hose provides natural hot water for a short shower. The distinguishing feature of this shower is that it is open on two sides, which provides a great view of the creek bottom while showering. However, I have to be aware of road traffic approaching our property because they may get a free show. The road drops below the view as the cars continue southward.

~~~ ~~~ ~~~

On the evening of July 23rd, I had an extended visit with Stan and Roxanne from town. We sat on their porch, watching the limited town traffic come and go. Roxanne said that during my few months of living here, reports reflect that I have fit in well with the local population. I was pleased and comforted to hear this.

With a great deal of personal relief, the work crew returned to the shop project on July 25th. They started an hour early, probably to avoid the hottest part of the workday, and continued to make good visible progress.

Today, they added the two-inch electrical conduit to the trench that I dug for them as well as the rest of the wood sheathing, which they will cover with insulation and metal clad siding panels.

On July 27th, we see good progress. Today, Dale and Dave finished half of the front end as well as the north half of the roof. For the first time, I could see full shade inside the shop.

We also set up the wood-burning stove, which was mounted on top of cement blocks and a metal platform. When I returned from my midday cooling time on the creek and approached my property from the east, I saw a fully enclosed shop.

Also, today, I cleaned up the old RV shower area since I now have a new separate shower location under the wood storage lean-to.

AUGUST OBSERVATIONS

As of August 1st, the work crew has nearly completed the shop. The metal-clad siding and roof are finished. Today, the contractor started to set up the extra-large garage door, and Dale also used his small tractor to level the final two gravel piles. At the same time, I finished the gate to nowhere, so that the internet antenna and satellite dish have a mounting point.

At this point, in the heart of summer, it is fantastic to have some shade finally. Dave expects to hook up the wood stove flue system in a day or so. Dale indicated that I should be able to start moving in by Friday. The only remaining step is to have the County Inspector come out for her final approval.

~~~ ~~~ ~~~
~~~ ~~~ ~~~

On August 3rd, I noticed a strange flight of different birds going overhead; two formations totaling around twenty birds. Their neck length and beak shape were different than any I'd previously seen.

My first impression was that I was looking at some sort of cormorant, but neighbor John later corrected me and told me this was a flock of white-faced ibis.

When I checked the field guides, I confirmed he'd made a good call, and it turns out that this ibis is the only ibis that lives in the western U.S. The primary visual factors included the dark feather color and the prominent hooked bill. This bird likes to feed in muddy pools and marshes.

Their flocks fly in a formation similar to the cormorants; however, they have some difficulty holding their formation, and I witnessed two smaller flocks merge into one.

~~~ ~~~ ~~~
~~~ ~~~ ~~~

By August 4th, the RV shop was ready for county inspection. It turned out that I had six discrepancies to fix before I could receive final approval. Until mid-August, the main focus was the completion of the RV shop and the subsequent move into this new structure.

I made plans to get the household effects moved from Reno storage to the ranch this coming weekend.

The move was a high tempo operation with two loads on Saturday and two more loads on Sunday. It was tough work made easier with a team effort of a father, step-mother, and son working together. The transformation from an empty shop to a very crowded shop was amazing.

In total, I moved six large truck and trailer loads from Reno to the shop. In addition to the RV, it is filled with household effects, dog kennels, shop equipment, a fridge and freezer, a TV, and more; the space is almost filled.

My quality of life quickly improved as I moved the RV inside and set up an office and a kitchen area; I have more shade and less dust. I have also added satellite TV service, so I no longer have to go to the town saloon to watch live baseball. My next task is to get organized and set up the shop area amid the storage mess.

Now the focus of my time is on getting all my stuff organized. At the same time, I am starting to add OSB boards to the interior walls and am beginning to develop my workshop area.

∿ ∿ ∿
∿ ∿ ∿

Last week, I learned that bureaucracy is alive and well, even in this rural Nevada county. I spent time responding to the inspection discrepancies and issues pointed out by the county building inspector. I also spent time finding suitable materials for my woodstove permit.

I was surprised to learn that I also had to apply for a motorhome permit, and the building inspector did show some reasonableness when it came to some of the motorhome particulars.

I also tried to apply for a permit to build my well-house. As it turned out, I did not have sufficient building detail to qualify for the actual permit, and I need to find a local expert who can help me finalize some of the details.

∿ ∿ ∿
∿ ∿ ∿

The first phase of my ranch development is basically completed, and now it's time to move on to other projects such as the ranch house construction, adding gravel, and starting the well-house.

By August 22nd, I had a long-detailed meeting with Roy, the house contractor. It looks like he will begin in a week or two. We have most of the details worked out; however, he still presented a half dozen questions or issues that I need to do homework on. I also gave a walking tour to Brian Curtis, the guy who will be responsible for the dirt moving and backhoe work—utility trench, foundation, and septic.

Brian Curtis and the Backhoe

In the past week, I have made progress on the first section of the shop workbench. I also moved the woodpiles to clear a path for the trench work soon to follow.

On August 29th, just as summer started to wind down, the heavy equipment arrived at the lower lot, along with Brian Curtis, who runs the dirt moving company.

Brian brought in a John Deere 710 D backhoe. He later explained that this was the largest and best rock digging equipment on the market. Brian was concerned last week that I may have too many large rocks to make this foundation digging a typical project.

As it turned out, because of his excellent equipment, Brian was able to dig through the rocks, and in many cases, he broke large rocks into manageable pieces. To create the space for the foundation, he had to dig approximately three feet into the earth.

After he and his helper Juan left, I gathered up many medium-sized rocks from the house foundation dig to create a new fire pit. Brian said that he would probably be able to finish tomorrow.

During the last week of August, the dirt moving subcontractor started. What would typically be a routine dig in the dirt was different on my rocky hilltop. As suspected before the backhoe showed up, my building site is all rock.

Most of the excavation amounted to moving rocks about the size of a medium-sized TV. About halfway through the dig project, I noticed that the crew was bouncing off a rock as big as my Land Cruiser.

My uneducated perspective told me that the project was in big trouble, but the professional crew simply banged on the rocks until large rocks turned into smaller rocks—no big deal. The sedan size boulder eventually disappeared. As the heavy equipment tore up the ground, two by-products were produced, rocks and fine powder. This dirt-moving phase took just over two workdays.

While this was unfolding, Dennis Heitman continued to bring in gravel. By the first week in September, most of the nearly half-mile circular driveway was groomed and graveled.

This project could have been completed earlier except that Dennis got himself stuck twice with the larger belly-dump gravel truck. He made two trips with the larger truck, and both times, he had to be towed out. He explained that he had learned his lesson after the second occurrence and started bringing a smaller truck, which prolonged his work here.

During the final days of August, I found a lady in Winnemucca, Valerie, who had a 14-week-old female kitten. I acquired this young cat to control the mouse population inside my shop; on the day before getting the cat, I caught two mice in house traps.

The new cat was appropriately named Minne the Mouser. I will try to feed her enough to put some meat on her skinny bones, but not so much that she has no hunger for mouse hunting.

EARLY SEPTEMBER

I'd been so busy through the summer that I didn't figure out the local church routine until September 10th. Town hosted two churches. The non-Catholic church is on the corner of Main and 3rd Street South. It looks like an old, small-town church should look; it has a bell tower on top, and spider webs drape the windows below.

Jerry Harper is not only a hard-working cowboy and rancher from the Owyhee Desert area, east of the valley, but he's also a lay preacher at the community church in town.

Our cowboy preacher conducts a wonderful freelance church service at 3:00 p.m. each Sunday, except on rodeo weekends. When time conflicts arise, church service is postponed until the next Sunday. As often stated, this is not your usual dose of "canned religion." Jerry has a wonderful gift of sharing the word of God through the cleansing filter of a hard-working cowboy.

On my first church attendance, Jerry came over to double-check my name so he could do proper welcomes during the early part of the service.

The old church bell signals the start of service, not when it is 3:00 sharp, but rather when everyone is situated in their seats after the obligatory chit-chat with neighbors.

Recently the service delayed its start so one grand old ranch lady could answer her cell phone. Who knows, it might have been an important phone call, and a few minutes would not matter much.

Jerry Harper, Cowboy Pastor

He did a simple introduction and asked who had read their bible this past week. He also took requests for both hymns and prayers.

His Sunday message is short, crisp, and to the point. If the spiritual point is beyond his understanding, he will tell you that upfront. In the same breath, he will tell you what is unequivocally simple.

Jerry also provides the musical accompaniment with a well-tuned 12-string guitar. It continues to amaze me how those beat-up ranch fingers can bring out such sweet music from a solo musical instrument. Even rough cowboy hands can excel here.

Jerry talks about Christian obligation based on the words of scripture. For some of us who consider ourselves luckier than most of the world's millions, comes a sense of obligation and responsibility to lead a good life and do what is right for our families and our community.

Jerry, our preacher, is fond of asking personal and pertinent questions to the members of the congregation. Some questions are rhetorical and do not demand a vocal answer; however, sometimes, he is looking for a comment or perhaps a show of hands. This approach works well in a small community where friends and neighbors have a closer personal relationship to the community and to each other.

Unlike the larger conventional churches, there is an ongoing comfortable verbal exchange between the congregation members and the pastor. Nothing is too thick or complicated, but rather basic and sincere lessons of life in the context of the good Christian teachings.

Gone are the trappings of the glitzy church ritual and the colorful sashes that reflect the seasons of the church cycle. Also, gone is the slick-haired TV evangelist who takes advantage of his tax-free income status and cares more about personal aggrandizement than the spiritual welfare of his flock.

Based on too many years of canned religion, I am not sure how many of these self-important clergy know the difference between their frock and their flock. Jerry knows the way to heaven and is willing to teach the rest of us.

The total attendance came to twenty-seven, and this included the full gamut of young kids, middle-aged folks, and some old-timers. This size crowd filled about forty percent of the pew capacity.

During communion, he served the blood and the bread to all twenty-seven people. He warned that if you understand the sacraments and are sincere, you were welcome to partake; however, if you are just doing it for the sake of doing it, then you would suffer the wrath of our Lord.

All in all, this first church visit was a good experience. It was basic and sincere, just like the lifestyle that pervades this valley. Over time my relationship with Jerry continued to grow as did my comfort level with the rest of his ranch family. I eventually became a regular helper on his branding crew.

∿∿ ∿∿ ∿∿

On September 15th, Roy, the contractor, told me the permits were approved, and he is about ready to roll on the house construction. I signed over the deed to the property as collateral for his construction work. He will hold this deed until the mortgage company pays for his construction loan. I had hoped for a summer start to the ranch house construction, but now it looks like it will be a fall project instead.

The shop cat is now old enough that I need to get the proper vaccination and deworming medication going, and Minnie's first vet visit is set for September 22nd. She seems to have adjusted nicely, and she and the dogs have a friendly and respectful relationship.

Between the shop construction and the house construction, I continue to work on my oversized workshop area, which includes a workbench against the wall and another island bench towards the center. I finally feel a sense of organization within this new structure. A mezzanine storage area sits overhead. Each trip to town to get building supplies cost at least another $300.

∿∿ ∿∿ ∿∿

Now that the summer heat is over, I've begun cleaning up the old orchard planted by the previous owners, which is now overgrown with sage. Some of the fence protection screens also need to be repaired, and the irrigation line does not make much sense because it does not cover all eight planting areas.

I need to get the watering source in place first, then dig out the planting holes, and finally get ready for fall planting of a few select fruit trees. Given that my dogs and I are so active on the ranch, I am not sure that I need the wire cage protection that was in place before.

I still need coaching help from Mike, the master gardener in town, both for setting up the drip systems and for the selection of fruit trees.

And so, summer comes to an end on September 22nd. It was hot but productive.

9: FALL SEASON

The first full day of Autumn was September 23rd. This is consistently a beautiful time of year, especially with the moderate daytime temperatures.

EARLY FALL

The first signals of a season change include cooler temperatures, shorter days, and just a few leaves turning yellow on the cottonwood trees in this creek basin. It seemed fitting that on this first day of fall, my wife and I watched a flock of geese circling overhead. It looked like they were looking for a wet or green place to feed.

Two days later, while riding my quad in the foothills northwest of my ranch, I spotted four male antelope in a ravine, and I often now see the solo coyote hunting just below my property in the Muffler Meadow.

As a side note here, I have learned that the locals use the name Muffler Meadow and the government officials prefer the name, Adams Slough. As a new guy, I found it odd that the same creek bottom had two different names. I was also curious about which definition would be most appropriate for this stretch of green land.

The *Common Ground* book defines meadow as land covered with grass, often along a river or a marshy region. It defines slough as a narrow stretch of sluggish water in a river channel. Of the two competing definitions, I think the meadow term is most appropriate.

I noticed that just three days into the fall season, the sunrise and sunset times were identical. On September

25th, the sun rose at 6:50 a.m., and it set at 6:50 p.m. For one day only, we have as much daytime as we have night time. Due to living in a valley, these times are shortened by a few minutes, especially as the sun sets over the high peaks of the Santa Rosa mountains.

Another sign of the fall season arrives in the form of consecutive cattle drives; this year, there were three different cattle drives managed by cowboys, horses, and seasoned cow dogs. Duane Boggio and the Cassanelli Brothers are the main moves for this drive. These range cattle come from the private and BLM or USFS grazing allotments in the upper flats behind Hinkey Summit.

Regarding dogs, this book would not be complete without paying homage to the loyalty and hard work of the ranch dog—these may be cow dogs or sheepdogs. Essentially they're the same; they just play different roles.

Loyal Tedi

In my case, I had three sheepdogs, mostly blue heelers. The oldest of my heelers was Tedi, who came to the ranch with me. While friends may come and go, even wives may come and go, but the typical working dog will show a degree of unswerving and unmatched loyalty to its owner.

On September 29th, I noticed that the large potato fields on the way to Winnemucca were being harvested. Harvesting was an impressive operation with around fifteen large produce trucks waiting their turn to match up with the half dozen new potato harvesting machines. This is the location that produces the potatoes for those Costco instant mashed potatoes—also, Pringle potato chips are made from these potatoes. The potato harvest in this region continued into the first half of October, as many fields had to be harvested.

Also, on the way home from Winnemucca today, on the section of road the last mile before my ranch entrance, I noticed abundant wildlife on or near the road. The wildlife collection included four young deer on the Sicking property, seven cock pheasants on the dirt road, followed by four wild turkey hens.

Later in the week, Joe Sicking and I had the chance to share our observations and found them to be similar. Joe mentioned that it was very unusual to see that many cock pheasants gathered in one place, especially the middle of the dirt road.

During my chat with Joe, I asked about the water flowing again in the canal. Joe explained that come September 1st, the water flow is redirected to allow fresh water to come in for livestock watering. It appears that the control of the water in the canal is on a strict schedule regulated by practical matters such as growing season and when the cattle are back from summer grazing.

In late September, Becky and I drove to the trailhead at upper Singus Creek. We used one of the hiking guide books by Mike White to check out the Singus Creek hike.

This trail is on the east slope of the steep Santa Rosa range, and it meanders through the middle of the aspen tree lines. Depending on the elevation and weather, fall is a perfect time of year to hike that trail. As we set out, the daytime temperature was in the 70s, and I'd say that the beauty on this hike was just past its prime by perhaps two weeks.

The lower elevation aspens were in full color, but the upper elevation trees had shed much of their foliage. We hiked south along the summit trail to Abel Summit. After gathering some trophy rocks at the summit, we turned around and returned to our vehicle. Next year we'll try this same hike, but go a week or two earlier in the season.

FIRE SEASON

Shifting gears from wildlife to fire season, we venture into an important and serious topic. While traditional natural disasters do not occur around here, fire is a different story. It tends to be a seasonal problem compounded by the near-perfect conditions for aggressive fire behavior, including dry sagebrush, low humidity, and wind.

The fire danger in this valley is listed between high and extreme for the past couple of months. All of the brush is dry as it hasn't rained for approximately half a year. Tonight was our turn for a close call on the fire danger.

I paid a visit to my cousin's ranch, which is one hour on the opposite side of the mountain. When I returned home after dark, I saw a fiery glow at the end of the valley, even though I was still fifteen miles out. Viewing a glow from this far away meant that good size fire was going.

From a distance, it looked like it might be centered at or near my ranch property. The closer I got, the worse the location looked. It was not until I was four miles out that I could tell that it was actually south of my place in the creek bottom. Even though the creek still flows, the surrounding brush tends to be dry at this time in the season. I was somewhat relieved that my place was not at the center and that ranch structures were not in danger.

As I traveled further on the county road, I encountered a good size traffic jam consisting of fire trucks and vehicles belonging to my neighbors. When I pulled over and joined the crowd, the first person that I ran into was Fred Stewart, the owner of the historic Ninety-Six Ranch. Fred said that it was his land burning; however, he did not seem too concerned since the only thing burning was dense brush and a few trees near the creek bottom.

The volunteer fire department surrounded the fire with older fire trucks, but they didn't attempt to fight the fire because it was not yet threatening anything important.

Considering recent temperatures, humidity, and wind, this night was a firefighter's dream with almost no wind, cool temperatures, and unusually high humidity. While I watched, the little breeze that pushed the fire north turned on itself and started to push the fire back onto itself. When I saw that good fortune, I decided to get back in my car and head on home.

Later, I learned that Joe Sicking took his tractor in the dark and ran his cultivator around the fire many times. Due to the darkness, Joe was not able to see where he was going until the fire flared up and provided slight lighting to help him find his way.

There will be a black creek bottom scar for a while, but because it is creek bottom, it should turn green again next spring. Most fires leave a black scar; however, I was surprised the following day when I drove by the scene. I saw absolutely no visible damage from the road, but I'm sure closer to the creek bottom, fire damage exists that is not readily visible from the road.

OCTOBER OBSERVATIONS

On October 14th, the chukar hunting season started. I can hear the gunshots throughout the day, and bragging rights begin in the evening at the local saloon. Often the victorious hunters buy drinks for the entire bar. According to the locals, the population of all the hunting stock has been way up this year.

~~~ ~~~ ~~~
~~~ ~~~ ~~~

On October 21st, I took the time to assess my current living situation. The temperature grows colder, and the days get shorter. My standard of living is more comfortable than when I started this adventure six months ago. While I do not have many of the conveniences of an ordinary house and home, I do enjoy the Spartan and austere lifestyle that I have selected for myself.

This current lifestyle not only makes me more appreciative of typical conveniences and comforts; but, it makes me physically stronger. With physical labor seven days a week and the Spartan lifestyle, I have a personal satisfaction that I am getting the best possible quality of life at this 10th hour of my life span.

When I can find an internet signal, I prefer to dial in CapRadio out of Sacramento and listen to their jazz program. This station provides good quality music, and it's good for the soul.

On this particular Saturday, October 21st, I spent extra time sitting in front of my woodstove. I prefer to burn the aspen firewood with the stove doors wide open. Usually, I have a sufficient draft that I don't have to worry about the smoke invading into the RV shop.

By late morning, I'll transition outdoors with an emphasis on taking care of those chores related to winter preparation. This topic reminds me of living in New England, where the locals claimed that they only had two seasons. The first one was winter, and the second one was getting-ready-for-winter.

I'll try to get as much orchard work done this fall as I can because when the snowmelt and rains start draining into the three canyons on my property, the ground will be wet and muddy. For the first few months of the spring, I will not have to worry about watering my new fruit trees.

᠊᠊᠊ ᠊᠊᠊ ᠊᠊᠊
᠊᠊᠊ ᠊᠊᠊ ᠊᠊᠊

I have kept daily notes on wind patterns because even after many months here, it seems hard to nail down the prevailing winds in this canyon and valley. During the final weeks of October, the winds were strong every morning and likewise every evening. The wind direction was almost always out of the north and east or coming down the canyon to the valley floor.

Wind speed above twenty miles per hour was often the norm. My ranch site may be an ideal location for the new style Mariah wind generator, which mounts on a thirty-foot pole and is a tall cylinder instead of the traditional bladed windmill. This style of wind generator started with much fanfare, but enthusiasm seems to have fizzled out. After months of consideration, I scratched this wind system off my shopping list.

NOVEMBER OBSERVATIONS

By early November, light rain begins to move through the region, and this is the first seasonal rain in nearly six months.

The early morning and late evening temperatures are chilly; however, the daytime temperature and working conditions are ideal. I think back to the hundred-degree temperatures in July and consider what a treat it is to do physical labor when the temperature is in the 60s.

Consistent with the cooler nighttime temperatures, the Santa Rosa mountain range to the west is capped with fresh snow. Unlike the snow from a month ago, this accumulation will most likely last into the winter.

The various hunting seasons are still in full swing, and I often see hunters driving around in their quads and pickups, and commonly hear gunfire. On this particular day, the gunshots from the valley echoed up into the rock canyon, and one occasion, I counted six gunshot echoes before the sound dwindled out.

On November 4th, the neighbor's cattle have been unusually vocal all day, even into the evening. I'm not sure what has prompted the extra mooing, but it is a noticeable change from the norm. I posed this question to my neighbor, and he explained that it was weaning time. As a former farm and ranch kid, I should have recognized this situation. The increased mooing continued into the third week of November.

During a weekend visit from my wife in mid-November, we looked down into Muffler Meadow and observed a vast number of wild turkeys. Since late spring, I have noticed a consistent flock of turkeys living and feeding up and down the lush meadow, and they consistently numbered seventeen.

On November 15th, that number jumped to around seventy-five! I tried to get an exact headcount, but it was hard to keep track as they walked around and foraged, one large group mixing and mingling with another.

THANKSGIVING

Three weeks before Thanksgiving, I received my first invitation to join a Thanksgiving dinner party in Paradise town. The reason for the Thanksgiving invitations is that most of the locals realized that I lived alone. This was the first time that I recall receiving such a warm welcome from people that I just recently met.

A week after that initial invitation, I received a second invitation from Tami Boggio. In the past, she described her place to me, and it was home to chickens, deer in the yard, wild turkeys, and many adopted cats. Her invitation was not only to dinner but also to come and check out the place that she was proud of. Tami told me that deer sometimes scratched on her back door begging for cookies. I figured that I had to see that for myself.

I shared the news with my next-door neighbor that I was pleasantly surprised to have received two such holiday invitations. My next-door neighbor assured me that there would be more.

A few days later, I was in town getting supplies when I ran into Joe Sicking, another neighbor. Joe asked if I was going to be alone for the holiday and then invited me to his house. The prediction was true; I did have more than two Thanksgiving dinner invitations. This situation was another example of local hospitality, especially while living alone at the ranch.

The Thanksgiving celebration began at noon when I drove to the Boggio ranch. It was a bustle of activity with guys working in the shop, and a few down the road at the hay storage spot. Tami raced around on her quad, trying to get people rounded up for the early dinner. Sure enough, I drove into a yard full of animals, including a small herd of deer grazing on the grass.

When I went into Tami and Duane's house, I found a maze of rooms and hallways. The house was full of charm, some of which was reflected through many framed pictures of family, local history, and animals that had been adopted by Tami over the years.

Apparently, the locals knew that if young deer had been abandoned or injured, they could be dropped off with Tami. And, while I was there, sure, enough one old deer did scratch on the back door with a begging look about him. This old guy showed some wear and hard times. His left ear was partially gone from the accident that caused him to be dropped off at this ranch. The family members knew the routine, and soon two fresh cookies were delivered to the back door for feeding time.

The actual dinner was a typical big ranch spread. Each course seemed to be prepared in two or three variations. For example, domestic turkey meat sat next to wild turkey meat. I assume the wild turkey came from the backyard. The meal was set out as a buffet with over twenty choices available. Including immediate family and neighbor friends, ten people were in attendance.

About the time I tried to excuse myself to join the second dinner invitation, Tami halted me with a deluxe plate of dessert. Rather than one piece of pie, I was presented with five large dessert servings, including homemade apple pie, homemade pumpkin pie, chocolate pie, banana cream pie, and cheesecake with raspberry sauce. Never in my life have I attempted five desserts after a meal. It took some time and an extra beer, but I managed. To use an old phrase, I left fat, dumb, and happy.

Oh yes, the charity was not done yet. As I left, Tami handed over a take-home plate with one more meal. Besides being good neighbors, Tami and her family seemed to have some sympathy for me and my temporary bachelor status. Being a slender guy, perhaps they think that I cannot cook for myself.

Even though I moved to the next dinner invitation, there was not much eating in store for me. This next step was for the company, conversation, and courtesy.

I did come home early so I could feed my dogs and turn off the water supply to the shop. The temperature really cooled off today; I woke to snow on the ground, and by evening, the temperature was already heading below freezing. It is now time to start a good wood fire in my shop and make sure that my three dogs, one cat, and myself, are comfortable.

The local hospitality has demanded that Thanksgiving events do not stop on Thursday. Following church on the 26th, Charlie found me at the saloon and invited me to his house. His wife, Liz, wanted to use up Thanksgiving leftovers. They had also invited Susan Kern, the lady who provided me with cured manure for my landscape projects.

We had a wonderful evening in their well-appointed large home. We started with wine, followed by dinner, then fresh pumpkin pie. After dinner, we shared a couple of hours of good conversation. Four people create the ideal size group for a worthwhile post-dinner discussion.

LATE NOVEMBER COLD SNAP
The long Thanksgiving weekend meant four days free from construction progress. During that period, we received our coldest weather of the season.

This morning, November 24th, when I awoke, the outside temperature was only 7 degrees, and the temperature inside the shop was 42 degrees, which is the coldest so far. I started an aggressive fire, and by 10:30 a.m., the inside temperature was up to 60 degrees.

During these morning hours, I tended to housekeeping and cooked a blueberry pancake breakfast. Late breakfasts seem to taste the best, and around here, they have become the norm. The outside temperature is expected to top out at only 45 degrees. The days are getting shorter now, and today's sunrise was not until 6:49 a.m.

The first heavy snow arrived during the afternoon of November 26th. By bedtime, we had four inches of snow on the ground, and another inch topped that the next morning. Since the bathhouse roof has not been finished yet, the morning chores included shoveling a few inches of snow off the sub-floor.

Since November 26th, the conditions have drastically changed. Before this, the weather was cold during the dark hours and workable during the sunny part of the day.

Now for the past five days, daytime temperatures have been extremely low, and there is little relief from either the evening cold or the daytime cold. My frost-free water spigot has frozen solid, so I can no longer draw water for doing dishes or flushing the toilet.

To get the shop temperature up to a comfortable level, I must feed the fire continuously. Even my pets now scramble for the warmth and shelter inside the motorhome. I have kept a heater going at a low setting all day long now.

I hate to leave the property because it means that the fire will burn out, which drags down the inside temperature. I can always re-start a fire and get back to normal, but it takes many hours to affect a real recovery.

These conditions cause me to tell friends and neighbors that I am ready for house construction completion. I asked the head framer, Dave, when he thought it would be my turn to install hardwood floors and ceramic tile. He predicted a couple of months with the caveat that this call needed to come from the contractor, not the framer.

With snow on the ground, we still have twenty-one days of fall before I change chapters to winter. Thanks to the snow and low temperature, it seems that we are already into the next season.

My frost-free water bib has been frozen now for a couple of days, and I have no water for the camp kitchen set up in my shop. I can manage for a few more days before I will have to find a water source.

WEATHER OBSERVATIONS

Discounting the storm fronts that move through, the weather pattern seems well established by early December. The night time temperatures for the past few weeks have dropped to the single digits.

Locally the cold morning temperatures are accentuated by the wind pattern that blows out of the northeast down

Martin Creek canyon. By 9:00 a.m. to 9:30 a.m., this breeze typically dies out as the temperature starts to work its way towards the mid-40s.

By 10:30 a.m., I am generally ready to start my outside chores. Often, by this time of the morning, the sky is clear, and temperatures improve to a point where you can work without gloves.

This pattern generally continues until mid-afternoon, when you can start to feel the temperature dropping quickly. From 4:30 p.m. until dark, it quickly becomes glove and hat conditions. The winds will stay calm until well after dark when they return from the northeast.

These conditions are tough on the house framers who start work by 7:30 a.m. They are usually cold and uncomfortable until mid-morning when conditions become more tolerable.

Snow has been on the ground as of early November, albeit only a couple of inches, and all of the surrounding mountain tops are well covered in snow.

As we get closer to actual winter, I look forward to observing weather changes and snow conditions. It will be my first opportunity to see this valley during the winter season.

I have observed and felt contrasting weather patterns through November and December. By late November, I experienced a cold spell with near-record low temperatures, and at my ranch, the temperature dropped below zero for a few nights.

By contrast, mid-December has found day and night temperatures to be above average. As of mid-December, the evening lows were in the low 30s, and the daytime high was flirting with 50 degrees.

As of December 13th, the temperature was so mild that I started to notice large flies inside my shop. There were not the common garden variety flies; instead, they were immense—B-52 bomber sized ones—and their flight skills were sluggish. They were so slow that they were easy to catch or swat. Yet, even during this mild mid-December spell, the snow refused to melt on the shady side of the shop.

This year, the late fall conditions have offered steady drizzle as opposed to regular rainfall. The cumulative effect of all-day drizzle was not only miserable for the outside construction workers, but it has turned the soil to mud.

On my ranch, the mud is the kind that makes you look taller; you can add a couple of inches to your height when the clay builds up on the bottom of your work boots. Local on-line weather tracking indicates only 0.32 of an inch of rain to date in December.

On December 20th, the fall season is nearly over. The official change over is 4:22 p.m. tomorrow and comes with a forecast of snow. The seasonal trend has cold mornings, warming days, with occasional storm patterns moving across the valley.

So far, in December, the average high temperature has been 45 degrees, and the average low has been 16 degrees.

As the fall season comes to an end, the valley floor is free from snow. On the other hand, the nearby mountains are all snow-capped. Ice clings to the edges of the canal running through the property as well as in the ranch ponds and the edges of Martin Creek.

My living conditions are consistent with 40-degree temperatures in the RV shop each morning. After starting the wood fire, I can easily get the inside temperature up to the low 50s. I favor opening the woodstove doors to appreciate better radiant heat; however, by doing so, I often end up with some wood smoke inside my shop area. The trade-off is worthwhile.

My dogs have learned that the inside of the motorhome is warmer during night time. When I go to bed, they line up waiting to get in. So far, the barn cat does not care or simply has not figured out that she has a choice here. When the shop doggie door is open, the cat seems to prefer night hunting outside.

So as the fall season comes to an end, the shortest day has concluded. The sunrise was at 7:12 a.m., and the sunset was at 4:24 p.m. The winter solstice has taken place, and the Latin word "solstitium" applies. This thirteenth-century word means that the sun stands still. For one day, the sun stood still, and now it changes its angle and works its way towards the longest day of the year.

10: RANCH HOUSE CONSTRUCTION

The change of season brings with it the first real progress on the ranch house construction. The first cement work is done, and I sense the promise that real headway will continue soon.

During the ground-breaking phase, I have done my best to use many of the exposed rocks. I started a curved walkway that has a rock landscape wall that is about a foot wide and a foot tall. If these rocks are not used soon, they will all be pushed back into the foundation hole as part of the fill process.

As the fall season starts, I continue to work on the orchard, clearing, or re-clearing planting spaces. I have set up a rudimentary irrigation line system that will handle the basic water needs. Early in the fall, I planted my first peach tree, near the existing peach tree that survived many years with no care at all. In mid-October, I added a third fruit tree, an apple, which, according to the tags, will provide good pollination for any future apple trees.

While I wait for the ranch house to get going, I have a good start on the mezzanine or loft section in the RV shop. The loft is set up with storage, a closet, and a bed. This extra living space will allow me to entertain my first guest on September 26th and 27th.

As fall sets in, the nighttime temperature is at or near freezing, I have started firing up the wood stove in the shop. I also moved a three-barrel wood storage system inside and set it next to the woodstove. The little addition of a fire goes a long way to make this temporary place seem like home.

RANCH RODEO

One of the significant local events each year is the Ranch Rodeo. This two-day rodeo is hosted by Woodie and Lilla Bell and is located just a mile north of town. The local Volunteer Fire District is the sponsor of this event, and they also host a midday BBQ feed. This group is so well organized that they even have their own liquor license. Locals are expected to contribute a dish to the pot-luck lunch. But, the primary purpose here is to stage a small-time rodeo for the benefit of the many local cowboys.

While I attended this event for the first time last year, I did not have a wife close by to help me cover the pot-luck contribution. As I move into my second autumn here, Becky was with me for the ranch rodeo weekend, and she put together a pasta salad.

What is most noticeable about the rodeo is how youngsters are incorporated into the competition. On the first day, there are horse classes, which included junior stock horse events for three age groups—the first bracket included newborns to five-year-olds, the second bracket included six- to ten-year-olds, and the final bracket included the eleven-to eighteen-year-olds.

One of the most popular spectator events is the barnyard scramble. An assortment of animals—chickens, goats, ducks, geese, rabbits, and pigs—are turned loose, and the objective is quite simple; kids, eighteen and under chased around after the stock and could keep whatever they caught.

The more traditional rodeo events had a strong emphasis on roping. These roping events were somewhat different from what I remembered last year, but it is clear that competition closely relates to what the local ranchers do as part of their daily ranch life. The first day ended with co-ed team branding, which used paint rather than a hot iron.

On day two, the kid events continued with events as goat tail untying, goat tail tying, dummy roping with a mechanical calf, sheep riding, calf riding, and calf undecorating. I was most impressed with the very young kids riding sheep. In reality, it appeared the kids were practicing a death grip drill where the kids were nose-down into the sheep's wool and had a death grip with both hands and feet while the adult sheep streaked across the arena.

In some cases, the eventual crash-and-burn dismount ended with brief tears, but in other cases, the toughness of ranch kids was apparent as the youngsters hit the dirt hard, rolled a couple of times, and came up looking very business-like. This event is also called Mutton Busting.

There is an end of event special youth award given to the kid who accumulated the greatest number of event points during the two days. Five-year-old Cade Bell was this year's winner of the Jim Angus Memorial All-around Award.

FIRST RANCH GUEST

On September 26th and 27th, I hosted my first ranch guest, as Dick Kirkland came to visit and explore the region. We plan to use our quads to get better acquainted with the streams and mountains.

On the 26th, we rode to Hard Scrabble as well as halfway up the side of Red Hills. Hard Scrabble is a location further up Martin Creek where there is a stone bunkhouse set up to support cowboys if and when they spend extended time in this area. This trip was well over ten miles, and the three dogs followed the entire distance.

Hardscrabble Cabin

That day we also hosted an impromptu meeting of a bunch of retired and current law enforcement guys. This group included the guy who would soon be elected as the new Sheriff of Humboldt County.

My guest, Dick Kirkland, and I met shortly after he was sworn as the new Sheriff in the Reno area. As the newly-elected Sheriff of Washoe County, he was a dynamo; I'll do my best to do justice to his description.

He took over a sleepy Sheriff's Office that suffered from years of neglect, and his new management style was bound to shake things up.

He had a gregarious, outgoing personality, a natural smile, and a way of getting his ideas accomplished. He was fond of saying that he couldn't do this alone, and he needed to assemble a new team that directly supported his plans. Less than an hour after he was sworn into office, he paid me a visit.

At that time, I was a corrections deputy in the felony housing unit at the jail. After a few minutes of chit chat, I asked him why he was visiting me. He said he had a job offer. He went on to ask if I would be willing to serve as his new Administrative Deputy. He said I would have an office across the hall from his office.

I asked why he chose me, and he explained that he had three-hundred-twenty deputies that could drive a patrol car and make arrests, but he did not have anyone who had proven staff experience. He was aware that I had worked in the Pentagon for four years and figured that if I knew anything, I knew staff work because that was all I did.

Minutes later, he had asked for a replacement deputy to take my jail assignment, and I followed him up to his office.

Initially, I had good intentions of becoming a regular patrol deputy and to do my part for providing law and order to our community. Instead, I started helping him with an endless array of projects, many of which involved writing and record keeping.

I was not alone in my new assignment. I shared an office with one of the brightest and most positive gentlemen I have ever known, named Mike G. He was a civilian recruited from Delta Airlines. The Sheriff's Office at that time had around one-thousand total employees. My partner Mike and I had just become the two busiest staff workers on the planet.

Starting from day one, we received work assignments that promoted the new direction of this agency. Little did we know that we would never catch up on our workload. We came to work early, we stayed late, and we often took work home, but we never caught up.

Most special assignments were changed every year or so. My job, apparently, was a lifetime appointment. I stayed with this inspired boss until he left to go work for the State.

He and I were the same age, and we had very similar interests. We accidentally became friends, which at times was somewhat awkward. At work, I always treated him as my boss, and I never let the friendship show. Other times, we were together socially, and then we could relax our respective roles.

At one point, years into my assignment, I was so far behind on my assigned projects that I went to his office and asked him to replace me. I said I wasn't capable of keeping up with his pace and that he needed to find someone that can work faster or harder to keep up with demands.

He told me to take a deep breath and relax. He said he never expected me to accomplish every task. He said he picked me because I could think for myself, and thus, I was expected to establish my own work priorities. In short, I had the freedom to get the important stuff done first and needn't worry about the rest. He told me to get out of his office and back to work.

I was also on the elected board for the Deputies Association. We were the union representatives, though not permitted to strike, that negotiated our contracts and represented deputies who were in trouble.

This, too, was a challenging position because often, the deputies association was at odds with the sheriff's administration. However, we managed to make this awkward relationship work to both his advantage as well as the advantage of the association.

So, in short, any visit from Dick Kirkland was a special event. As a boss and as a friend, I adored him. Over the years, he also was generous with his compliments and anecdotal stories. We have stayed in touch.

In total, I worked directly for him for nearly six years. These were the hardest working years of my adult life, but they were also the most rewarding.

Dick was always fond of travel in his retirement years, but he told me if he had a place like my ranch, he would be inclined to stay home a lot more.

During the second day of Dick's visit, several friends—Kull, Kilgore, Casey, and Kirkland—stopped by for a visit and a chance to enjoy a few beers.

CONCRETE FOUNDATIONS

It has taken a few days to build the forms for the concrete stem walls. This wood frame assembly is more complex than I imagined. Even if this phase of work is completed this week, the work crews say that I am on a waiting list for concrete delivery, and that may not be until next week. One thing we all agree on is the view from my upper-level is grand.

While I waited, a recent job involved crawling to the top of my RV shop roof so I could add canvas covers over the new roof vents. I anticipate that these covers should help keep out some of the winter moisture and maybe even stop the vibration noise that has persisted since they were installed.

On September 28th, I received the second concrete delivery. This phase included the concrete fill on the stem walls. It also included the final sections of mid-footprint foundations. I still had 1.4 cubic yards leftover, and it had to be dumped around the foundation. It is getting late in the season, and the contractor voiced his concern about possible weather coming around the time of the next concrete delivery.

I continue to hand-dig the foundation trench for the future well-house. This pick and shovel work is difficult for an older guy, but that seems to be part of ownership to do this kind of manual labor.

COMMUNITY MEETING

After being a full-time resident for six months, I attended my first community meeting, a rather informal governance comprised of appointed representatives from the local 4H, the PTO, the volunteer fire department, and the Recreation Board. These principals can then appoint at-large board members during their annual December meeting. I was asked to attend in support of two controversial issues. One issue involved the thirty-three percent rent increase for a nice couple living in a mobile home at the RV park.

The other issue had to do with the recent treatment of the saloon manager Nita. The primary issue here is that someone made a formal complaint to the county health department that their outdoor cooking operation was not legal or in compliance with health regulations.

This complaint was a sore point because it forced the shut down of the very popular Saturday night cookout, where 60 to over one-hundred members of the community gather to eat, drink, and catch up on the news. These cookouts, which provide a welcoming and warm environment, are where I met most of the local residents. Without this social gathering, I would not know many neighbors yet.

During the meeting, the locals spoke emphatically and emotionally about the current issues. There was strong support for the folks who had been mistreated as a result of board actions. Even the legal standing of the governance board was challenged, and as a result, the board did not take any formal action. Because this gathering had no agenda, minutes, or board vote, the meeting served purely as a healthy place to vent, followed by the plea to take better care of one another.

Perhaps the most influential dissident voice came from Chris and Fred Stewart, owners of the old Ninety-Six Ranch. Chris had done her homework and was clear in her presentation without getting personal or emotional. I sat next to Steve Lucas, a long-standing resident and businessman. He also made an impassioned plea about the problems at hand. Steve and I continued our chat once we adjourned to the bar.

I found this community meeting experience interesting as I viewed it as a western version of the New England town meeting. It was also illustrated how local residents want to control their own community without input from the county, attorneys, or any other outsiders.

The meeting adjourned with a comment from the crowd that we should now depart and finish the conversation at the saloon. True enough, most of the attendees—except for a few of the board members who were ideologically roughed up—walked down the street to the saloon where the discussions continued.

I found some of the post-meeting comments to be interesting. Mike E. told one of his relatives that he was sorry that I had to witness this tense community meeting; he did not like the idea that problems were being worked out in front of a new resident such as myself. Another report from Stan J. indicated that some of the board members didn't know who I was and wondered why I was taking notes during the meeting; apparently, some found this intimidating, as they thought I might be a spy or an attorney of some kind.

Strange reactions, I would say, but I am learning about small-town politics and internal dynamics. One source suggests that the board, in accordance with its by-laws, will not take any further action until its annual December meeting when formal appointments are made. As one person pointed out, the good news here was that after the heated exchanges in the meeting, the majority of the folks moved to the saloon to sort things out in a healthy way.

CONSTRUCTION CONTINUES

October 4th was not only an ideal workday, but significant progress was made on the backfill. My neighbor Joe K. offered dirt fill from his property. Since we already have a short cut road to his place, this transfer of fill dirt was relatively easy.

On the 5th, Brian used his heavy-duty backhoe to dig the utility trench that connected the new ranch house with the power and water connections about eighty yards down the hill, approximately three-hundred-twelve feet to the water source and around four-hundred feet to the electrical source.

At the crest of the hill, Brian, as he expected, hit large rocks and boulders. However, he is skilled at chipping away at the rocks and continued changing the angle of his attack, eventually finding a way to win the battle.

As of October 10th, we are ready for the final cement delivery on the ranch house, which will take care of the patio and sidewalk sections under the extended roofline.

The weather has become much cooler in the past couple of weeks, and this date is about as late in the season as my contractor is comfortable pouring concrete.

In anticipation of possible extra cement, I also finished setting up the cement forms for my well-house project, which I'm constructing on my own. With help from the ranch house construction crew, Marcus and Jose, I used the extra mud and completed the slab work on my well-house.

In an effort to get the feel of the finished house project, at the end of the long workday, I carried a plastic lawn chair and a cold beer to the back porch of the house-in-construction. This was my first chance to sit on the back porch and relax for a few moments, soaking in the view of the Muffler Meadow and the Old Mill Ranch. Oh, what a sight.

During the following few days, I removed the forms, backfilled the dirt, and built a two by six plank floor covering over the actual well hole.

On October 15th, Becky helped me cut the planks, mount the insulation, and install the wood covering. This should provide sufficient protection to get us through the winter. I will try to find $4600 to pay for the Tuff Shed well-house next spring.

My new shop cat does her job well as she has caught two mice in as many days. The first one was more of a game of play. The second night's hunting was more efficient as she ate half her catch.

By early evening on October 15th, my mother's birthday, we have a light rain shower. This is only the second time it has rained since I moved here in April. It turns out this rainy pattern has continued into November with about one shower per week. Most of the rain is light and measures between a trace and one-quarter of an inch.

As of October 20th, the electrical sub-contractor had connected power to the house site, no small feat, because it had to be pulled approximately four-hundred-fifty feet through a three- to four-foot deep trench. The game plan is to have power on the job site before the framers start.

The two framers showed up late in October, and by the first weekend in November, they already had six of the eight walls up. A large stockpile of fresh lumber is stacked around the job site, including trusses for the bathhouse. It will be comforting to see the structure enclosed so that I don't have to worry about rain and water damage on the fresh wood.

By November 10th, the house framers had all of the roof rafters in place. They also had the cross-support beam dropped in that will provide some wall stability during any future high winds. This cross beam will support the bedroom loft section.

By Thanksgiving weekend, my ranch house construction had progressed to the point that the roof covering was in place, and the bathhouse roof was well on its way to completion. The loft support system was finished, and the loft stairway was half-finished.

LANDSCAPING

In my eagerness to get projects underway, I planted trees and shrubs on November 4th. Although it seems a little late in the season, the weather is still fine, and many of the Reno nurseries are having end of season sales.

Today, at the beginning of the driveway, as it comes off the county road, I planted four Lombardy poplars, the most traditional large trees in and around the ranch sites. They are slender and easily the tallest trees around. Eventually, I want to plant them all the way up the drive to where the bridge crosses the canal.

I am pleasantly surprised to find a fair amount of subsoil moisture on the entire lower step of the property. The moisture level looks good enough that I may not need to provide an irrigation line to reach these trees.

I also planted a locust tree, opposite the existing one at the front entrance gate, and at the upper step, behind the house on the east side, I planted three sea-green junipers. They are intended to provide ground cover and soften the rock-lined pathway out the back door of the house.

Finally, I planted my first Miss Kim lilac, which is a smaller variety of lilac that should not exceed three- to four-feet and thus not block any of my beautiful views.

To prepare the poor soil around the house site, I made arrangements with a neighbor, Susan Kern, from the HS Ranch, to pick up a trailer load of manure. I was fortunate enough to get access to well-cured manure that looks more like topsoil than it does manure.

While at Susan's ranch, I was invited in for afternoon coffee and pumpkin pie. We discussed many ranch topics, including care and maintenance of old tractors. She explained that I did not need to buy new front tires for my Farmall because I could put on older worn-out pick-up tires that would be functional.

RANCH ARCH

I have long admired ranch entrance arches as I travel across the west. During my last trip to Montana, I stopped at many ranches to take photos of different style entrance arches.

One of the nicest examples was found north of Missoula. This one was made out of three timber pieces, and the top section had a slight arch, giving it distinction and good looks. Although I could purchase something similar, I ran into two problems, the price, $1500, and the logistic challenge of transporting it to Nevada.

Once I got access to a post hole digger, I started to work on my entrance arch. I bought two twenty-foot treated six by six posts from the local lumber company. I also put together two ten-foot planks, two by six in size, for the top crosspiece. To add a little ranch flavor, along the top plank, I mounted a mixed blend of old rusty horseshoes that I found at the Upper Willow Creek Ranch on the Orovada side of the Santa Rosa Mountains.

Ranch Arch

Fortunately for me, the framing crew offered to loan out their Hyster forklift so that I can place the top arch seventeen feet in the air. I need the forklift's help to get both cross pieces up that high so that I can bolt them securely in place.

The final step in the entrance arch will be building two-panel wood gates. These will be the old-style ranch gates with a high support on each side that permit the long cross brace to help stabilize the gate and provide some weight distribution for the hinge system.

This project unfolds during the second week of November, and my working conditions are starting to get cold. I still need to tamp in the dirt around the tall posts so that they are stable, and this needs to get this accomplished before the ground starts to freeze solid.

Thanks to a late and warm fall season, I had time to start adding the fence posts and the lodgepole rails that adjoin the arch and gate complex. The lodgepole rails were sixteen-feet long and cost $13.39 each.

I have built one side of the wood ranch gate, and I found it to be heavier than expected. It takes two people just to lift it so it can be turned around. Some of my neighbors have warned me that I will need to add a caster wheel for the side opposite the hinges, to help support the gate weight. I was also told that I would need a guidewire cable on the side opposite the gate. Thanks to adjoining railroad tie posts, I will have something to anchor the guidewire to.

On Thanksgiving morning, there was a light dusting of snow on the ground. This cooler temperature was an excuse to do minimal work on the entrance arch. I did unload the four lodge pole fence rails, and the task of mounting them can wait for warmer conditions, perhaps even next spring.

As of December 5th, I added the hinge hardware and hung the second wood gate. I still have some fine-tuning to do, but due to the winter conditions, I have decided that this can wait for spring's warmer temperatures. I think the project turned out well, and it adds a visual appeal to the entrance to this property.

MARINE CORPS BIRTHDAY

For a few moments and a few paragraphs, I would like to step away from my new rural life and my quest to build a ranch house.

Tonight is November 10th, a sentimental and special date for me. On this date, my beloved Marine Corps is two-hundred-thirty-one years old. Not a bad lifespan for a bunch of patriots who met in a bar, Tun Tavern, in 1775 to form a fighting group that became the Marine Corps. Remember, 1775 is one year before America became a country. Tomorrow is Veterans Day. It seems fitting that these two special days fall next to each other.

The Marine Corps may be the only military service that even knows when to celebrate their birthday. Over the years, I have asked fellow veterans, that are not Marines when their service celebrates their birthday. The answer seems always to be the same, "I just don't know." Because I know the Marine's birthday, I had to pause and pay my respects to the greatest military institution ever formed.

Eleanor Roosevelt once said that she had never seen a group with such low morals and such high morale. I have heard that she also wanted to abolish the Marines and just lump them in with U.S. Army soldiers. Not.

On CNN TV news, the Lou Dobbs show paid special tribute to a cross-section of young men. Some of these featured warriors have recently been killed in combat, while others have survived their battles. In every case, these stories remind me of the truly important issues of our day. My situation is minor in comparison, and I acknowledge this openly.

I realize that no matter how chaotic our world situation seems to be today, the fact is crystal clear that we have young men, both officers and enlisted, who are so well trained that I can rest assured that our military is in good hands. Our country is in good order to have these people fighting for our national goals.

The 2006 election seems like a soft victory for some of the enemy, as it seems our country has voted for a change, and the enemy has already commented on the signal that the 2006 election appears to send. While the political message is unsettling to me, the fact that we have honorable and brave men serving in our military helps make up for any political weakness.

I am proud that I had the chance to serve my country in combat back in 1970-71. Times have changed, but the characteristics that are worthy of our recognition remain the same.

At least in this current Iraq war, our country seems to provide better care to its servicemen and servicewomen, and their service is certainly better recognized, compared to the way Vietnam veterans were treated when we returned home.

NOVEMBER CONSTRUCTION PROGRESS
At the time of the Marine Corps birthday and Veterans Day, construction on the ranch house has reached the point that the outside frame is complete, and my roof line eves are being prepared with eight by eight timbers placed today.

These twelve outside timbers provide the support structure that completes the 12/12 pitch roof that seems to appear more like a church roofline than a traditional ranch home.

Outside Framing Complete

On November 19th, Becky and I had been doing some site clean up when my next-door neighbor walked over to the job site with three cold beers. Although it wasn't even noon, we stopped our work to enjoy the quenching treat.

Joe wanted to invite us to the first birthday party for his son, Ethan. As it turned out, many neighbors were invited, and the crowd was large.

Also, during the gathering, we had the first opportunity to meet Duane Boggio's delightful wife, Tami. She is a classy lady and fun to talk to. It turns out that she is from the same town in Montana, Havre, that my aunt was from; this commonality provided grounds for a long chat.

It was impressive to see this community gathering to celebrate something as simple as a child's birthday.

FALL'S FINAL TASKS

As November comes to a close, many outdoor chores remain, most of them are related to preparing for winter and getting items put up so that they are not covered in snow in the coming months. One of the chores is placing blue plastic tarps over my wood piles behind the shop.

I have already finished the soil preparation in the proposed flower beds next to the ranch house. This task was a long and challenging chore because I had to dig up a bed of rocks, and once they were removed, the soil level was much lower than when I started. On the other hand, now that I'm done, these new planter beds will be ready for spring soil augmentation and rotor-tiller work.

I continue to work on the entrance arch, wood gates, and lodgepole connector fences. My work is currently stalled because I need to buy a cordless drill so I can drill holes to set the lag screws in place so that the rails can be supported into the railroad tie posts.

As of December 1st, the house's main structure is almost completely enclosed from the weather. The only steps pending for total enclosure are two skylights and three exterior doors. All of these items are on-site, and I expect to see full enclosure by the end of the first week in December.

One of the challenges of moving here has become one of the great joys, the task of meeting the people of this valley. Last night, December 4th, I attended Monday Night Football at the saloon. I sat next to Jason and Char, my near neighbors on Deputy Lane. They are conversant and agreeable people. Later in the evening, Davy and Kati took their place at the bar, and the visiting continued.

Back at the job site, I met Tom Brophy, the older guy plumber who is helping with the house construction. Actually, Tom can do plumbing and a whole lot more. We eventually became very close as we would be work partners for the local Weed Control District.

It turns out that he lives a couple of miles to the west, on the road to Spring City, an abandoned mine. He is part of that pattern of older folks bailing out of places like Gardnerville, to move here. It seems that increasingly folks are tiring of the rapid growth of previously small towns in western Nevada.

As the fall season comes to an end, the only crew working is the roofing crew. They will finish the roof shingles on the final day of the fall season.

By this point, the interior rough wiring and plumbing are also complete. Two of the three heating stoves have been installed, but there is no sense in firing them up yet because gaping holes still exist where the roof rafters meet the side walls.

I believe that the next interior work will be the insulation phase, followed by the sheetrock crew. When the sheetrock guys are ready, I will fire up my heating stoves.

By mid-December, the backhoe guy was filling his utility line trenches as well as working on the installation of the septic system. The contractor expects to see the stucco crews arriving soon.

On February 9th, I took inventory of my working hands. I was now done with the wood flooring project and just starting the tile flooring.

As I look down at these working hands, I can see better why they hurt. On my left hand, I have two bloody wounds on the back of the hand, caused by errant hammer blows this morning. On that same hand, I have a fresh sliver into the thumb. On this same thumb, I have a dry skin split along the thumbnail. On the index finger is a day-old blood blister, again thanks to a hammer blow. My middle finger has a cut on the tip. The remaining two fingers are still okay.

On the opposite hand, I have an extended sliver wound in the little finger. This wound got infected a couple of days ago, and thus the middle finger joint is swollen and does not bend well.

Why would I go into such detail about wounded hands? Recalling this past summer's observation about the appearance of the rough hands of the working cowboys, this discussion of my hands helps illustrate that now I look a bit more like the rest of the hard-working people in this valley. About the only thing missing on my hands is a couple of black fingernails. I have considered going out back and whacking a couple of fingernails, just to get it over with.

11: WINTER SEASON

My first day of the winter season had a lazy start. I've been getting up later than usual, with the excuse of waiting for the temperature to warm up, both outside and inside the shop.

DECEMBER NOTES

When I got up this morning, the temperature was 20 degrees outside and 40 degrees inside, and a fresh couple of inches of snow coated the ground.

On a few particularly cold occasions, I have gotten out of bed to let the dogs out, start a wood fire, and get the coffee going, then I go back to bed for a few minutes, allowing time for things to warm up. This luxury routine is most common when I hear and feel the sleet on my metal roof and sidewalls.

The day's first chore is restarting the wood fire, and as it got going, I brewed a fresh pot of coffee. To speed up the heating process inside the shop, I ran the propane heater for a bit.

My morning's next routine is to read the Reno paper online. I have to say, drinking coffee and reading the internet version of the paper is not quite the same as actually turning the pages. I understand that the newspaper business is slowly dying; however, reading a physical newspaper was one morning habit I enjoyed.

When the outdoor conditions are extra cold, I try to focus my time on inside projects. At this point in the season, I have more projects pending inside the shop than outside.

However, once the temperature outside reached 40 degrees, I'd start any required outdoor work. Today, with fresh snow on the ground, I determined that it would be safe to burn sagebrush piles that were close to standing live sagebrush. I discovered that even with my favorite accelerant, it was difficult to get a fire started.

~~~ ~~~ ~~~
~~~ ~~~ ~~~

Later in the day, when I arrived at the saloon, the bar was nearly full of the usual customers. I enjoyed the usual exchange of buying drinks for one another and sharing good healthy conversation.

Steve Lucas, who operates a B&B, which is the only overnight guest accommodation in the valley, was kind enough to extend an invitation to his Bed and Breakfast Christmas Open House. His B&B offers a pleasant place to stay with first-class hospitality extended all of the time.

~~~ ~~~ ~~~
~~~ ~~~ ~~~

I realize that the house will be completed within four to six weeks. The mortgage rollover is coming soon, and the reality is that my budget is about maxed out. Many items that will help with property development will take time to acquire. Most likely, I'll spend the next couple of years with a strict budget and some austere spending practices. Much of the work ahead will be simple manual labor, especially for the house landscape work.

As an example, a new forty-horsepower tractor is over $21,000, which means that I will need to find a way to get the old Farmall tractor running well. After the new year, I was able to get the starter rebuilt for $67, as opposed to purchasing a new one for $400. This old tractor will be a great help in digging post holes for fence posts as well as prepping holes for tree and shrub planting.

I have come to realize that I will soon need a portable generator for multiple projects on the property. At the moment, I need this tool for remote fence work and will most likely need this power when it is time to start pumping water out of the shallow well. I have learned that I will need a five-thousand-watt generator if I expect to power a water pump in the 1.25 hp range.

Perhaps an austere budget will be a practical excuse to spend more time next summer hiking, camping, and exploring the national forest that is my backyard.

My psyche seems to welcome this change, of course. I firmly believe that people who live in conditions other than the typical warm and cushy are more inclined to hone their senses and enjoy taking time to observe the world around them. Also, my own experience of living alone has offered pleasant changes in the areas of observation and self-awareness. Alone is okay.

Interestingly, the winter isolation issue seems to be of some concern to my city friends. The common question is, "What do you do with yourself and your time during the winter months?" I am afraid that my answer probably comes back with a wry smile and the proud explanation that I enjoy every moment to the fullest.

∿ ∿ ∿
∿ ∿ ∿

My woodstove is often a sort of magnet, especially during those cold days when the wind howls. I have discovered that my new purchase of a hooded sweatshirt sewn inside a flannel shirt is the best protection that I own. Most of us will eventually find that favorite jacket that follows us most everywhere. I like the hood up, as head protection has become more common than not.

After being outside for a period, it is comforting to hustle back to my white plastic lawn chair, which sits directly in front of the stove.

Woodstove

This routine is singularly peaceful in my shop shelter, and that particular chair has been in that position for so long now that the white plastic has become discolored and is now a dirty shade of gray, smoke gray to be precise.

THE NEW YEAR BEGINS

This year, the local snowpack seems to be behind normal, and our region is consistent with the entire northern part of Nevada.

By the first week in January, we received only three measurable snowfalls. The local snowmobile guys say that even in the mountains, the snow depth is not sufficient to make the sport worthwhile.

This snow trend is unfortunate for the snow sports guys; however, it has been helpful for my construction progress. By the first of the new year, I have only lost one day of construction work due to crews not being able to get through the steep snow-covered driveway.

ᴍᴍ ᴍᴍ ᴍᴍ
ᴍᴍ ᴍᴍ ᴍᴍ

The morning hours are the best time to pay bills, get other paperwork done, and catch up on house planning and budget considerations. Instead of working out of a typical office, I work out of a shoebox.

As a matter of personal choice, I now eat my breakfast around mid-morning, instead of in early hours, as was my practice when I was in the working world—breakfast alternates between oatmeal with blueberries, and buttermilk pancakes, also with blueberries. The delayed breakfast hour heightens my appetite and appreciation for this meal.

ᴍᴍ ᴍᴍ ᴍᴍ
ᴍᴍ ᴍᴍ ᴍᴍ

Usually, by mid-morning, the working conditions outside are suitable. There have been few days when wind and temperature drove me indoors, and it is rare for me to confine myself all day inside the shop, even when the winter conditions are oppressive.

More often than not, regardless of weather, the work crews make progress on the house exterior. In recent weeks, this has included roofing and stucco preparation.

As the winter season started, I made a note to save a spot in this book to describe the worst of the seasonal storms. I looked forward to chronicling the worst of winter conditions. I envisioned describing the pain and suffering from being snowed in for a week and running out of supplies.

I set this writing space aside in November when the temperature dipped into seasonal norms. But for weeks now, the pattern has been a low around 20 degrees and a high of around 40 degrees. This temperature difference of 20 degrees has been easy to deal with so far.

As of January 7th, we are now seventeen days into the winter season. For seventeen days, the sun has started working its way back to the higher arc.

During the summer peak months, the sun rises above the upper rock canyon. Now it appears well south of the creek canyon. I find comfort in knowing that it is working its way back to the warmer arc. I'm particularly happy to know we're moving toward summer as the temperature in my shop when I wake in the mornings is consistently 40 degrees.

The average temperature spread for this particular date, January 7th, is 23 degrees. The normal highs are 40 degrees, and the normal lows are 17 degrees. With that said, the local weather report is calling for a cold storm starting in four days.

On the topic of the return of summer, I want to express appreciation for the sun and how it heats our dwellings and our bodies. Additionally, other life, from the pesky flies to the growth of gardens, all await the same change in the sun's path.

There is an adventure in chasing the solar calendar. It is the core of all things natural. Living it fosters the awe and appreciation that other naturalist authors have written about. When the temperature permits, I want my door to be wide open so that I can remain close to both the sun and the nature that it supports.

It is more difficult to get out and study the work of nature in winter. It has been a long time since I checked the flow of the creek through the canyon. Likewise, it has been months since I moved in close to the wild turkeys for a more intimate look. Most of my days are spent making progress on the house construction. Perhaps subsequent winter visits to the local nature will be different.

FIRST WINTER STORM

The first bitter cold weather arrived on January 11th, 2007. The temperature has been at or around 0 degrees, and the daytime highs are not able to reach 30 degrees. The wind picked up and steadily blew ten miles per hour, which helped to make matters worse. The forecast indicates that there will not be any temperature relief for at least a week.

It would be one thing to just hunker down during these cold snaps; however, in my case, work still needed to be done on the house construction and outdoor projects. For example, it was not until January 12th that we finished the dirt fill on the final sections of the utility trench. Multiple times the young fellow, Josh, who operated the skid-steer, had to come indoors to warm his hands near the wood fire.

Three days into this cold snap, the routine has changed radically. My hands are full, just keeping the heat going—at this point, my primary job is to keep the heat going in both my RV shop as well as the house under construction.

I prefer not to wander too far from the source of heat. I catch myself spending more hours sitting in front of the wood-burning stove—the practice is more pleasant with the stove doors swung open. Previously, I found that smoke often floated into the shop when the doors were open for a long period. Now, I joked with my wife that the barn temperature was so cold that the smoke did not want to enter. She laughed, but it took her a second too long.

Early this morning, the temperature inside the barn before starting the wood fire was down to 35 degrees. It dawned on me while I was making breakfast that the temperature inside my fridge was warmer than my make-shift home.

On January 13th, the Harpers, living on the Owyhee Desert, reported 31 below zero. Their generator froze up and shut down. Neighbors along Martin Creek reported temperatures from zero to minus 12 degrees.

CHURCH IN WINTER

This cold spell has lasted ten days, with some relief on January 21st. Today the temperature broke 40 degrees. Because of the sunny sky and no wind, the day seemed even more comfortable.

As a sign of the cold spell, the community church met at the Sicking home on January 21st, where thirteen adults and five children were present. This gathering was led by the Sicking's son-in-law, Kyle Moore. He led the service, which was more of a bible study than a traditional service.

Services that day were moved from the old church because the building is hard to heat, and once the church heater blower kicks on, it becomes hard to hear what the preacher is saying.

Also, with the cold spell, the rancher/pastor Jerry Harper had his hands full. His ranch is remote, and the low temperatures hit him particularly hard. His house power comes from a generator that has frozen up during these last few days.

ɯɯ ɯɯ ɯɯ
ɯɯ ɯɯ ɯɯ

As January comes to a close, local ski area employees talk about the lack of a normal winter. Though we had a week and a half of unusually cold weather, we've had little precipitation to speak of this winter, and particularly this month.

According to normal weather patterns for this community, the average high temperature is 41 degrees, and the average low point is 18, resulting in a normal monthly average of 30 degrees.

As February is right around the corner, the average high will increase by 8 degrees, and the average low will be 6 degrees warmer. The February average temperature will be 36, as compared to the January average of 30.

Tomorrow will be the last day of January when the sunrise is 7:04 a.m., and the sunset is 5:01 p.m.

WINTER WILDLIFE AND BEAUTY

I have long realized that I live in an area abundant in natural life, which displayed its wonders non-stop. While nothing can compare with the summer wildlife viewing, the winter offers its own spectacular version.

I have enjoyed my winter wildlife observations. The scores of redtail hawks have shrunk to an occasional few. The magpies appear to maintain a similar population as in other seasons because they do not migrate. The wild turkey population in Muffler Meadow has exploded to over five times the average summer population; my hunch is that the valley population did not change one bit, but rather, various flocks may have moved to this portion of the valley. It would be easy to calculate that the winter conditions around Muffler Meadow may be ideal for winter feeding and protection.

The deer population appears to be consistent with summertime. The local herd seems to favor the same winter alfalfa fields that are so popular during summer feeding. The high sage and scrub brush of the meadow and the valley, in general, offer some protection from the cold winds that most often blow out of the east.

Though in most cases, the wildlife population numbers are down in winter, the joy of being so close to so many different animals and birds continues to add value and interest to my new lifestyle—and it was only when my way of living slowed down that I began to observe details of wildlife and my surroundings in earnest.

Only those who have lived in nature would understand what I mean. I now look forward to purchasing a spotting scope so that I can continue to observe the wildlife.

A similar story of local beauty and appreciation took place a few weeks ago when I was driving north out of Winnemucca. It was late afternoon, and the sun was setting.

As I neared the Chevron turn off to Highway 290, I noticed that the entire Paradise Valley was already in the shadow of the Santa Rosa Range, for my valley neighborhood, sunset had already taken place.

On the opposite side of the mountain range, the sun found an opening under the clouds so that the west-facing slopes were brightly lit. Not only were they bathed in the late afternoon light, but they were vibrant and alive in that unique purple color that many of us believe is unique to Nevada. Many call this color "Nevada purple."

The contrast in lighting was so awe-inspiring, I wanted to stop and just let that brief moment soak in. As I turned eastbound, I left that postcard setting and drove into the darkening valley. I thought to myself if any visitor or stranger came to me and asked, "What is this 'Nevada Purple' thing?" all I would have to do is point to that scene, and no descriptive words would be necessary.

One of my neighbors, Bill Arant, stopped by for a progress check on my house construction. In the course of our chat, Bill explained the brief history of a development plan that seemed to go sour. It's an interesting story of what might have been. Apparently, several well-to-do guys from Winnemucca decided that it would be a good idea to sell some one-acre lots along the bank of Martin Creek. The theory was that they would build a creek dam to attract land investors. These land investors would probably be outdoorsmen or at least fishermen. The dam would be a draw, as it would offer good fishing. The proposed site of this dam would be exactly the same place that the pioneers used over a hundred years ago. It turns out this idea was fairly well hatched before these real estate investors realized that the landowner, Les Stewart, would not sell them the land for the dam. In this case, Les (less) is more, because the decision not to sell helped preserve the creek bottom.

FEBRUARY OBSERVATIONS

This chapter is entitled "Winter," but today it is not winter-like. It is now February 4th, Super Bowl Sunday, and the weather is so nice it's almost spooky.

When I got up, the thermometer said 30 degrees. That is 30 degrees better than a month ago. By mid-morning, the sun is shining, the air is calm, and the temperature is now shirt sleeve weather. The weather is so nice that I see my dogs lying in the shade as opposed to the normal quest for a warm sunny spot.

It is so nice that I took time out from the house construction, poured a fresh cup of coffee, grabbed a lawn chair, and sat on the front porch on the sunny side of the new house, which will likely be my favorite place to sit and soak up the natural beauty. The front side of the ranch house is sunny in the morning and shady in the afternoon and offers the best view.

This morning my neighbor has his John Deere tractor running and is feeding hay to his cattle. This feeding crew today consists of the tractor driver and three fellows on the hay trailer. The tractor sound is occasionally interrupted with sounds from the gobbling turkey flock, which is feeding on my side of the creek for a change. Both sounds are emitted from the bottom of Muffler Meadow. Everything else is quite silent.

Looking in this direction, basically south, the morning sun angle is such that the sunlight reflects off of Martin Creek. From this angle and elevation, it is the only spot on the creek where I can see the water running. The rest of the creek is shrouded with willows and the like.

This spot where the water is visible is also the location where the creek has a four-foot waterfall, a continuous source of a steady water sound. At this location, the creek starts to split to the south, and the water canal, rancher lifeblood equally shared thanks to old water rights, splits to the north toward the Sicking.

As another indicator of the unusually warm weather is the surprise sound of a large fly buzzing around my head while I type out these words. Even the fly critters must be confused

As of February 9th, the conditions are more like spring than winter. Today, I got up to a damp and calm morning where the temperature started in the 40's. By mid-morning, I was sitting on my porch in shirt sleeves, enjoying the wonderful weather. This past week, Reno weather recorded the highest temperature on record for this date at 69 degrees.

The birds and insects must be as confused as I am pleased with these conditions. I accidentally dug up a bulb from my front yard. I could see that it already has a green bud showing.

Winter weather returned to more normal conditions by the third week in February when temperatures went below normal. For example, on February 23rd, the high temperature was only 39, when 51 is the long-term average. The overnight low temperature dipped to 15 when 25 degrees is the norm.

EARLY MARCH

By early March, the temperatures are back to being unusually warm, and consequently, the bird population is starting to increase. In particular, I see a large number of small bird flocks on the nearby roads. I am not sure what the attraction is to the road, but when you travel at high speed, you disrupt these flocks, and often the car will hit one or more of these small birds.

On March 6th, I noticed the flock of wild turkeys moving quickly from the creek bottom towards the foothills. It is not clear what would get them to move away from their feeding areas and also their night time protection areas. Later in the day, one of these large birds entered my property, just behind the house. My cattle dog felt it was her duty to chase this solo turkey, but I called her back.

On the following day, I noticed some male strutting going on in the flock just below my property. I counted twenty-two total turkeys with four males in full dress, strutting around with their best feather dress. Shortly after, I drove my quad down to the orchard and encountered a full-size flock, approximately fifteen to twenty birds. When my dogs got too close, they took flight and headed for the safety of Muffler Meadow. It is quite a sight to see such a large bird get airborne.

The winter season officially ends around 5:09 p.m. on March 20th.

I have waited all winter for that memorable storm and its momentous challenges, yet it never arrived. This year hosted a very mild and easy winter, not counting my general conditions living in the shop.

I have waited for months to describe for you the first really big storm of the winter season. Instead, the weather gods have spread out mild weather for weeks now.

Rather than describing an icy weather pattern or storm, I find myself detailing warmer than typical situations. For example, the local TV weather predicts that the Reno area will get into the 70s by this weekend, March 11th and 12th.

If this forecast is accurate, it will be the second time this season that new record high temperatures have been recorded. On this date, March 7th, the Reno high temp is supposed to get to 60 degrees. By contrast, the Winnemucca high is forecast to be 54 degrees today. Further north, the Paradise Valley temperature is supposed to be 52 degrees. The norm for this date locally is 53 degrees.

The weather has been so beautiful the past few days that I found myself outside, starting to develop my new yard landscape and garden. Most of my spring and summer efforts will be on establishing a perimeter fence around the garden to keep the pests out—dogs, deer, rabbits, and Mormon crickets. This perimeter fence will be a massive project that will take me years to finish.

At this point, if there is a memorable storm, it will be in the category of spring storm and not a winter storm.

12: TRANSITION TO THE NEW HOUSE

As luck would have it, the first day of winter offered three inches of fresh snow for the roofers to contend with, but they only had half of one roof left to shingle. After they swept off the new coat of snow, they finished their work by early afternoon. The tasks of sheetrocking, painting, and flooring are coming upon us quickly.

After living in my motorhome and RV shop for nine months, I am ready to move into a real house. The best guess at this point is that I still have five to eight weeks before I can move in.

In recent days, I have wrestled with a few different landscape plans to fit inside my large front yard fence and the smaller backyard fence. Given all of the work pending on these projects, I reckon that it may take most of the next summer to finish this step. It is daunting to think of how much work remains.

From a philosophical standpoint, I have found comfort by focusing my time and attention on local issues with less concern for the international problems that often seem beyond solution. I am still a news junkie, and my evening routine includes some time on both CNN and Fox News. The contrast is good.

∼∼∼ ∼∼∼ ∼∼∼
∼∼∼ ∼∼∼ ∼∼∼

As mentioned earlier, Dyn-Corps International asked if I was interested in a police training position in either Iraq or Afghanistan. At that point, my priorities shifted to ranch matters rather than international issues. Further, I have no comfort level that the actual training mission is well-conceived and operating with any degree of efficiency. The recent Iraq Study Group had little good to say about the years of training effort with Dyn-Corps at the lead.

JANUARY

During the first week of January, two work crews worked concurrently. On the outside, the stucco crew prepped the exterior with tar paper and chicken wire. Now we need to wait for warm enough weather to apply the stucco mud. On the inside, a crew has installed the sheetrock and applied the tape and mud. This step has required propane heaters so the mud can dry.

We had trouble with the shower pan because the piece that I picked up from Reno was cracked. The company that did the man-made marble has agreed to remake the piece and deliver it all the way to the valley.

My contribution has been multiple trips to Reno to pick up products, such as flooring, ceiling fans, gas range, range hood, fridge, windows, etc.

Early January presented multiple opportunities for trips to Reno. I am near the end of the product pickups. I have scores of items on hand, waiting for the appropriate cycle of the house construction.

During one recent trip to Reno, it appeared that my cattle dogs wanted to supplement their free-feeding dog bowls. When I returned, I found a freshly killed rabbit on my shop sofa. Given the amount of meat missing from the rabbit carcass, I assume this hunt was more than just for sport.

ᴧᴧ ᴧᴧ ᴧᴧ
ᴧᴧ ᴧᴧ ᴧᴧ

Also, during the holidays, I had my first opportunity to sit down and visit with an older gentleman by the name of Frank, who comes with a great reputation as an "old salt" in the valley, capable of endless stories. As I was prepared for the storyteller to do his thing, I was not disappointed when we sat down for an hour-long visit.

He was not only a great storyteller, but he covered a tremendous range of subjects. Because of his age and the associated failing hearing, he often walked over my comments. While this habit can be annoying, in his case, it was excusable because his stories were better than anyone else in the conversation circle. Frank used to be the cow boss of the largest ranch corporation in the valley, Nevada First Corporation.

I found that his topic areas included: 1) ranching, 2) hunting, 3) guarding federal prisoners at Fort Knox, 4) flying, 5) the difference between herding cattle with a quad versus a horse, 6) drilling wells, and 7) finding water with the art of a willow branch.

You quickly realize that a guy with this personality and wealth of stories is, in fact, a national treasure. It would be a shame if someone did not sit him down with a video camera to capture a sample of the stories before Frank dies. One thing I did learn was that when Frank was in the storytelling mode, don't even try to get a word in edgewise.

᭺᭺᭺ ᭺᭺᭺ ᭺᭺᭺
᭺᭺᭺ ᭺᭺᭺ ᭺᭺᭺

At this point, I have spent time tracking those extra expenses that were not included in the contractor's budget. Some of the basic items such as floor covering were not included, and therefore, it has become my responsibility.

While waiting for house progress, I have been surprised at how much firewood I've burned. When I did my summer and fall firewood gathering, I thought that there might be enough wood for two winters, but that was not based on any actual experience.

By early January, I struggle to find storage for those house construction items that will be needed soon. For the house, I now own ceiling fans, a refrigerator, washer and dryer, window screens, light fixtures, sixty-one boxes of oak planks, forty-one boxes of ceramic tile, a gas range, a hood vent, and the like. These items, along with my trailer, take up valuable space in my shop. Within two months, I hope to have all of those items moved and hooked up in the new house.

〰 〰 〰
〰 〰 〰

One of the milestones for my house construction progress was January 6th when I fired up the pellet stove for the first time. This step was critical for the proper drying and curing of the finish sheetrock work. My burn rate has been on "high" as I try to get as much heat drying as possible.

After one day of operation, it has proven capable of heating the entire house as well as part of the adjoining bathhouse. This rate of burn means that I am going through one bag of pellets per day.

On January 8th, I drove to Winnemucca, expecting to buy a good number of pellet bags. My first stop was Brown's Hardware, where they explained that they had none in stock—this was similar to my recent check at Lowe's in Reno, where they have been out of stock all winter. The personnel at Lowe's indicated that they did not expect a shipment until the end of February.

I did find that the local feed store was selling pellets on a ration basis. They only permitted five bags per customer until they get restocked. The price per bag has gone from $4.35 at Lowe's to $5.75 per bag at the feed store.

It seemed fitting that the Reno evening news did special coverage on this topic of the shortage of pellets. They blamed it on supply and demand; however, the word on the street around here is that the problem is related to the recent changes in allowing Canadian lumber imports. Apparently, this has slowed down or shut down U.S. wood production. When there is not enough sawdust and wood waste, there is nothing to make pellets out of. Reno TV reported predicted that this problem would self-correct, but only after one year.

Later an employee at the local lumber yard had an insider explanation that made more sense than the evening news report. This fellow indicated that other products are now being made out of sawdust and other wood cutting waste products, and now the pellet producers compete for the wood waste, and they are behind.

∿∿ ∿∿ ∿∿

I have come to learn that the only time to try controlled burns is in the middle of winter. Those sage piles that have grown during the past ten months need to be removed.

On January 15th, I did a large controlled burn on the lower level of the property, burning dead sage that was leftover from a previous fire. Also, this past summer, I cut a lot of sage from the upper lip of the canal, which was scattered along the canal bank.

During this latest cold spell, I decided to get a fire started and then feed it with the deadwood lying around. Once I got the fire started, the cheatgrass burned out to a twenty-foot diameter circle in a slow burn that allowed me to stomp out any section gaining too much momentum.

As usual, a hot sagebrush fire kicks out a lot of burning embers. During the windless conditions, these embers climb into the sky with the thermal heat of the fire. When these embers fall into the grass and sage, they pose no burn threat.

After a couple of hours, the hot ember bed was kicking off a tremendous amount of heat. I tried to spread the coals so the fire would cool off before bedtime; however, the heat was so intense that it was difficult to stick a rake into the coals without getting a face burn.

The area where this sage burn was taking place is where I hope to build my corral next summer. I also hope to make a fire break/motorcycle racing track in this same area. I plan to wait for the gift of a Caterpillar dirt mover from Cousin Chris before I start ripping up sagebrush. On this lower step of the property, the sage grows up over six feet tall.

I have an even larger burn pile waiting near the orchard. I may take a fire there tomorrow if the winds cooperate.

〰 〰 〰
〰 〰 〰

January 21st was somewhat significant in that I got heat to the bathhouse for the first time. Last week the gas company installed the LP tank and hooked up the line. With this prep work done, I started the gas log heater for the first time. It is a small heating stove, so I am anxious to see if it can provide sufficient heat to that space of just under 500 square feet. The inside temperature was only 51 degrees after burning all day.

〰 〰 〰
〰 〰 〰

While the Santa Rosa mountain range is impressive during the summer, it's grandeur increases when winter adds snow caps. At a recent steak dinner at Bill Arant's house, my friend Liz went outside for a smoke. When she returned, she approached me, asking if I had seen the mountains in the moonlight. Having missed this perspective, I admitted not, and we both went outside.

She pointed westward at the peaks of Abel, Singus, and Cottonwood glowing in the moonlight. Against the darkened sky, the mountain tops reflected the moonlight as if they were generating the light themselves.

It was so impressive that we stayed a while and let it soak in despite the 20-degree temperatures, while dressed in shirt sleeves. Clearly, we both appreciated this local beauty.

〰〰〰
〰〰〰

As January comes to a close, the work phase is now painting, followed by flooring. Those projects will close out this month.

As of the last day of January, house construction is down to finishing details. I have spent the last two days installing dark oak, five-inch wide planks. The process is not difficult, even considering that this is my first time doing any floor installation. While I lay the floor, the finish work continues on the main exterior doors, the window trim, and the last electrical work.

While many local folks are concerned about the lack of winter precipitation, the lack thereof has been a blessing to my house progress.

The contractor is now projecting a completion date between thirty and forty-five days out, which is good because I am running low on firewood due to keeping the house warm for texture and paint curing.

FEBRUARY

As of February 4th, I work on my oak plank flooring project at the same time as I make progress on my ceramic tile project. I spent the first part of the morning cutting and laying out the planks for the loft closet. When that project hit an obstruction, window trim pieces drying, I shifted to the bathhouse tile work.

Yesterday, I laid down the first fifty-six squares of Italian ceramic tile. This was the first tile work of my life, and I found the work to be hard on the knees, hands, and back; however, I found it to be rewarding to the eye. It was so satisfying that I found myself returning to this particular room repeatedly to check my work.

~~~ ~~~ ~~~
~~~ ~~~ ~~~

While sitting in front of an open fire, you can only be mesmerized by the flames for so long. Finally, you have to find a book. In my case, I have carried around a book for a few years, waiting for the right opportunity to begin.

The book is *Icebound*, a doctor's incredible battle for survival at the South Pole, written by a wonderful lady named Jerri Nielsen.

To make a fireside reading spot work, I had to configure a desk lamp on a stand so I could have some over the shoulder reading light.

I learned a long time ago, growing up in North Dakota, that cold temperature is relative. If properly dressed and satisfactorily disciplined, it was easy to work outside in sub-freezing temperatures.

Yesterday was just another example. The point of this relative comparison is to consider the fact that the coldest recorded temperature on earth was recorded in 1983 at the Russian outpost, Vostok, on Antarctica. The temperature was minus 129.3 Fahrenheit.

I prefer to think in contrasts. I often think of the 110 degrees Fahrenheit reading this summer and how we are already headed for that season. I have just another month or two of winter temperatures to deal with.

~~~ ~~~ ~~~
~~~ ~~~ ~~~

244

When it comes to cold weather adventure stories, I am proud of my Norwegian roots. Not only did a Norwegian first find the South Pole, but my cousins, the Plaisteds, made the first snowmobile expedition to the North Pole. Roald Amundsen was the first to the South Pole in 1911, and the Plaisted expedition was the first undisputed snowmobile journey to the North Pole in 1968. An insurance guy, by the name of Ralph Plaisted, led this well-covered expedition.

Ralph Plaisted, accompanied by three others, accomplished his goal in April 1968. CBS News did a documentary of the trip with Charles Kuralt tagging along. Later, Kuralt wrote a book about this event called, *To The Top of The World*.

It was a four-hundred-twelve-mile, forty-three-day journey, resupplied by DeHavilland Twin Otter turboprop aircraft. Their destination was confirmed by a military C-135 weather recon plane that flew over the ground crew and communicated by radio as to their location, the North Pole.

I think Scandinavians have a genetic disposition not only to handle the cold but to thrive in it. That helps explain why so many chose to homestead in North Dakota after Lewis and Clark made the journal entry, while at Mandan winter camp, that "The Dakota Territory was one of the most beautiful stops on their 'journey of discovery;' however, it was unfortunate that white men would never be able to live in those winter conditions."

~~ ~~ ~~
~~ ~~ ~~

I used my best Spanglish last Friday to determine if the large Mexican stucco crew would work this weekend. I thought I heard that they would skip Saturday, but work Sunday. Normally they are on the job site by 9:00 a.m., but it now looks like they took off for Super Bowl Sunday.

While Super Sunday is a great excuse for a party, I regret that they are not working on a day when the temperature is so pleasant. The stucco work is complete, save for the final two walls on the shady and cold side of the house.

~~~ ~~~ ~~~

House construction has reached that point where many things converge. The paintwork merges with the window trim application. The gas log installation holds up the oak plank work. The ceramic tile work is affected by large man-made marble slabs hogging up half of the floor space in the bathhouse. The mortar work for the HardiBacker boards is delayed, so the paint guy, Devon, can install the final outside door into the laundry room. Devon has been staining and sealing these doors at his place, a process that ensures the doors are properly stained and dried without being affected by all the dust and abuse of ongoing construction.

The house interior looks a mess with flooring partially down, flooring material stacked against the opposite wall, multiple saws on the main floor, scaffolding erected in the middle of the great room. The cement porch on the exterior is covered with dried stucco mud and leftover prep material.

The Mexican crews have been impressive workers; however, I can barely keep up with the food and drink trash that is scattered around the job site. The subtle clue of adding a large trash can has somehow been missed. I guess as the property owner, it is my job to gather up the burrito wrappers and the empty energy drink cans.

~~~ ~~~ ~~~

The first half of February was focused on adding the oak and tile floors as well as finishing the trim work. By

February 24th, the cabinets and countertops were in both the kitchen and bath. All of the doors and windows have been trimmed.

I spend about twelve and a half hours a day working on the house. This is the only structure with continuous heat, and the heat provides a comfort excuse to put in long days.

My most significant contribution to the construction has been the floor installation. I put in the wood floors by myself. My wife came in from Reno to help with the tile in the bathhouse. These two projects took weeks of continuous work.

Both projects tended to destroy my hands. There is certainly a pride factor in looking at a day's worth of work. This is the sort of satisfaction that you can't get by working in government, where the days bleed together, and seldom is there a real sense that you might see the fruits of your labor.

The only drawback of long workdays is the realization that there is less time to slow down and enjoy the clean air and beautiful views. I vow to get most of the work done, so when springtime arrives, I can balance my time and activity.

The contractor expects to finish his work by March 9th. I will then have to wade through the mortgage loan process.

MARCH

On March 2nd, a couple of key things happened. The finish carpenter arrived to finish his work. At the same time, the winter conditions seem to be turning to spring.

Today, the seam on the kitchen counter was sanded out, and the counters buffed to their finish condition.

Also, Chaney and I finished the antique bath door, an old door that I have been dragging around for years. It was installed on the toilet closet with a heavy-duty metal sliding door apparatus. The door is old and warped; however, it has some appeal with its age and the fact that there is a small hatch opening at the top with an aged glass door—in case you want to check who might be using the toilet.

13: SPRING AGAIN

On the weather side, I can't help but remind myself that March may signal the end of winter and the beginning of spring, yet today's eight inches of fresh snow reflects a lingering winter. However, as the day warms, the new snow melts quickly.

Also, the temperature has improved with a forecast of a warming trend to continue for the next few days. Daylight saving time is right around the corner, which is another indicator that spring is coming. I still feel that DST is a foolish idea. Arizona seems to have it right.

Today, March 2nd, I called the small local phone company to establish service. The fancy high tech internet phone—voice over IP—has proven unreliable and impossible to repair. While it has some attractive features, the fact of the matter is that it is not working, and I need a more reliable phone service. I am too far out in the country and too far away from family and friends to put up with the so-called high-tech and unreliable phone system.

~~~ ~~~ ~~~

The snowstorms of the past week have set back my house construction because the work crews cannot make it up my steep snow-covered driveway. The recent eight inches of snow means that I've lost a week's worth of construction progress. We are now down to nitty-gritty final projects that we hope to finish within the next week.

As I look back on the past four months of winter, it kind of seems like the "winter of my discontent;"

however, this term may not quite be appropriate. It has been a winter of hard times living in the motorhome inside the shop.

Most of my mornings greeted me with shop temperature in the low to mid 30's as I stepped out of the so-called comfort of the motorhome shell. I still had to cook and live in those shop conditions when I was not working on the house.

I like to think that this past winter has been about building character. One thing that is for sure is the fact that I will appreciate the comforts of a normal home here shortly. I value the fact that I stuck out this winter, so I could be a part of the house construction and to prove myself worthy of this ranch setting.

The first good target date for completion of the house construction was March 9th and was the date the contractor would call the county inspector to sign off the project. This date was scheduled before the eight-inch snowstorm that scared away the contractor workers. The new target date for completion will be closer to mid-March.

The spring temperatures, now getting into the 50s, will be ideal for the stucco crew to finish the exterior on March 7th and 8th.

The official beginning of spring is late afternoon on March 20th. This date also marks the eleven-month point of living on this new property. I look forward to that date as it signals my quality of life is about to change for the better; much better, I should add.

As the cool spring days slowly add a bit more warmth, the ranch house construction draws to a close. Somehow these work crews have found a way to either work around the coldest part of the winter construction or, in most cases, how to deal with the reality that they are working outdoors in the construction trade.

At this final stage, it helps that the house has been enclosed for a couple of months, and I have done my part to ensure constant heat.

MOVING INTO THE HOUSE

On March 23rd, Becky joined me to help with the house set up. It was an important day for our mental calendar. After sorting priorities, we moved the heavy log bed from the shop to the loft section of the house, and this step allowed us to spend our first night in our new place.

The next day, my older son, and my middle son and his girlfriend drove out to help with the heavy lifting. A couple of days ago, it was flat out cold. Now the temperature has climbed to 69 degrees, about as nice as it gets for moving furniture household effects from shop storage up the two hundred yards hill climb to the new ranch house.

This step can't help but provide personal gratification. There is the anticipation of how the new home will be organized and set up, and there is an appreciation for the reality that my standard of living will be greatly improved.

My grown sons came in handy when it came time to move the heavy furniture and appliance items. In most cases, I was told to stand back and get out of their way as the young and strong backs went to work. This experience reminded me that it was nice to have the child-rearing done with and better yet to have them grown and strong, chipping in where their help was needed most.

While the house was the clear priority, other ranch projects needed the man-help of an extra set of hands. This included adding the lodgepole rails to the fence and arch at the entrance driveway. Steffen held the poles straight and steady while I drilled holes to mount them securely into the waiting railroad tie fence posts.

Since others took care of the heavy lifting, I focused on sorting out the smaller and more personal items, which included books, photo albums, wall hangings, personal papers, and other "stuff."

My life long collection of books is extra special. Most have been read at least once; however, many await future winter reading opportunities. I have learned by now that my summertime is too busy with ranch projects to find time for reading. Winter is much more suited for fireside reading.

Because the new ranch home is only one bedroom and much less square footage than my previous home in Reno, my challenge will be to sort out the smaller items so that only the best pieces make a move from storage to house.

After family members returned to their respective jobs, I concentrated on moving the smaller personal items. On the first day on my own, I sorted through six cardboard boxes full of books. I now had to sort out the books that I wanted in the limited bookcase space inside the house. The rest would go back into the boxes until I could figure out what to do with them. I do not throw out old books, so that was never an option.

That same week, I hauled out rocks that were discarded from the landscape area. I also planted my first shrub, a small barberry, in the side yard. And, though the day's weather was cold and windy, I had already made arrangements to pick up a load of old manure, so I took care of this chore despite the conditions.

While planting, I continued to look around for my cat; she has been gone now for three days, and I am starting to worry that a coyote or eagle may have found this young and skinny cat. It turns out she came back the next day.

So as the new spring seasonal changes take place, my home set-up is taking shape. Some of the immediate improvements include sleeping in my large and comfortable log bed. The cooking and eating arrangements are more suitably situated. Bath comforts, such as showering, are so much better and more convenient. Perhaps the winter living in the shop was good from the perspective that I will think fondly of the quality of life improvements that are now before me.

〰〰〰
〰〰〰

My winter was spent in a large shop without any windows, and I was reminded of my many years at sea, where I lived in a stateroom below deck without the benefit of windows.

Now I am in a new home, built on the west bank of Martin Creek, which has commanding hilltop views over the creek meadow to the south and east. With careful forethought, this house location took full advantage of the wonderful view.

The focal point of the view is out of the three large south-facing windows; however, each side of the house provides a contrasting view perspective.

To the north are the snow-capped Santa Rosa mountains. To the east are the foothills leading up to the national forest mountains, and further east are the magnificent rock canyon walls that allow Martin Creek to move from its mountain headwaters to the drainage into the valley floor.

Southward, I look out over the Old Mill Ranch, whose meadows are complemented by a large number of tall trees at the perimeters. This pastoral setting always includes cattle grazing accompanied by wild turkeys, and at times other visitors, including birds, coyotes, and deer, make use of the pasture as well.

What makes spring so special is the rapid change in color. Spring green replaces the gray and brown tones that underlie the pristine white snow. By this point in the season, the snow is mostly gone, except for the mountain tops to the north. This color change signals a change in personal mood. Plenty of work remains to be done, but I am reinspired and see new opportunities for projects.

~~~ ~~~ ~~~

On the one hand, I have many major projects pending, and on the other hand, I have been pondering the possibility of going back to work.

The work option is viable only if the job meets certain criteria. As far as the Forest Service is concerned, the reality of my new ranch location is that I have thousands of acres of public land right out my back door. In my time here, I have been too busy working to find sufficient time to explore these mountains and valleys and canyons. Could it be that I might find a job opportunity that would allow me to work and explore these spaces at the same time?

I am not willing to drive long distances to find suitable work. I am not interested in returning to the demands of managerial responsibility. Starting the learning curve of a new career does not entice me. I would like to find something in or around our small town, and I would like to find something that takes advantage of the great outdoors. In short, I am interested in a job that will provide personal satisfaction without traditional job-related stress.

So back to my dilemma, do I pursue a summer job or stay close to home and continue to work? I believe that I have the luxury of a couple of months to sort this out.

As far as the job prospects are concerned, I have visited a neighbor who is employed by the U.S. Forest Service. I asked pointed questions about working conditions and what is available. In showing this interest, I inadvertently planted a seed that would eventually bear fruit.

〜〜 〜〜 〜〜
〜〜 〜〜 〜〜

To this point, I have spent my entire two-year retirement, fixing up homes and readying them for sale. This was true for my large log home at Lake Tahoe and then our smaller cottage home in old Reno. Now here I am working on the third home in less than three years.

I would be remiss if I did not say that I enjoy this kind of labor. Why else would a person beat up his hands and wear out his back if he wasn't motivated by the work? Unlike many other tasks, this kind of work generally provides a strong visual reward that goes beyond salary or compensation. So, while I ponder these questions and decisions, I find ease and relaxation as I cast my gaze to the greening of Muffler Meadow below.

〜〜 〜〜 〜〜
〜〜 〜〜 〜〜

Even now, it is plain to see this spring is much drier than last. The general drought conditions affecting many western states have been compounded by the lower than normal snowpack in our mountains. Watershed off the mountains is critical here, as this factor changes the scenery and affects the growing conditions for the farmers and ranchers. They can gauge the impact of this condition much sooner than the rest of us.

Two strong visual clues indicate this year's dryer condition. First, unlike last year when the Humboldt River crested its banks during the spring and early summer, this year finds the river volume to be considerably less. You can see the difference when you drive to Winnemucca and observe the water level below the main highway bridge. Second, you can't help but notice with some concern the dust cloud kicked up when local farmers hit their fields for the first time this spring. Last spring, these same fields were extremely wet.

Over the long haul, Paradise Valley has averaged 10.14 total inches of precipitation. The wettest months, thanks to snow, are December (average of 1.51 inches) and January (average of 1.39 inches). Traditionally July and August have been the driest months of the year (0.28 inches and 0.32 inches, respectively).

As March comes to a close, I notice not only the change of color in the meadow below, but I also find tufts of fresh grass growing in and around the sagebrush. The mature trees in the meadow below show hints of green, and some are leafing out well ahead of other trees in the same general location.

As the month comes to an end, the only vegetation that has gone through the budding process on my property is the lilac bush near my shop—this is the lilac that survived years of neglect from the time the previous owners left to when I moved in.

∾∾ ∾∾ ∾∾

By early April, the temperature reluctantly becomes more comfortable. The morning low temperatures are generally in the 30s, while the daytime highs are in the 60-70-degree range. For now, I hold off on outside chores until mid-morning when it starts to get comfortable out. This pattern has served me well for all of the seasons except summer.

∾∾ ∾∾ ∾∾

Early April provided enough warmth that I dared to pour a cement entrance walkway. As a way of creating visual interest, I wanted this walkway to have more texture than plain concrete, and so I incorporated some of the river-washed flat rocks that were hauled in when the driveway was graveled.

Some of the flat stones were not suited for traditional driveway cover, so I collected the best pieces for other use. This project will also use some of the leftover pavers from my landscape project at the Reno house. The entrance path will have a railroad tie border to offer even more texture contrast and provides an opportunity to show some design creativity.

Also, today, I drove my pickup and trailer to the HS Ranch to pick up another load of well-aged cow manure. Susan came out to help and used her front-end tractor loader to help load my trailer. As is often the case, my neighbors seem to have ample time to stop and visit when we do cross paths. Susan has been one of the most supportive neighbors in my brief time here.

She commented on the fact that I have been around for almost a year now, and moreover, it was her observation that I have made a good transition to the neighborhood. While this kind of comment is always welcome to a newcomer, I tried to explain that I grew up in a similar rural situation, and my time spent here was really quite comfortable, a sort of homecoming to the same kind of "salt of the earth" people.

In many respects, Susan has gone out of her way to make me feel welcome and to take steps to help speed up this transition. I will be long indebted to her for this support role.

〜〜 〜〜 〜〜
〜〜 〜〜 〜〜

Just as I was getting settled into my new home, my good friends, the Lee Webb family, from Reno asked if they could come out to spend a weekend. The answer was easy because my place was now sufficiently civilized to host guests properly, and further, I could not wait to show off my ranch development so far.

I had not only bragged about my rapid ranch development, but I was fond of sharing stories about our community social center, the Paradise Saloon. The Paradise Saloon is western culture is at it's best with its Saturday evening cookouts and comfortable setting in which neighbors could socialize.

Paradise Saloon

When I proudly took Lee and Arlene to the saloon, it lived up to its billing. They were greeted and welcomed by my new-found friends and neighbors. It was good fun.

On April 4th, I saw a new sight. Around mid-morning, I looked down towards the arch at the main entrance of my property and spotted twenty-six wild turkeys marching up my driveway like they were on a mission.

I grabbed the camera for a photo about the time that the dogs spotted the same strange sight. Unfortunately, the dogs chased them back into the meadow before I could shoot any photos.

Later I learned that mid-April was a special turkey hunting season associated with special hunting permits offered by local ranchers.

It was up to ranchers to determine who they permitted to hunt on their property. They, in turn, can demand a tag fee that they think is appropriate. I never understood the normal thrill of the hunt for something as tame as a wild turkey; however, I learned that big-time hunters from far and near would take advantage of this special hunt.

I met one such guy at the saloon. He was not just a big-time hunter in the west, but he traveled the world in pursuit of hunting trophies. He said his next trip in two weeks would be to New Zealand, where he would be hunting stag.

From my house, I could see the hunter foot traffic up and down Muffler Meadow. The shotgun noise was clear evidence that a new hunting season had started. The meadow is close enough that I would often see hunters with a dead turkey slung over their shoulders. While I understand the values of hunting, it did strike a chord that these were the same turkeys that complimented the natural scenery below my house.

Now I know why this flock of turkeys left the once safe meadow location to move up the west bank towards my house. Run for your lives.

14: ONE YEAR ANNIVERSARY

April 20th, 2007, is the anniversary date of living here. Now the priority shifts to finding suitable work.

SPRING'S OFFICIAL BEGINNINGS

Now that the spring season has officially begun, I need to embrace the mix of nice days and cool and windy days that mark the seasonal transition. The first day of spring was cold, and emphasis was placed on the task of financing the loan for our new home.

While tending to the paperwork, I still move items, such as the pantry shelf system, into their new places. If this was not enough to fill a day, I also started paying more attention to potential job leads.

On this first day of spring, I also drove to the other side of the Santa Rosa's to check with Morris Ag Air to see if they needed any help with their crop spraying business. Though I had a cordial meeting with the owner, he informed me that all of his positions have long since been filled. I am not even sure why I bothered with this job search, perhaps just curiosity.

CALF-BRANDING

During the second week of April, my wife and I attended our first local calf-branding, thanks to the invitation from Kris Stewart at the Ninety-Six Ranch. The day started cold, with temperatures starting in the high 30's.

The Ninety-Six Ranch, established in 1864, has a rich local history, and its proud start date is listed on their ranch entrance sign. As the crow flies, it is located a couple of miles south of our property, along Martin Creek, but by dirt road, it takes six miles of driving to reach it. After arriving at the historic Ninety-Six Ranch, we found the cowboys out gathering up the mother cows and their young calves from early this spring.

The casual start to this process turned scary as Grandma Cook was bucked off her horse a couple of hundred yards from the ranch house. After the horse threw her, we saw her land on her left ear. Many of us sprinted to her crash site, and the earliest arrivals found her unconscious. Only after her son, Joe, and I arrived did she start to stir. Because she suffered from short term memory loss and nausea, concussion symptoms, she was taken to the local hospital for a check.

In the meantime, the branding fire was started in a converted fifty-gallon oil drum. A square hole had been cut in the side to handle the numerous branding irons. Thanks to metal corral panels on the north side of the corral and the strategic parking of pickup trucks and horse trailers, we had the livestock well cornered.

The most talented crew consisted of Jerry Harper and his two young sons. Joe is the oldest of the two, and Sam is the youngest. They were responsible for roping and dragging the calves close to the branding fire.

Sometimes, they brought the calves in solo, and sometimes they would team rope. Team roping meant that one rope was on the two rear legs while the other was around the calves' neck.

Step two of the process was when the two of the crew, sometimes called "muggers," called out bull or heifer, drop the calf on their right side—since all of the brands would be placed on the left side—then twist and pull up on the front left leg. The term mugger was used by a fellow ranch hand; however, I have since been told that this may not be the proper term for this particular branding chore. In any case, this process allowed for step number three when Nancy or Kris vaccinated the calf with a quick injection from a large needle and gun.

Joe Harper

In step four, Fred cut off a long section of the right ear and then would make a careful cut on the throat that would leave a "wattle" hanging down from the calve's neck. This marking step provided time tested identification of the livestock that belonged to this old ranch. Ear tags have become common for cattle, but over time these tags may fall out, and then the only proof of ownership goes back to the old fashion brand, ear notch, and skin wattle. To keep track of the day's work, Fred put the notched ear pieces in his Wrangler rear pocket.

Step five was applying the Ninety-Six-brand on the left hindquarter. The only exception was when Fred's daughter's few calves were branded with the JD brand—

another old family registered brand. All of the heifers got a second brand, which was a "7"—a reminder that these particular heifers would be culled out and sold in seven years. The young bulls did not get this second brand.

The branding step is very precise because the hot iron needs to burn through the hide into the skin, and it needs to sear the skin without burning too far into it.

Fred explained that the signal for the completed brand is when the burn smoke turns yellow briefly, and then the color changes to a sort of blue color. When you spot the bluish tint, it is time to remove the branding iron. There is a very exact science in how the brand is applied, not too little and not too intense.

The final step was the castration of the young bulls. The person responsible for this chore is called the "knifeman," or in this case, the knifewoman. Kris took care of this step. Proving that nothing goes to waste, the testicles were placed in a cooler for future gourmet cooking.

The total time for these six steps, five steps for the heifers, took less than two minutes. The whole process involved a team effort and was very efficient. It was a no-nonsense process even when some first-time city observers were present. Most of the members of the Cook family took turns with most of the steps, including the teenage daughter, who was a good sport and took a turn at each of the six steps.

After a couple of hours, the herd of fifty-two calves was completely processed. In the finest tradition of ranching, the hard work was followed by a tasty lunch spread, which included BBQ beef, beef chili, fresh bread, and multiple homemade desserts—to die for.

The eating was followed by good wholesome conversation. Much of the discussion included real-life ranch stories from the cowboy participants.

My wife and I went home full, and the young calves returned to their pasture a bit sore for the time being. I should also add that by the time the lunch was served, the grandma and the son returned from the hospital with a good report that she would be okay. It would take a couple of days for her to regain her short-term memory loss.

As an indicator of the color and flavor of the branding event, I took a close look at my blue jeans when I got home. They were covered in blood, dirt, soot—from the branding irons—and of course, a good dose of yellow-green calf shit. It was a colorful reminder of a fun day of ranch work.

NINETY-SIX RANCH HISTORY

The host ranch is one of the most historic properties in this valley. It was started by Fredrick William Stock, who was born in Germany in 1837.

After time in New York, Ohio, and California, Stock homesteaded in the valley in 1864. In 1879 Stock returned to Germany to marry Wilhelmina Christina Wahague, then they returned to the ranch, and six children were born during the 1880s.

After Fredrick Stock died in 1898, his wife incorporated the ranch operation as the William Stock Farming Company. At that point, the ranch included three-thousand cattle, six-thousand sheep, one-thousand horses, and 17,560 acres of land.

After 1910, the ownership and control of the ranch reverted to the three of the children, William, Edith, and Minnie. Soon the operation was under the control of Edith and her husband Fred Stewart Senior and remained the case from the 1920s into the 1950s. Les Stewart was born in 1920. Fred died in 1959, the same year that Les and Marie were married.[1]

In 1979, the final share, belonging to Minnie, was purchased, and the operation changed names from William Stock Farming Company to the Ninety-Six Ranch. Today the ranch is alive and well under the ownership of Fred and Kris Stewart. Marie still lives in one of the ranch houses, while Fred, Kris, and their young daughter, Patrice, live in a newer ranch home.

The host family for the branding not only has many relatives across this valley, but they are also sister to the family that sold me my ranch property.

HUNTING REVENUE

My television is hooked up and working. Through the marvels of satellite technology, I now get the local news stations from Reno.

While watching one of these local channels in late March, the spokesman from the Nevada Division of Wildlife (NDOW) discussed numbers for the antelope population in the state. His point was that NDOW was doing a fine job of managing these numbers.

He set the stage with a population number of ten-thousand back in 1980 then went on to explain that the population doubled in twenty-six years. He also said that NDOW issues two-thousand-eight-hundred hunting tags per year; the hunter success rate for antelope is now at 68%, so around one-thousand-eight-hundred hunters went home with a fresh kill. Some of those hunting success stories unfolded in this valley.

Financially hunter and angler contribution is no small matter for the state. Records indicate that there are 182,000 hunters or fishermen in our state. While that number seems significant enough, the real issue boils down to the dollar and cents.

This large number of outdoor enthusiasts contribute more than $417 million to our state economy. The Department of Wildlife makes enough money off its hunting tags and permits that they don't need any help from the state budget; it might be the only part of state government that is self-sufficient.

LANDSCAPES AND JOB APPLICATIONS

During the construction process, the contractor asked to hold my property title as collateral for his construction investment. At the end of March, I recovered this title as the loan process has been completed.

As the calendar page turned to April, I continue to plant a few token shrubs in my side yard, which included a couple of burning bushes, some boxwood, raspberry, holly, and lilacs.

I haven't developed a master plan to work from, but rather an instinct of what will fit where. I have tried to be mindful of sun exposure and other factors that will promote some degree of success. I have an image of how I want the perimeter yard fence to work. My early plantings have stayed clear of this future fence location.

With a fence to define the yard boundary, I can focus on improving only the enclosed section of yard. On the warm days, I dig in the dirt and as happy and content as a former farm boy can be. On the cold or windy days, I shift my work projects to house organization.

These chores are tedious and labor-intensive, but I love this kind of manual work, for example, hauling silt topsoil from the edge of the irrigation canal. This is dark rich soil that needs to find a new home.

I have over twenty five-gallon plastic buckets leftover from the stucco work crew. These buckets, along with my quad and trailer, provide the means to move this dirt. I know that this kind of work will be slow, and that is fine because I can see the progress even when it comes in five-gallon increments. I may be the only guy in the world who has measured dirt progress by the gallon.

While in the midst of this chore, my neighbor, Lisa, called to inform me that the time is right to go to town and make an application for the Forest Service job. Apparently, she worked behind the scenes to keep track of a couple of job prospects. By this point, I was mentally ready to shift my work efforts to something else.

Having worked for the federal government before, I had some idea about the bureaucracy process. Now for the first time, all Forest Service job applications were being submitted online and away from the control of local district officials.

There seemed to be a sense of urgency in filling a handful of positions, so I thought I might hear something before the month was over. It turns out I was wrong for as early April turned to early May, and I received no indication of my new hire status. The local Forest Service guys could not offer any insight.

In the meantime, I had plenty of projects to work on. I continued to move manure to the job site, and I continued to plant things outside the house.

In addition to the landscape work next to the house, I also had a favorite ravine site a couple of hundred yards downhill, where I was pursuing an orchard. The prior owners had selected this particular site; however, all but one of their fruit trees had long since died. There was one sole surviving peach tree.

I had to set up a new drip irrigation system and prepare some spots where I could add another five fruit trees.

SPRING CONDITIONS

In the passing of one year, I see a sharp contrast in spring water conditions. The 2006 spring season was wet; the mountain snow accumulation was well above normal, and thus the mountain streams ran fast and high. The local farmers and ranchers had an abundance of water to irrigate their fields and pastures.

By contrast, the spring of 2007 reflected the mild winter and the scarcity of mountain snow. As of mid-April, the creeks are running low, and the soil is dry. The concern about the dry season is evident in most conversations. The farmers that rely on irrigation ditch water will now be forced to pump water from the deep wells, and pumped irrigation water makes for higher operating. As a result, hay and alfalfa production will be reduced this summer.

To help illustrate the dryness of this season, I noticed that the irrigation canal that runs through my property no longer flows, a sharp contrast from April a year ago.

The meadow below the house is still green, but not the kind of lush Irish green from last year. I am not sure the birds know or care about this matter because they still sing loudly at the moment.

〜〜 〜〜 〜〜
〜〜 〜〜 〜〜

As a matter of spring perspective and contrasts, I find myself sitting at the view window all comfortable and warm while I watch the snow swirl outside. I watch the cattle grazing on the fresh spring grass, while the snow falls around them. I also see the new rose bush, recently planted, with its three fresh red flowers starting to bloom. It looks uncomfortable with the snow on the leaves.

Enough snow is in the air that I can barely make out the Mill Ranch below, and the temperature hovers around 30 degrees. Fortunately, the flowering plants I bought yesterday sit in the shelter of my pickup.

Even my mouser cat, who prefers to run outdoors during the day, has decided that today can be better spent curled up in a quiet corner.

As of mid-April, we have a forecast of three storm fronts passing through in the next ten days. These fronts bring threatening skies and wind, but precious little moisture. I am talking about the slow, soaking rains or heavy wet snow that help replenish the topsoil moisture, the kind of moisture that will kick-start the crop seeds that local ranchers and farmers have recently sown. Without this help from Mother Nature, their seed will be a wasted investment.

My cousin Chris called from his Willow Creek Ranch with a report that he now has three inches of fresh wet snow on his side of the Santa Rosa range. He fears that his freshly planted garden will suffer some damage.

We agreed that this is a good day to put on a second pot of coffee and focus on indoor projects. As I savor this second pot, I have the urge to fry some eggs and sausage to keep this aging body fueled up. In the background, I have blues playing on the Sirius satellite radio.

However, by April 9th, it seemed that spring was finally getting to the point where I could count on mostly warm days. Then came the worst weather day in the past two months. It was downright cold, and the wind made things worse. This is the seasonal pattern that adds interest but also tends to drive you crazy when there is lots of work to do.

ANNIVERSARY

Shortly after waking up on the morning of April 20th, it dawned on me that this is a special anniversary date. As of today, I have been on this property for exactly one year. I can't help but reflect on how much has been accomplished in just one fast-paced year.

The most significant change is that I now sit in the relative comfort of my new home, looking down at my finished shop, the wood ranch arch, and the green meadow below. It is still early enough in the spring that warm days are not yet guaranteed, and accordingly, the trees in the meadow have not yet fully leafed.

This extended spring cold spell right now feeds my itch to get out and tackle the many remaining outdoor projects. Like a bad habit from my working days, I have a long list of things to do. I like crossing tasks off the list. It provides a sense of accomplishment and personal rewards when reviewing the list and seeing the fruits of my labor. Unlike office work, there is generally a visual reward following hard labor, which at times, is grueling before the task is finished.

THE MARTIN HOTEL

After many weeks of hard work, I decided to attend a Celtic music concert at the Martin Hotel, the only regular live music venue in Winnemucca.

They have an intimate performance space that seats around ninety people. When a headliner comes to town, such as Don Edwards, they will squeeze in another ten seats.

The venue creates a close and personal experience for both entertainers and the audience, and everyone seems to enjoy this cozy opportunity for music appreciation.

One of my close neighbors, Bill, is the former owner of this establishment, and I thought it would be nice to offer him a ride as he no longer drives after dark.

As a side note, Bill Arant distinguished himself in WW-II, especially in the Battle of the Bulge. He was so good at his job he received a battlefield commission, from sergeant to lieutenant. The military liked him so much that they called him back so he could fight in the Korean War.

Bill told me that both combat experiences were in the coldest conditions recorded in both locations. He said the problem was that when you got cold, there was nowhere to go to warm up. You just stayed cold.

Also, after some research by a small local committee, it was determined that when WW-II broke out, thirty-three young men left Paradise Valley to fight the war, a lot of men from one small community. The incredible statistic was that all thirty-three made it home alive. What are the odds of that?

LATE APRIL OBSERVATIONS

Assuming that there might be a job in my future, I have decided to move quickly on establishing my perimeter fence. For the most part, the temperature is now cooperative enough that I dare to pour concrete.

The rocky hilltop has precluded all attempts at post hole digging, so the next best plan is to pour a concrete footing and add a cinder block fence base. This base will be three courses high so that it has sufficient depth to drop in round metal posts and cement them in place.

These posts provide vertical support, to which I attach horizontal redwood two by fours. With this support in place, I can then finish the top half with traditional redwood pickets. While this will be more work than any normal fence, it should accomplish my goals.

In addition to defining my garden space, I hope this perimeter fence will keep out critters that may interfere with a productive yard, such as dogs, rabbits, deer, and the dreaded Mormon cricket (if they should return).

Just a couple of days ago, I was complaining about the miserable working conditions; now, the spring conditions are near perfect with a temperature high of 69 degrees. This is my kind of weather.

Oh yes, just after I report a near-perfect day, we get three inches of snow two days later.

While I labor with this book draft, I try to keep my ears open for any advice on how to get published. I have to admit that I don't have a clue where to. I came into this effort with eyes wide open, as I know that the odds are not good for any kind of success.

Years back, I had this conversation with Dale Brown, the successful suspense author, and he explained that if you are established, you can get anything published, and if you are not established, it is near impossible to break through those barriers.

Recently I listened to National Public Radio, and the story suggested that prospective new authors find a publisher or company that specializes in the kind of book that you are writing. This is fine advice, except for the fact that I have not yet defined what type of book I am writing. Finding the category here may be difficult.

The NPR advice also warned to avoid those agents who want to charge for their service. These are worries that can wait for now. The combined effect of the above advice was intimidating. As it turns out, many years would pass before I found a good connection on how to get published.

~~~ ~~~ ~~~
~~~ ~~~ ~~~

By the third week in April, my friend Mike from town offered to give me the "mother of all rose bushes," as he called it. He wants to get rid of it because it grows so fast that it takes over the entire fence line between his cottage home and the street.

We decided that a good new location would be the front entrance fence line, where the lodgepole fence transitions into the ranch arch. The root mass was so large that it took two of us to dig it and lift it out of the ground. Time will tell if Mike's prediction is accurate about the rose eventually taking over that entire fence section.

As it turned out, this rose bush adapted well and is now a major landscape feature at the front entrance to the ranch. Thanks, Mike, this was a nice gift. Kind of like VD, the gift that keeps on giving.

〜〜 〜〜 〜〜
〜〜 〜〜 〜〜

I tried to get creative with a tile project in my new home. I wanted to take the decorative and colorful Mexican hand-painted tiles and dress up two risers on the stairway to my loft. The first section marked the top of the short transition to the 90-degree stairway turn, and the second decorative section sits at the top riser on the longer section of stairs. I had no real experience with this kind of work, but I fumbled my way through it, and the result was even better than expected.

〜〜 〜〜 〜〜
〜〜 〜〜 〜〜

Near the end of April, I got an urgent phone call from Kris at the Ninety-Six Ranch. She asked if I could help search for a downed cowboy.

She had received a broken cell phone call from her husband that said that one of the cowhands had been bucked off and that he was in bad shape. The cell call broke up before she could hear the location of the accident.

Kris had me search a sector over the east bank of the creek. I used my quad to sprint to this search site. Other folks helped explore other sectors.

While I found no sign of a cattle drive, someone else did have luck and rushed the busted up cowboy to the local hospital. He suffered many broken ribs and other internal injuries as the horse bucked him off on a steep rocky downhill section. This was my first search and rescue effort, even though I came up empty.

MAY LANDSCAPING

The song of a western meadowlark signaled the start of May. The bird sat on a large rock in my front yard east of the house. My windows were open to the fresh air and the sweet bird song. It seemed to be a fitting signal that we were finally getting to the real springtime. By this time, the daytime temperatures approached the low eighties.

Knowing that I would someday be clearing the brush on the lower fields, close to the county road, I also took the trouble of transplanting some of the healthy clumps of Great Basin wild rye. I transplanted these grass clumps from the lowest part of my property to the highest part. At this point, I am intent on moving in anything green.

Just as I report temperatures in the 80s, I also need to say that on May 3rd, we had a fresh snowfall on the top of the Santa Rosa Mountains. The next day was shrouded in an uncommon blanket of fog. At this same time, I took some pleasure in writing my first mortgage loan payment check on my new home.

My chores now range from transplanting cottonwood trees to troubleshooting the old Farmall tractor that is nearly as old as I am. I continue to haul in more manure from the HS Ranch.

So, what am I trying to accomplish with this yard project? I have long been a believer that a good yard is an extension of your normal living space. I intend to spend as much time outside enjoying this favorable weather and beautiful views as I would spend indoors, being a lazy house mouse.

My goal here is to enclose and green up a yard at least as large as the square footage of indoor space. I have a picture in mind of a low profile, green space full of shrubs and flowering plants. This green-zone needs to be low profile, so it doesn't hinder the panoramic view.

The front yard, on the south side of the house, already has a rough design as I took thousands of rock pieces from the house excavation site and built curved rock walls that defined a pathway through this long section of yard. I desired to create a landscape that draws the eye through the yard towards the connecting path to the lower shop area.

A few of the rocks in the front yard are oversized discards from the foundation digging. Simply, many of them were too large to move by hand, and it was easier to incorporate them into the master design than it was to relocate them.

Since I do not own the preferred new tractor or other heavy equipment, I knew that my landscape work would have to be done the old fashioned way, by hand and with a strong back. I have done enough landscape projects in my day to appreciate the challenge here. When all the work is done, I have a vision of turning this rocky hilltop into a lush green garden. Little did I know what I had gotten myself into.

Being unaccustomed to gardening in this sort of rocky terrain, much of what I have to do will be by trial and error. While the terrain is not in my favor, other aspects of this project are. I have found friends and neighbors willing to share transplants, so I do not have to spend large sums of money at the nursery.

As mentioned, my friend and neighbor Susan is essential to this project since she kindly shared with me as much cured manure as I can use. My friend Mike has offered both expert advice and numerous transplants— roses, raspberries, and a few plants that I don't know the names of—to get me started.

The story of Mike's help is a prime example of good old fashioned barter. Some time back, I helped Mike side his cottage house in Paradise town, and now he is trading his time to help with my garden project.

FOREST SERVICE NEWS

These types of projects continued until Friday, May 11th, when I received an urgent phone call from a Forest Service employee out of Minneapolis. He made me a job offer after nearly seven weeks of waiting in suspense. To demonstrate how government works—or does not work—he instructed me to take care of all the prerequisite steps that day so that I could start the following Monday.

These steps included a doctor's physical, physical fitness testing, fingerprints for a background check, completion of many government job-related forms, and so on. With seven weeks of available time, it would have made more sense to make this decision earlier and give me sufficient time to accomplish these steps. However, I got the important stuff done and was on the job by Monday the 14th.

15: THE UNEXPECTED JOB

The last chapter ended with the start of a Forest Service job, but here are more details.

Shortly after my first full year here, in 2007, I received a phone call from a Forest Service Range Management guy, Boyd, asking if I would be interested in driving a quad around the national forest this summer. I replied, "Yes, what is the catch?"

He said he wanted to hire a senior local guy to work with the seasonal weed crew. This local guy would start earlier than the seasonal college help and stay later than the college kids had time for.

He also said the local guy provided continuity to this seasonal job. Additionally, he mentioned that I would be free to cross-train as a wildland firefighter, which would involve a full week fire academy that the fire community calls Rookie School.

I felt compelled to say yes to both offers; however, I was concerned about the issue of a guy my age going to a place called Rookie School. I took the flippant attitude that I was never too old to be a rookie, and it is never too late to try one new adventure. Maybe I developed this attitude from Burt Munro, mentioned in chapter one.

~~~ ~~~ ~~~

This new routine started mid-May. Once the activity began, it came fast and hard. I had one week of miscellaneous chores before the two schools. This week included everything from early weed spraying to fence repair in the high mountain pastures, or as the Forest Service calls them, grazing allotments.

This first week provided an opportunity to get to know the new college batch of seasonal hires. This seasonal help included two fire crew members and two weed crew members.

For the most part, this group proved to be good kids willing to work hard to help with their college tuition. I can only assume their reaction to seeing an older guy as part of this team. In years past, this weed team was made up exclusively of college-age kids.

⁓⁓ ⁓⁓ ⁓⁓
⁓⁓ ⁓⁓ ⁓⁓

The first school was two weeks of weed training in Elko, and it ranged from ATV training and certification, to weed identification, to proper spray chemical handling, to how to work a PDR/GPS—the hand-held device that allowed us to plot every weed spray location with supporting details. This data is then downloaded onto a Forest Service "Rangeland" software program that keeps track of our progress on the war against weeds.

I was slightly aware that there was an organized effort to fight the invasive, noxious weeds, but before this summer, I did not have any idea how this worked. At the end of the training, I came out as a state-certified weed sprayer. I was now approved to handle restricted chemicals—like Tordon, Escort, Transline, Plateau—for the sake of killing weeds. This list of chemicals includes the now-famous Roundup.

The next school was the Rookie School, kind of like a fire boot camp; we managed to cram in ninety hours of instruction and practical field training into a normal forty-hour week.

My only concern about attending this training was that I managed to throw out my back just before the first day of school, and I knew I was not going to have a comfortable experience ahead of me.

I not only survived the training, but I also managed to get the dubious award for the oldest rookie, for which there was little competition; the closest competitor was still twenty years my junior. At the end of the week, I came out as a certified wildland firefighter.

Daryl Reirsgard Firefighter

Now that the training is complete, the actual work has begun. My team meets at 6:00 a.m. each morning at the Forest Service Compound in Paradise Valley town.

This compound is a delightful and historic campus of old white and green buildings located on the south end of Paradise town. The front sign clearly indicates its Forest Service connection, complete with a full size cut out of Smokey Bear—not Smokey the Bear as many people believe.

The Forest Service office is well situated, considering that it has been charged with managing the nearby forest land and maintaining relationships with the ranchers and farmers in the region. Throughout the summer, I grew to appreciate the close working relationship between the local ranchers and farmers and the handful of land management specialists who were doing their level best to be good stewards of this government-controlled land.

With this local and federal connection in mind, I headed off to work each morning, and my short commute each day allowed me daily moments to contemplate the good fortune of this ideal job at this point in my life.

It was rare in my life to have such a short work commute. Rather than dogging traffic in five lanes of madness, I was now only worried about hitting a deer on the drive to work.

*** *** ***

Regularly my crew and I loaded up two pickup tankers and two quad sprayers, and we then drove up into the forest. Based on observations by the district ranger and my boss, we were assigned priority creek locations covered with problematic weed patches.

Generally, we parked the trailer at the bottom of the foothills and started working our way up the canyons. Eventually, we progressed our way to upper elevations, and in some cases, we sprayed and worked either summits or meadows at the upper reaches.

Every day of work presented new sections of the forest for us to explore and to work. With each new location came the benefit of unfamiliar scenery and, in many cases, new wildlife to observe. Through most of the summer, I felt the appreciation for this kind of work and enjoyed knowing that we were getting paid for this outdoor experience.

I expected some direct supervision from the Forest Service bosses; however, they were busy with reports, office work, and some special environmental impact studies. I think I work well without direct supervision, and they seemed confident that the three of us would figure out a plan to spray weeds and cover the 400 square miles of forest land. Their supposition turned out to be valid as we found our way just fine.

A few times, we placed phone calls to clarify certain "how" or "where" questions. I can say that it was refreshing to find so many pleasant and laid-back professionals in the ranks of the Forest Service. Most of my life had been subjected to working in and around type-A personalities who would just as soon stab you in the back if it would promote their personal or professional interests. The attitude here was much more gentle and easy-going.

Besides doing what we were paid to do, we were subjected to fresh air, sunshine, green scenery, wildlife, rich riparian zones ripe with assorted vegetation growth, and remarkable scenery.

Oh yes, we also developed an eye for spotting and spraying invasive and noxious weeds such as white top, Scotch thistle, Canadian thistle, Russian knapweed, leafy spurge, and medusahead. As the season progressed, we focused on twelve to fourteen primary weeds that pose the biggest threat to the native vegetation and the quality of the national forest watershed.

Before training, I did not know one weed from another. Still, it did not take long to develop a visual scan that allowed me to identify a given weed positively, and not long after, I could predict what weed may be around the corner based on terrain and other natural features.

The simple goal for the Forest Service is to preserve and protect the natural vegetation in the upper elevations so that when the watershed flowed from mountain to valley, it would not be transporting weed seeds to the productive land below.

The federal weed program has no false assumptions that we will ever win the weed battle, but it is determined to establish some degree of control, so the weed infestations become smaller rather than bigger. We share this same goal with the local weed control board that performs the same function in the private lands in the valley.

When the summer began, it was my goal to discover my large 400 square mile backyard, and it turned out to be an attainable goal. Throughout the summer, I traveled or hiked every single canyon and creek bed in the entire forest. In many cases, our weed crew worked a particular canyon for up to a week.

This experience was made even better considering the scenery and the abundant wildlife. It was common to chase up chukar, pheasant, sage hens, and the like. It was also common to chase up antelope, deer, and bighorn sheep. The first half of the season was made even more beautiful with the abundance of higher elevation wildflowers. Yellow and blue seemed to be the dominant colors. While wildlife spottings became the norm, it is worth mentioning that we occasionally spotted a few humans as well, very few.

As I have since learned, the Humboldt-Toiyabe Forest, located in different sections across this state, is one of the largest forests in the national system. By contrast, our forest has the fewest number of visitors.

I appreciate this truth because it makes it easier to protect the pristine beauty, and it is easier to practice sound forest management with less human traffic. Most of the forest traffic starts arriving in mid-August when the first of the hunting seasons begin, and hunting continues until early winter.

I enjoyed the opportunity to work outdoors and soaked up as much sun as possible. During my annual VA medical check-up, my assigned doctor chastised me and told me I needed to be more careful about sun exposure. He observed that I was overdoing my time in the sun. With this kind of job, it is impossible to avoid the sun, so I opted to buy a wider brim hat.

The sun I enjoyed so much eventually dries out the forest and increases fire risk. By late summer, Mother Nature provided dry lightning storms that tested the skills of the local wildland firefighters.

~~~ ~~~ ~~~
~~~ ~~~ ~~~

One of our seasonal teammates was a talented young lady named Kati, from Gonzaga University. She came up with the idea of a team dinner once per week, which meant that one person had the responsibility to plan and cook a meal for the rest of the team.

Since their crew quarters were old and small, I offered my new commercial kitchen at the ranch house. Here we practiced the art of community cooking. It was a fun social touch, and it went a long way to build team continuity. These social outings often went late into the evenings, well past my normal bedtime. One of the side attractions for the college kids was the fact that I had a new batch of new pups, and they were the center of attention.

~~~ ~~~ ~~~
~~~ ~~~ ~~~

The only downside to the seasonal job change of routine was the fact that I had less time to mess around with my ranch projects.

I did manage to find a few extra hours at the end of the ten-hour work shift to get some work done here. I couldn't help reflect on the major difference of this kind of low-key job compared with the normal stressors of previous government jobs. No longer do I need to lose sleep over budget woes or personnel issues for my workforce. This new job was as close as I will ever get to a no-stress job. The biggest things I have to worry about each day would be what to wear and what to pack in my lunch.

~~~ ~~~ ~~~
~~~ ~~~ ~~~

My first-hand observations throughout the summer made it clear that we were dealing with ever-increasing drought conditions.

As I worked the canyons and stream beds, I found less water. Many of the springs still produced, but the water flow didn't last long before it dried out. Some of the creeks, such as Martin, Rebel, and the Quinn South Fork, still flowed by the middle of August; however, other streams such as Cottonwood, the main Quinn River, and Singus stopped flowing.

It appears that there isn't sufficient water for the grazing livestock on the forest land. The large wild mammals use the same spring-fed drinking troughs as the cows and horses, and there isn't much water to go around.

The most obvious visual change is that the green grass had dried up except for the riparian areas and around active springs. These late-season conditions make ranchers and firefighters nervous since they're happening far too soon.

~~~ ~~~ ~~~
~~~ ~~~ ~~~

I augmented the Forest Service fire engine crew only twice during the summer fire season; however, when the large firestorm swept through seven counties in Southern California, FEMA officials did call in resources from all of the western states, plus many other resources from as far away as Minnesota and the Dakotas.

Thanks to an extended fire season, and in part due to the large firestorm in Southern California during late October, I stayed employed with the Forest Service well into November. When I signed up, this was supposed to be a limited seasonal job; however, this year's fire season stretched the timeline. This extra work used up the better part of the warm days of late fall. Now that my seasonal lay off has started, it is time to start enjoying the quiet time of the winter months.

The fall transition was marked by community concern about the drought. While dry conditions during the summer and fall were the norm, this season was worse than normal. With this reality upon us, the fire-season was even more dangerous than normal.

By late summer, the fire condition was officially listed as "extreme." This point hit home when a fire mysteriously started a couple of miles north of my property. The fire was pushed north, away from my house, by the prevailing winds. The majority of the fire was on BLM land between the Forest boundary and Martin Creek.

In one full day of uncontrolled burn, it consumed nearly 8,000 acres. The fire suppression included smokejumpers and bulldozers. Because well-established roads don't exist on the east side of the fire line, the bulldozers refreshed some old cowboy trails and, in a few cases, established new access close to the fire line.

By the second day, unlimited air resources were called in, and they hit the fire line hard—a large part of that air assault unfolded from Muffler Meadow below my house. With permission from my neighbor, the fire crews set up a helo port south and west of the Old Mill Ranch. For the next couple of days, non-stop helicopter traffic dumped water on the fire line.

My house is high enough on the west bank of Martin Creek that I would often look down at the helicopters as they made the transition from their grassy take-off position up the canyon to the fire. At the end of the second day, thanks to water dumped by aircraft, the fire was under control.

Later, one of the BLM supervisors, Derek, told the local community weed board meeting that if they did not have the air resources, that fire could have burned all the way to Boise, Idaho.

While this fire scar is obvious when you get up into the hills, it is not visible from the valley floor or my property. The vast majority of this fire scar is on BLM land. Only a small portion of Forest Service land, near Spring City and Goal Pit, burned.

EXPANSION

Concurrent with the Forest Service job, I am developing the backyard at the west end of the house, where the main entrance is located. The key to the future success of this landscape project is cured manure mixed with topsoil, a combination I'm moving by hand.

I hope this mixture will augment the rocky clay soil that I inherited. Instead of waiting for my landscape master-plan to fall in place, I plan to plant a few shrubs and flowers as soon as the season permits. For every bucket of good soil that I carry in, I tend to carry out a similar size bucket filled with leftover small rocks I've dug out. Already I see how much manual labor lies ahead.

The goal is to add the cozy comfort of grass, green vegetation, flowers, shrubs, and fruit trees. Realizing that time will be required to cultivate a mature yard, I have tried to get a lot of plants and trees into the ground so they can start to grow.

Being unaccustomed to gardening in this sort of rocky terrain, much of what I do will be trial and error. Living in this remote area, I have found the internet to be a valuable resource. I can get Mike's garden newsletter, and I can find seed catalogs that will mail me the plants and seeds that I cannot scrounge locally.

While it would be nice to have an instant yard, I have resigned myself to the fact that both front and back yards will take me at least a couple of years. This way, I get to spread out the personal pleasure of watching this project take shape. This extended time frame will be a good excuse for quiet time, with a coffee in hand, to ponder both the planning and the progress.

$$\sim\!\!\sim \sim\!\!\sim \sim\!\!\sim$$

By design, my ranch house only included one bedroom. This feature was driven by the quest for a simple and affordable home.

Once the house was completed, I started to entertain both friends and family, and it soon became clear that I needed an extra bedroom for guests. The simplest fix for this problem was to plan and build a small guest house near the shop or a larger bunkhouse very close to the ranch house.

By mid-September, work began on this one-and-a-half story structure. This building has a dual purpose. First, it protects the sunken well hole and provides weather protection to the well pump and water tank that serves the entire property. Second, it provides a guest bedroom. This building becomes my third ranch structure.

Once this structure was completed, I made an effort to finish the interior so that it would have some guest appeal. The building has a sleeping loft on top and a den below. The interior finish work is not yet complete, so it will be a while before guests have their first opportunity to stay in this new space.

Well-House

Once this structure was completed, I made an effort to finish the interior so that it would have some guest appeal. The building has a sleeping loft on top and a den below. The interior finish work is not yet complete, so it will be a while before guests have their first opportunity to stay in this new space.

Throughout the summer, I had the chance to plant both cottonwood trees and willows around this guest house. It has already established itself as a new green-zone.

～～～～～～

This account has exceeded the anticipated nature year time frame. Over the past twenty-one months, all the large scale construction projects are complete, and all that remains are the ongoing countless little projects.

The events of this past summer, particularly taking a seasonal job where the season extended longer than anticipated, were not foreseen, but do remain as part of this story, proving that you can plan and control most activity, but you can't control all of the unexpected things that pop up along the way.

16: SOJOURN INTO WINTER

So, what does one do to prepare for the final few chapters of life? Well, from my perspective, the answer centers around the quality of life, starting with making life simpler.

Place has to be considered, and it is one of the things that we can control to make our lives better. If you select the right place, then you increase your satisfaction. By doing so, stress reduction a guaranteed byproduct of fulfillment, simply outweighs the conditions that induce stress.

It was indeed a fortuitous chain of events that brought me to this valley, and to my way of thinking, most things in this world happen for a reason. I believe finding this valley and ranchland is my reward for my life's hard work and my history of risk-taking.

Perhaps it is karma, perhaps good fortune, or perhaps even a grand design by our maker. I am the right person in the right spot at the right time. I am totally at home and at peace living in this community.

Unlike many of the authors mentioned throughout this book, I did not come to this place just for a one-year experience. Rather, my move had much longer or broader implications. This place is now home, and it will get the full appreciation that it deserves until it is time for my inevitable long dirt nap. Then perhaps someone in the family will follow in my footsteps, to keep the ranch alive.

The lifestyle in this valley is one of beauty and simple living. Thoreau once said that "he lives best whose needs are the simplest." This is my context when describing simple life.

I find myself being somewhat maudlin—perhaps overly or foolishly sentimental—about any attempts to capture and celebrate this way of living close to the land. Trying to record this lifestyle was certainly a noble effort from the Smithsonian research 27 years ago. In the present, celebrating this way of life is also a full-time effort of the Western Folklife Center in Elko, Nevada— home of the annual Cowboy Poetry Gathering.

For some, this celebratory effort is a conscious endeavor, but often it seems that working ranchers who *live* this life may be oblivious to what others are trying to accomplish.

One of the subtle challenges for my rural life adventure was to slow down and regain my appreciation for both nature and this simple rustic style of living.

After spending my adult life in and around medium to large cities, my sense of values, my pace, my quality of life expectations had all changed. It was the natural course of things to get used to long commutes. Bad neighbors became the norm and not the exception. City noise started to become commonplace. Tight fenced yards restricted the freedom and spirit of my dogs, during the times it was practical to own a dog. Feeling hemmed in and restricted was part of normal city living. Enjoying nature was difficult to accomplish.

It long seemed that this was just the price you had to pay when you were employed and locked into a particular geographic location. All of these limitations went away when the move was made to these wide-open spaces.

As a reinforcement of my hunch about city living, one of my couple friends from New Mexico recently cited reasons why they were disappointed with their relocation to a large city suburb there. The very issues of their concern were the same issues that contrast favorably here. I could not help but share a side by side comparison for them to consider as they are planning to sell and move to a smaller town as soon as the market permits.

During my recent time with the Forest Service work and with quiet, contemplative time at home, I've had the opportunity to sort through some of the important things in life.

I consider these things important to my quality of life: 1) family, 2) health and vitality, 3) reasonable financial security, 4) any kind of new enterprise or challenge, 5) pets to keep me company, and 6) enjoyable work.

Of these six points, perhaps only work needs a better definition. I refer to work as not what you do for a living but what you do with your living. As Aristotle once pointed out, happiness resides in activity, both physical and mental.[1] Our talent and character are expressed through the projects we choose to endorse.

In the past year or so, I have had the time to look back and consider how my life has treated me. While there have been ups and downs, the vast majority of my experiences have been positive and rewarding. I look back at the difficult times and write them off as life's little challenges to see how durable I really was.

Some of those stressful challenges were probably intended to test me, then toughen me up a bit. I never expected life to be limited to just the good things. The tough times made me more appreciative of my current comfort and tranquility.

∿∿ ∿∿ ∿∿
∿∿ ∿∿ ∿∿

I am often reminded that I am part of that large baby-boomer generation that is about to make the transition from careers to retirement. We make this move in large numbers. I have been told that there are seventy-eight-million of us in the boomer category. While I tend to think of myself as one unique individual, it is impossible to ignore the reality that I am one of many with similar aspirations about quality of life and general peace of mind as I move towards the tenth or eleventh of my life. Some boomers can afford to make a move; others are stuck where they are.

During the time frame of this book, I have pondered my ability to slow down and absorb the full measure of peace and tranquility of this special place.

A challenge I've set for myself is to consider how I see and appreciate time. With more focus on the present, I find less need to ruminate over the past and, moreover, I worry less about anything the future might have in store. To appreciate this place to its fullest, I am training myself to dwell more on the present. It has so much to offer.

Another challenge I've set for myself in this special place is to also absorb and appreciate every aspect of nature, along with the magic of every bird and wild animal within my view. I strive not to be that sleepwalker who walks through the choir of bird sounds and hears nothing. It has taken the discipline of a novice Buddhist meditator to transform my internal thought process into one that experiences nature with the same freshness as when I was a kid growing up on the rural prairies.

～～ ～～ ～～
～～ ～～ ～～

I had lived in this community for only a few months before my neighbor Joe S. pointed out that there was a non-denominational church service in town each week. He welcomed me to join them the following Sunday to check it out. As mentioned before, I found much to enjoy in these simple services led by Jerry Harper.

I have long held the belief that there is a logical connection between spirituality and nature. Often, my favorite authors have been those that wrote about things natural. In many cases, the topic matter lends itself to philosophical and introspective thinking.

Some of my favorite writers have examined some of these weightier issues. I use the word weightier because there is significance to what is important to our life: appreciating nature, good clean living, and showing respect for the western lifestyle.

Barry Lopez speaks about the importance of balancing introspection with community engagement for aspiring authors. He also talked about the obligation and responsibility, which may or may not be related to any political expression, to address the values of the current locale. In my case, I see this concept represented by discussing the values of the Intermountain West.

When I moved to this rural location, I had every intention to avoid political issues. I needed to respect the fact that I simply did not have any seniority here and that I still had a lot to learn before I opened my mouth. Perhaps over time, my role as a proponent of cultural and conservation matters will change.

Barry Lopez talks about a separate continuum linking that loosely knit group of men and women, intent on sharing a story. He spent time paying tribute to Wallace Stegner, and he recognized that valuable trait of making time for other people, pointing out that Stegner felt that the West would be a better place when people were generous with what they had.

Part of this generosity includes giving of one's time as well as making an effort to find some common causes within different factions—such as ranchers, farmers, loggers, developers, Forest Service, BLM, rangeland advocacy groups, mining interests, hunters, and so on.

This perspective, if enacted, would help reduce the present-day animosity and distrust that exists between old-time ranchers and the large public land holdings of the government, especially the BLM.

In Nevada, either BLM or the USFS manages eighty-six percent of the land. And yes, there is still the matter of the Sagebrush Rebellion, but without the fervor of a few years past, the current focus may be towards sagebrush solutions as opposed to fighting.

Some of the ongoing issues lend themselves to federal-level solutions, for example, wildland fires and forest management. In contrast, others fall under state purview, for example, managing scarce water resources and urban development. It has been said before that just because you love the West does not mean that you may not be dangerous to it.

The community may have a clash of its ecologies and its cultures, but the point here is that we must strive to find ways to trust our neighbors and invest in them.

It can be argued that since Ronald Reagan left the White House, there has been a shortage of a strong political voice concerned about the unique issues of the Intermountain West. Today it can be asked, what are the reasons for the West's marginality in the national political scene. Considering the current crop of Presidential contenders, this will not soon change. But, I digress.

~~~ ~~~ ~~~
~~~ ~~~ ~~~

Much can be said about the quality of Stegner's writing from the 1930s into the 1990s, and the ideal lifestyle that promoted his writing discipline.

Similar to the pattern of Thomas Jefferson, Wallace Stegner focused on his writing in the morning and on work around his place in the afternoon. It was said that he would start to pound out the keys on his typewriter as early as the birds would start their singing in the morning. The work he performed around his property, he called "idiot's delight," and outdoor work seemed to bring out the poetry in him.[2]

I am not sure if I unconsciously copied this routine or if this routine just comes naturally, especially on cold winter mornings when the open fire and a good book seem like natural partners.

I think of Stegner's contribution when I look up into the Wilderness Area of the Santa Rosa national forest. One of the first written arguments for this kind of environmental protection came by way of Stegner's "Wilderness Letter" dated 1960. In fact, this famous letter contained five references to the word spiritual—spiritual resource, spiritual health, spiritual losses, spiritual refreshment, and spiritual renewal. He provided arguments that supported the significance of wilderness areas beyond their natural beauty.

I find Stegner's writing easy to connect with and easy to follow. Despite three readings of Thoreau's book Walden in my life span, I never felt like I connected with the heart of that story or the continuity of his content; I enjoyed the Walden idea, but any deeper connection escaped me. In contrast, I found a passion in Stegner's theme of not abusing the Western land that was missing in Thoreau's account at Walden Pond.

If any reader here is unfamiliar with Stegner, then consider and digest the following two-line description from fellow writer Ivan Doig, "In person, Wally, of course, looked like a one-man Mount Rushmore. And his solidarity, that Scandinavian-Iowan-Saskatchewan-Montana-Utah-etcetera mien of flat-footed common sense and endurance, went much more than skin deep."

I first read Stegner during a solitary three-day hike, with my oldest cattle dog, into the wilderness of Jarbidge, Nevada. This sojourn, in late October, was an ideal setting in which to read his. It was a kind of spiritual trip, alone other than with the company of my dog, sleeping out even when the temperature dropped below freezing. My feet never froze because my sheepdog crawled to the bottom of my sleeping bag. We both benefited.

I don't know if Stegner was driven by Christian thinking or just common sense, but he spoke eloquently of loving your neighbor and loving the people around you.

It is of equal importance to love each other, as it is to love the earth. I have witnessed the best examples of this love of earth in my newfound valley home. The ranchers and farmers here are the best examples of land stewards and spend much of their working day outside in the elements, surrounded by the best and worst that nature has to offer.

These very issues of love help perpetuate and support two of the most important things, 1) our children and 2) the place where we live.

As Lopez said, it is love, and all that love contains—passion, awe, allegiance, ecstasy, respect, selflessness—that carries us in the direction of something good that we call God.[3]

Recently I saw a local example of ranchers and farmers demonstrating good stewardship. This past summer and fall have been dryer than normal.

As part of the natural course of things, the drought conditions affect the population of birds and mammals for hunting, and this season has been especially bad for upland game birds, a consensus found when talking to any of the outdoors people. I also noticed the low populations of upland birds when doing my seasonal forest work. However, I have heard the State Department of Wildlife will not alter the hunting season just because of lean years.

Instead, I now see private "no hunting" signs where they are not normally displayed. They're now common around the alfalfa fields that are especially abundant in both birds and wild mammals. The point here is that if the government does not make adjustments, the locals will.

Along the same lines, the author William Kittredge talks about responsibility, especially as it relates to our Western values. He shared an interesting perspective, which is that many people, like gardeners and cowhands, are artists in the long run.

In terms of writing, this art appears in a most basic form as writers try to share stories that recognize the best humane and compassionate impulses, in the stories that we write and share. The Kittredge home of Warner Valley, Oregon, is not that far from this particular valley that I call home. Both Kittredge and Stegner have been influenced by the geography and lifestyle of the Great Basin.

Kittredge is also fond of defining and writing about those things that some of us hold sacred and taking those steps necessary to preserve them. I hope that this account will be my token effort to carry out the Kittredge challenge. Further, my goal from this point forward will be to become the consummate citizen of the West.

There is a common denominator with these skilled authors mentioned above, and that is time spent with and hard work on developing their craft. Achieving their literary standing was not easy.

Unlike the contemporary TV commercial, with the "easy button," these accomplished writers spent their time in nature, honed their descriptive skills, studied such matters to be better caretakers of the land, better keepers of the truth, better brothers to each other, and thus better writers.

〰〰〰
〰〰〰

My neighbor Bill has a bumper sticker that reads, "RURAL NEVADA, Leave it that Way." This message is more than a sticker on a bumper; it is a plea to allow the locals to enjoy this lifestyle without change.

Nevada Bumpersticker

This community seems to grow by a couple of new families each year. Concurrently, we see occasional new house construction as a signal of slow but healthy growth. This pattern represents growth; however, I believe this to be a healthy and limited growth.

I fear that the day may be coming when some of the landowners will be tempted to subdivide their pasture land to make way for small acreage sub-divisions. It will be interesting to see how much unofficial influence that the local population can yield on the land sale process.

If this should ever happen, the below warning/pleading from Wallace Stegner will haunt any such development effort:

Something will have gone out of us a people if we ever let the remaining wilderness be destroyed; if we permit the last virgin forests to be turned into comic books and plastic cigarette cases; if we drive the few remaining members of the wild species into zoos or to extinction; if we pollute the last clear air and dirty the last clean streams and push our paved roads through the last of the silence so that never again will Americans be free in their own country from the noise, the exhausts, the stinks of human and automotive waste. And so that never again can we have the chance to see ourselves single, separate, vertical and individual in the world, part of the environment of trees and rocks and soil, brother to the other animals, part of the natural world and competent to belong in it. Without any remaining wilderness, we are committed wholly, without chance for even momentary reflection and rest, to a headlong drive into our technological termite-life, the Brave New World of a completely man-controlled environment.[4]

There now seems to be a limited consensus concern as to whether local families will be able to maintain their rural ranch lifestyles. It goes without saying that there is a quest to promote the best of this lifestyle and allow for the healthy interaction of the good folks who live and work here.

This topic of community and lifestyle causes me to consider questions such as, "Who am I?" and "How do I effectively fit in here?"

When people are busy making a living and doing the eight to five routine, it seems rare to find space and time for reflective thinking. The transition from regular work to retirement is a great opportunity to sort through these questions, and possibly one may realize that there may be a gap between who we are and who we want to be.

In going full cycle, I see myself starting as a rural tyro—a beginner or novice—armed only with a few life experiences and good intentions. I still have much to learn, and that learning curve will have to be compressed into a limited number of years. I will make the most out of this ranch life experience.

∽∽ ∽∽ ∽∽
∽∽ ∽∽ ∽∽

Some of my life experiences, especially as shaped by my time on this property, have helped me formulate some thoughts that now seem appropriate.

Over the past twenty-one months as I've developed this ranch property, a large portion of my effort has been spent on fitting into this community, and this community is rural and well established, the process of fitting in takes time.

Even after all these months, this is still a work in progress. Connecting with the community has been a reminder of the value of humble manners, not coming across too fast, or trying to be too important.

This effort has also included a sincere appreciation for the locals that call this home. These are good, hard-working, salt-of-the-earth people that make this place special, long before I showed up—and some are better than others.

Each new introduction requires time, not just for the first meeting but for many of those subsequent visits when paths do cross. For instance, when you come across your neighbors on the back-country roads, you learn to stop and visit rather than just waving and driving on by. They have the time, and thus you need to learn to take the time for a five- or ten-minute roadside visit.

It seems that each little visit provides an opportunity to learn something new, and each visit is another opportunity to hone those country gentleman skills.

~~~ ~~~ ~~~
~~~ ~~~ ~~~

During my hurried years in college, when there was never enough time to do anything well, it was tempting to rush through my English major reading assignments. I read through many topics and concepts but did not fully understand them. One example was the concept of existentialism.

Now a lot older and a little wiser, I have a better grasp of some of the precepts. Translated into plain language, I find some important existential points show up in my life here, such as 1) freedom of choice, 2) personal responsibility for your actions, 3) creating your own moral values, and 4) determining the future that works for you.

Free choice and free will are so important to the Western way of thinking. There are large numbers of independent-minded thinkers and voters in these parts. You can be an independent person without being an angry person; however, I will be the first to admit that a little anger can go a long way to develop a passion for something.

Part of this independence is to be responsible for your own actions. To me, responsibility should eliminate the need for many petty rules and laws that box us in. Too many regulations create a situation where we all act alike.

In the process of being boxed in by rules, the real characters of the world often get eliminated. They are eliminated because of the consequences that arise when people push the envelope and do things differently. And in many cases, done in moderation and thoughtfully, the individual choices do no harm.

Heaven forbid that we should drive the back-country road to check our mail in town, without wearing a seatbelt. Even though it is against the law, we might drive our off-road quads on the pavement or on the streets of Paradise. Or, we might drive our quads off the established roads/trails in places such as the national forest.

Perhaps the worst examples are the hundreds or thousands of pages of environmental regulations that govern what a person can or cannot do at Lake Tahoe, my home for fourteen years, thanks to the governing body called the Tahoe Regional Planning Agency (TRPA).

Following the large forest fire at South Lake Tahoe last summer, some of the burned-out residents finally lashed back to say that TRPA was partially to blame for the scope of the fire because there were too many rules about what the property owner could not do to protect their homes in respect to clearing trees and brush to minimize fire danger.

This list of petty little examples could go on indefinitely. So, if there are enough rules and laws, we will all have to act and think exactly alike, and thus we will all become vanilla flavored. I like the idea that some can be chocolate flavored or Cherry-Garcia flavored.

Much can be said of the concept of pushing the envelope or simply finding a newer or better way to live your life.

Other parts of the existential argument are easier to deal with, such as establishing your moral values and determining the future that works for you.

When these points are considered, I remind myself of how important nature has been to me. During those years of large city living, I tended to head for nature each and every weekend.

It may have been as simple as hiking the C&O Canal to Harper's Ferry, or camping in the Black Rock Desert, or riding my dirt bike in the deserts of Southern California, or weekend drives to the most rural haunts of Vermont or long, slow distance jogging (my version of LSD) outside the congested spots where I lived. I often justified these outings as preserving my sanity.

Now, these outings are just outside my back door. Nature has been an important part of my life because it often helped to find the answer to life's questions and finally for the aesthetic rewards of being close to those good and wholesome aspects of the non-urban environment. As Wallace Stegner once said about wilderness, you don't go there to find something, but rather you go there to disappear.

So, finding a location close to nature was a no-brainer for me, and that is why I feel a sense of *place* is so important. Most of us have favorite spots to visit and recreate, but finding the ideal spot to call home is more complicated than that. The place where you end up living may end up being different from the place that you occasionally visited because of subtle factors that you never thought to consider.

Moving around is fine, I suppose. When you move around, you end up adding interesting new chapters to your book of life experiences. In my case, I have moved around too much. For example, during my twenty years in the military, I had twenty-four different mailing addresses. These addresses included five different continents and countries.

But eventually comes a time in your life when you need to settle down in that last ideal spot. Most of us know when that time is right. As I have said more than once in this book, I have found my perfect place. And, yes, *place* is important.

My final thought or perspective on living a quality life is the value of hard work. Hard labor is healthy, both physically and mentally. It tends to keep you lean and mean. It offers untold rewards after a project is completed. Work adds purpose to your life. As I analyze my faults in life, I must admit a consistent lack of tolerance for those who shun work, those couch-potatoes who tend to be lazy and overweight.

Regarding the topics of nature and hard work, consider this old quote from Teddy Roosevelt about the time he was leaving his North Dakota ranch, "We love a great many things—birds and trees and books and all things beautiful; and horses and rifles and children and hard work, and the job of life."

~~~ ~~~ ~~~

While winter is not my favorite season, it does provide certain opportunities that the warmer seasons do not. The most obvious advantage is the change of pace. I get to sleep in longer in the morning. My early morning activity includes time for both reading and writing.

These activities often suffer as a result of major projects during the spring, summer, and fall. It takes a short while to get used to the changes to my daily routine. It is pleasant in the morning to sit close to the open flame, pellet stove. It is the warmest place in the house, and the seat is in view of morning TV news.

I have an east-facing window over my shoulder, so the early morning sun angle not only helps to warm the house, but it provides just the right lighting for quiet reading.

This morning routine centers around that first pot of coffee. After rolling out of bed, making coffee is job number one. From my reading perch, the top of the tepid to warm pellet stove is so close that it serves as a place to rest my coffee cup. This way, the fresh cup is not only close but stays warm for an indefinite period. This morning routine suits me even better when I look outside to see snow falling or fog shrouding the foothills and mountains.

On the subject of reading, I feel that I am still playing catch up on my lifetime reading. I have carried around scores of books for most of my adult life. Many of these books date back to college when I had good intentions to read some of the classics, but other activity got in the way, and the well-intended reading was postponed. As often stated, there is much to be said about the benefits of reading. William Bennett, in his *Book of Virtues*, provides an appropriate argument made by Francis Bacon for this endeavor:

> Read not to contradict and confute; nor to believe and take for granted; nor to find talk and discourse; but to weigh and consider. Some books are to be tasted, others to be swallowed, and some few to be chewed and digested: that is, some books are to be read only in parts, others to be read, but not curiously, and some few to be read wholly, and with diligence and attention... Reading maketh a full man; conference a ready man; and writing an exact man; and therefore, if a man write little, he had need have a great memory; if he confer little, he had need have a present wit; and if he read little, he had need have much cunning, to seem to know that he doth not.[5]

Even though Francis Bacon made this argument in 1597, I find it is still sound reasoning today despite the distractions of available other entertainment such as television and the internet.

On the subject of warmth, this is the season to take advantage of the four-person sauna that I included in my house plan. This idea came in part from my Scandinavian heritage and part from one winter spent in Japan where bathhouses were common. The one-hundred-thirty-degree sauna is not only a peaceful respite from the outdoor chill but is also a perfect step just after my shower, for if a chill is in the air, the sauna also provides a comfortable respite while my body gets toweled off.

Because of the cold winter nights, my three dogs decided to overnight in the house, inside their respective wire mesh kennels. While they are high strung and full of daytime energy, they do seem to appreciate the good fortune of a warm night indoors.

Despite this comfort option, my male dog sometimes signals that he prefers the outdoor dog house on the front porch. I guess he is just tougher than the two female dogs.

My cat, Minnie the Mouser, is a bed companion except for the nights when she is out hunting and doing whatever cats do in the middle of the night. Her favorite sleeping position is when she can position herself nose to nose with me. This proximity seems to offer some sort of security blanket for her purposes. My cat has become a trusty companion, both indoors as well as outdoors, and I'm not even considered to be a cat person.

On the topic of warmth, the winter season has proven to be ideal for stews and homemade chili. Author, Bernd Heinrich, has a suggestion that works well when the outside temperature drops.

He described making a beef-vegetable-potato stew in a large cast-iron pot. After the enjoyment of this fresh stew, he allowed the pot to cool down, and when cool, the pot would be placed outside in Mother Nature's fridge. It would stay chilled until the next dinner when a simmer flame could heat it, and the meal is enjoyed again and again. If and when the appetite tires of stew, then it is time to switch to homemade chili. As a cooking challenged guy, this routine has proven to be both practical and easy.

My appreciation for these newfound home comforts is fresh in mind because last winter, my quality of life was different while subsisting in my shop. I have to say, I enjoy this new routine. As winter settles in, it is my first winter here with a real house to enjoy, and this is my only season when going to work for the forest service is not a factor. Now is the time for the luxury of getting up later than during my summer workdays.

While I look forward to enjoying the comforts of this warm home in the winter conditions, I have already laid out some plans that will kick off when winter gives way to spring. These plans will try to make the best possible use of my available acreage, and will hopefully warrant another story.

ᨠᨠ ᨠᨠ ᨠᨠ
ᨠᨠ ᨠᨠ ᨠᨠ

By tracking the weather forecast via the Reno news, it is possible to know in advance how my next day will look. When the weather is decent, I make progress on my list of outdoor projects, which at present includes doing finish work in my new guest house, working on the dog run alongside my shop/barn, and setting up lower pastures for my first goat or sheep venture come next spring.

Also, restoration work continues on my very old Farmall tractor, which is almost my age. Right now, the fuel governor has been removed to swap out with a neighbor Farmall collector. If this throttle problem gets fixed, then my tractor will again be functional. As another repair step, the oldest front wheel/tire went to town for a replacement. The old tire rubber was cracked and nearly falling off the rim. For just over a hundred dollars, this problem was quickly fixed.

Farmall Tractor

On the days when the wind is blowing, the temperature is below the mid-thirties, or it is wet out, it becomes time to stay close to the fire and make progress on paperwork and other inside chores. These are the mornings when the routine calls for a late but large breakfast. Buttermilk pancakes have been a lifetime favorite.

〜〜〜

Now that my seasonal forest service job is complete for the year, it's time to get back into a consistent workout routine, a refreshing mix of running and hiking.

On the anniversary date for Pearl Harbor Day, I created a new running course that followed an old established BLM trail to the north of my property that had somewhat overgrown.

The trail starts out over rough terrain covered by sagebrush; then, it heads north until it crosses the first dry ravine. On the other side of the ravine is a ridge top trail that moves from sage fields to open grassland, and this section heads due east until it finds the easiest crossing of the larger ravine, called Dry Creek. This drainage is deep enough that a quad can only cross in certain select spots. Once this crossing is made, the trail heads uphill towards the geographic feature called Red Hills. At the base of these foothills is the prominent China Grade—the terraced rock trail that was described earlier in this book. The China Grade is the first section of trail suitable for a jeep or four-wheel-drive pickup, and it is the best stretch of the trail to enjoy easy running. This is also the high point on the run and provides a wonderful panoramic view of the entire Paradise Valley.

I follow this trail to the east until it joins the rock canyon section of Martin Creek. From this intersection, it is an easy jog back to my property. This route takes just under forty minutes, which is about the right amount of exercise time.

∾∾ ∾∾ ∾∾

I try to finish my walks or runs by sunset, so I'm home in time for the evening news. I have long considered myself a news-junkie; however, in recent years, I've tired of the sensational, re-run news stories such as the Scott Peterson murder case and the Anna Nicole Smith (who's the daddy?) story.

Now there is another Peterson murder case that Fox News will beat to death. This time the conduct of the former police officer suspect is just too weird to watch. Currently, the news is dominated by the Presidential primary campaign. I can only handle so much of this game where the candidates are expected to say what they have to say in each state to garner political support; it just seems to be political glad-handing and not much more.

In the summertime, it is easy to watch an evening baseball game, thanks to a special TV sports package.

Baseball is low-stress entertainment. Other programs like PBS, Discovery, Speed Channel, and music concerts offer a suitable reprieve from the poor taste re-run news.

Many evenings, my quality of life increases by joyously shutting off the TV and put on some music. My Sirius radio offers a great choice with excellent reception. If not Sirius, then back to jazz from CapRadio. If I rely on my car or home radio, I can only get two stations until I reach town. Certain technological advances—satellite TV, satellite radio, and the internet—have improved my situation.

As part of the end-of-day routine, I eat a late dinner. Consistent with many runners, the day's end also calls for a cold beer or two—a simple reward for a hard day's work or, as is the case now, a hard day's retirement. When it is time to put the day into the history book is also a good time for a beer.

About once a week, I plan a trip to town for supplies. I have a constant need for building supplies, spare parts, tractor equipment, and even some groceries now and then. I never expected to be a Wal-Mart shopper, but that is the best large store in town for one-stop shopping. It is amazing how often we run into our neighbors while shopping here. I have become a familiar face at the local hardware store and the local lumber yard.

One cold morning after Christmas, a hunter and his dog strode across my property. When I approached him to inquire about his activity, he explained that he was tracking a mountain lion and her cub, and he had lost the track between my property and the neighboring property.

This small story gained traction in the community, and subsequent accounts of this tracking story were exchanged at both church and the saloon.

This realization of large cats as part of the local wildlife provides a sobering thought to my future intent to raise some combination of Soay sheep, Boer goats, and BLM wild mustangs. Of the trio of choices, I ended up with a rare breed of sheep called Soay.

ᨃᨃᨃ ᨃᨃᨃ ᨃᨃᨃ

January 1st, 2008, will be the last day covered by this story. This date in history is of interest to me because it is the same day that Hank Williams died at the tender age of twenty-nine.

He had hired an eighteen-year-old kid to drive his new blue Cadillac to Canton, Ohio, for a New Year's Day concert. While the driver pulled over in Oak Hill, West Virginia, for a rest, the country legend died. He's proof that the significance of a life's contribution can be compressed into a few years.

Not only do I enjoy the quality of Hank Williams' songwriting skills, but I admire how he led his hard-living life and how he did things his way.

Over the course of the past twenty-one months, much has happened. My property went from nothing but a dilapidated well and a tilted power pole to a functioning ranch property with multiple buildings. This time frame was also my transition period in this community.

New-found self-discipline has taught me to slow down and enjoy every precious moment of this beautiful life. I have also learned from this experience that everything has value, and everything has beauty. What a ride this has been.

This place has become my sanctuary, my green-zone, my respite, my haven, my escape, and my dream. As I ponder these terms to describe my contentment, it is now the first day of the new year and a good time to close this account. Around me and before me is the product of careful planning and the hard work of my own two hands.

〰〰〰 THE END 〰〰〰

SELECTED BIBLIOGRAPHY

Bennett, W. J. (1993). *The Book of Virtues: A Treasury of Great Moral Stories*. New York, NY: Simon and Schuster.

Beston, H., & Finch, R. (2006). *The Outermost House: A Year of Life on the Great Beach of Cape Cod*. New York, NY: St. Martin's Griffin.

Chouinard, Y. (2016). *Let My People Go Surfing: The Education of a Reluctant Businessman, Including 10 More Years of Business Unusual*. New York, NY: Penguin Books.

Ehrlich, P. R., Dobkin, D. S., & Wheye, D. (1988). *The Birder's Handbook: A Field Guide to the Natural History of North American Birds*. New York, NY: Simon and Schuster.

Heinrich, B. (1999). *A Year in the Maine Woods*. Reading, MA: Perseus Books.

Hubbell, S. (1999). *A Country Year: Living the Questions*. Boston, MA: Houghlin Mifflin.

Jenkinson, C. (2002). *Message on the Wind: A Spiritual Odyssey on the Northern Plains*. Reno, NV: Marmarth Press.

Kittredge, W. (2000). *The Nature of Generosity*. New York, NY: Knopf.

Long, J. (1985). *Outlaw: The True Story of Claude Dallas*. New York, NY: Morrow.

Lopez, B. H. (2006). *Home Ground: Language for an American Landscape*. San Antonio, TX: Trinity University Press.

Marshall, H. W. (1995). *Paradise Valley, Nevada: The People and Buildings of an American Place*. Tucson, AZ: University of Arizona Press.

Nielsen, J., & Vollers, M. (2001). *Ice Bound: A Doctor's Incredible Battle for Survival at the South Pole*. New York, NY: Hyperion.

Sibley, D. (2016). *Sibley Field Guide to Birds of Western North America*. New York, NY: Knopf.

Stegner, W. (1969). *The Sound of Mountain Water*. Garden City, NY: Doubleday.

Stegner, W., Stegner, P., & Stegner, M. (1996). *The Geography of Hope: A Tribute to Wallace Stegner*. San Francisco, CA: Sierra Club Books.

Thoreau, H. D., & Cramer, J. S. (2004). *Walden*. New Haven, CT: Yale University Press.

Udvardy, M. D. (1994). *The Audubon Society Field Guide to North American Birds: Western Region*. New York, NY: Alfred A. Knopf.

White, M. C. (2006). *50 Classic Hikes in Nevada: From the Ruby Mountains to Red Rock Canyon*. Reno, NV: University of Nevada Press.

Zarzyski, P. (2003). *Wolf Tracks on the Welcome Mat: Poems.* Carmel, CA: Oreanabooks/Carmel Pub.

ENDNOTES

INTRODUCTION:

[1] Thoreau, H. D., & Cramer, J. S. (2004). *Walden* (p. 19-20). New Haven, CT: Yale University Press.

[2] Thoreau, H. D., & Cramer, J. S. (2004). *Walden* (p. xxiii). New Haven, CT: Yale University Press.

[3] Page 36-37 In Zarzyski, P. (2003). *Wolf Tracks on the Welcome Mat: Poems* (p. 36-37). Carmel, CA: Oreanabooks/Carmel Pub.

CHAPTER ONE:

[1] Thoreau, H. D., & Cramer, J. S. (2004). *Walden* (p. 9). New Haven, CT: Yale University Press.

CHAPTER TWO:

[1] Marshall, H. W. (1995). *Paradise Valley, Nevada: The People and Buildings of an American Place* (p. 13). Tucson, AZ: University of Arizona Press.

[2] In Lopez, B. H. (2006). *Home Ground: Language for an American Landscape* (p. 45). San Antonio, TX: Trinity University Press.

[3] Thoreau, H. D., & Cramer, J. S. (2004). *Walden* (p. 119). New Haven, CT: Yale University Press.

CHAPTER THREE:

[1] Thoreau, H. D., Homer, W., & Sargent, J. S. (1992). *Henry David Thoreau--the Poet's Delay: A Ccollection of Poetry by America's Greatest Observer of Nature* (p. 105). New York, NY: Rizzoli.

[2] Thoreau, H. D., & Cramer, J. S. (2004). *Walden* (p. 241). New Haven, CT: Yale University Press.

CHAPTER FIVE:

[1] Ehrlich, P. R., Dobkin, D. S., & Wheye, D. (1988). *The Birder's Handbook: A Field Guide to the Natural History of North American Birds* (p. 11). New York, NY: Simon and Schuster.

CHAPTER SEVEN:

[1] Thoreau, H. D., & Cramer, J. S. (2004). *Walden* (p. 202). New Haven, CT: Yale University Press.

CHAPTER FOURTEEN:

[1] Fleischhauer, C. (n.d.). The Founding Years, 1864-1910: A History of the Ninety-Six Ranch: Articles and Essays: Buckaroos in Paradise: Ranching Culture in Northern Nevada, 1945-1982: Digital Collections: Library of Congress. Retrieved August, 2006, from https://www.loc.gov/collections/ranching-culture-in-northern-nevada-from-1945-to-1982/articles-and-essays/a-history-of-the-ninety-six-ranch/the-founding-years-1864-1910/

CHAPTER SIXTEEN:

[1] Bennett, W. J. (1993). *The Book of Virtues: A Treasury of Great Moral Stories* (p.347). New York, NY: Simon and Schuster.

[2] Stegner, W., Stegner, P., & Stegner, M. (1996). *The Geography of Hope: A Tribute to Wallace Stegner* (p.80). San Francisco, CA: Sierra Club Books.

[3] Stegner, W., Stegner, P., & Stegner, M. (1996). *The Geography of Hope: A Tribute to Wallace Stegner* (p.119). San Francisco, CA: Sierra Club Books.

[4] Stegner, W. (1969). *The Sound of Mountain Water* (Ref. Wilderness Idea, originally a 1960 letter to Outdoor Recreation Resources Review Commission). Garden City, NY: Doubleday.

[5] Bennett, W. J. (1993). *The Book of Virtues: A Treasury of Great Moral Stories* (p.423-424). New York, NY: Simon and Schuster.

Made in the USA
Middletown, DE
03 January 2023

21157133R00179